THE

CARIBBEAN

A Walking & Hiking Guide

3rd Edition

Leonard M. Adkins

HUNTER

HUNTER PUBLISHING, INC,
130 Campus Drive, Edison, NJ 08818
732-225-1900; 800-255-0343; Fax 732-417-1744
hunterpub@emi.net

1220 Nicholson Road, Newmarket, Ontario
Canada L3Y 7V1
800-399-6858; Fax 800-363-2665

The Boundary, Wheatley Road, Garsington
Oxford, OX44 9EJ England
01865-361122; Fax 01865-361133

ISBN 1-55650-848-4
© 1999 Leonard M. Adkins

Cover photo: The Baths, Virgin Gorda
All photos by author

Maps by Kim André, © 1999 Hunter Publishing, Inc.

1   2   3   4

Acknowledgments

I used to wonder why authors needed to thank so many people. Now I know. To the following go my most heartfelt thanks and appreciation for their invaluable assistance and for the sharing of their knowledge.

On St. Croix – Nancy Buckingham, St. Croix Environmental Association; William Cissel, National Park Service; K. Olasee, I. Davis and Rudy G. O'Reilly, Jr., University of the Virgin Islands; Susan Ivy, Colony Cove; Kathy Weaver, Barker, Campbell & Farley; Liz Wilson; Bill and Betsy Gladfelter.

On St. Thomas – Julie Lentz, Secret Harborview Villas; Lyla Naseem, Laura Davidson Public Relations; Monica Leedy, Barker, Campbell & Farley.

On St. John – C. Weiker and D. Near, National Park Service; R. Miles Stair, Holiday Homes.

In the British Virgin Islands – Keith Dawson, Tourist Board; Janine Cifelli, Resorts Management, Inc.; Eugenia Martac, Elizabeth Beach Resort; Kathryn van Kampen, BVI Press Office; Simon Owens, Paradise Beach Resort; Helen Bayne, Biras Creek; John Moorly and Katherine Dickens, Guana Island; Nicolas Drayton and Veronica Champion, National Parks Trust.

On Sint Maarten/St. Martin – Myron Clement, Clement-Petrocik; Bernadette Davis and Silvianne Hill, Tourist Office; Eric Dubois Millot, Action Nature.

On Anguilla – Bob Conrich; Pam Berry, Carimar Beach Club; Elizabeth Mason and Amelia Vanterpool-Kubish, Tourist Office.

On St. Barts – Ellise Magras and Marielle Greaux, Tourist Office; Hotel Yuana.

On Saba – Glenn C. Holm, Saba Tourist Bureau; James Johnson, Saba Nature Guide; Ton van't Hof, Saba Conservation Foundation; Captain's Quarters.

On Statia – Roland Lopes, Dept. of Tourism, Raphael "Charley" Lopes, Statia Nature Guide; Golden Era Hotel.

On St. Kitts – Timothy Benford; Greg Pereira, Greg's Safaris; Ocean Terrace Inn.

On Nevis – Pam Berry, Golden Rock Estate; David Rollinson, Eco-Tours Nevis.

On Antigua – Ann Marie Martin, National Parks; Chris Lafaurie, Long Bay Beach Hotel; Matt Seminar, Trombone Associates; Desmond Nicholson, Museum of Antigua & Barbuda.

On Guadeloupe – G. Claude Germaine, Tourist Office; Touring Hotel Club de Fort Royal; Wilfred Demonio, National Park.

On Dominica – Janice Armour, Dominica Tours and Anchorage Hotel; Ken's Hinterland Adventure Tours and Taxi Service; Floral Gardens; Marie Jose-Edwards and Magdeline Jervier, National Development Corporation.

On Martinique – The staff of the Tourist Office; La Bakoua; Michael Tanasi, National Forest Office; Primereve.

Others who deserve a big thank you are:

Ann Mesick – for resource materials.

Barbara Schober – without her the French island chapters would never have been completed.

Denny Messick – skipper of *Rebel Ann II*.

Dr. Stephen Lewis and Caroline Charonko – thank you for giving me a new lease on life.

To my wife Laurie – thanks for doing all of the daily hum-drum of life that I neglected while writing the book.

Contents

Maps

Montserrat

Montserrat's Soufrière Hills volcano began erupting in the mid-1990s, eventually covering much of the island in lava and/or a thick layer of ash, destroying the capital city of Plymouth and forcing the evacuation of nearly the entire population. Because of this, the island is, at present, no longer a tourist destination.

We hope that the extremely friendly people of this once-beautiful island may one day return to their homeland.

Read What Other Folks Say About This Book:

Introduction

Thoughts of the Caribbean bring to mind images of lying on sun-drenched beaches with a gentle surf lapping at your feet or of dancing to the rhythms of a calypso band at a world-class resort. Yes, the islands of the Caribbean are this, but they are also so much more!

Beyond the glitter of the casinos, the temptations of the duty-free shops, and the passive pursuit of a golden tan is a unique and fascinating world that is best discovered on foot.

Nowhere else is it possible to experience, in such a small area, so many different cultures and social conditions, such diverse vegetation, and such varied landscape as in the Caribbean. Even the most casual walker can step out the door of a luxury hotel onto a palm-lined beach to search for conch shells and hermit crabs, pass through the center of a busy and historically-rich port town, then enter a cactus and boulder-strewn landscape. From there, you can walk among stalks of sugarcane, or up the slopes of a lush, rain forest-covered volcanic mountain to discover crashing waterfalls and thousands of multi-hued tropical flowers. All of these delights can be experienced in less than an hour's walk from major towns and tourist spots.

The Virgin and Leeward Islands have never been so accessible. The increase in adventure travel and ecotourism over the last 10 years has attracted a different kind of visitor; this new breed is no longer content to sit on the beach soaking up sun. Rather, they want to experience and come to know the lands and the people. This active tourist has not gone unnoticed by the islanders. The tiny island of Saba has rebuilt and now maintains the handcarved step-trails that once were the only links between the four villages of the island. Montserrat has not only embarked upon a vigorous campaign to promote its walking and hiking opportunities, but has even employed civil servants to clear trails of obstructing vegetation. The National Park Service of Dominica is upgrading a network of pathways through the rugged mountains into areas that have active volcanoes and are rarely visited. The British Virgin Islands National Parks Trust has sparked a renewed interest in protecting ecologically fragile areas so that current and future generations can enjoy walking in unspoiled tropical terrain.

Having been somewhat neglectful in protecting their history and culture, many islands are rediscovering their rich and colorful historical backgrounds and are restoring old forts, revitalizing whole sections of their villages, returning the great houses of former sugar plantations to their original grandeur, and establishing walking tours of these sites.

The well-defined trails in the national parks of the French islands of Martinique and Guadeloupe and of the United States Virgin Islands have been around for years – leading visitors deep into the rain forests and up to volcanic craters. But new trails and parks are being established every year. One of the most exciting developments for serious walkers and hikers was opened to the public in 1994. A pathway, known as the Grande Randonnée G.1, now makes it possible to hike along one continuous route from the southern end to the northern tip of Guadeloupe, enjoying a full week of backpacking and camping without ever leaving the trail!

At one time, if you wished to travel off the usual tourist routes, the best you could do was to hire your cab driver's brother, who would merely show you a way through the rain forest. But there are now many well-established, professionally-run (and prosperous) companies, whose employees are well versed in the flora, fauna, geology, and history of their homeland.

The Lay of the Land

On the North American continent, the general rule is that vegetation deteriorates as one gains altitude, changing from lush foliage to open, treeless mountaintops. Almost the opposite is true in the Caribbean. On islands such as St. Kitts, Nevis, and Statia, it is the norm to begin in dry, scrub-brush country and ascend to the vine-covered giant hardwood trees of a deep and dark rain forest.

In contrast to the wet, mountainous islands, there are the numerous low-lying, dry, deserted islands that dot the Caribbean Sea. The rock-littered moonscape of Ile Fourchue near St. Barth or the scrub-brushed flat lands of Petit Terre off the coast of Guadeloupe often see days go by without a single visitor. About the only company you would have on these and other deserted islands would be a herd of wild goats or the seldom seen – but often heard – iguana slithering through the cactus and underbrush.

All of this is not to suggest that the beaches of the Caribbean should be overlooked. Sint Maarten/St. Martin boasts of 36, while Antigua claims to have 365 beaches. The north coast of Anegada has a stretch of unbroken, undeveloped, and unpopulated beaches that continue for almost 20 miles! All of the islands have beaches to be explored and these can be as varied and as interesting as any inland walks. Some are in heavily developed areas, with high-rise hotels crowded closely together, while others are hidden in bays and coves that may not see a person, tourist or local, for days on end. Narrow strips of golden sand, bordered by sandstone cliffs pockmarked with small caves, lead to wide expanses of coral-pink sand lined with swaying palms and tangled sea grape. As nothing like them exists in North America, black sand beaches can be a startling discovery as well as a gentle reminder of the volcanic origins of the islands. There are even some well-established topless – *au naturel* – bathing spots.

One of the more fascinating aspects of the Virgin and Leeward Islands is the great diversity of cultures that exist within close proximity of each other. Only a 20-minute flight separates a walk in chic, French-speaking, sophisticated, and modern downtown Fort-de-France, Martinique, from a stroll on the dirt streets of Portsmouth, Dominica, lined with sheet-metal-roofed, one-room houses. On Sint Maarten/St. Martin it is even possible to be on Dutch soil and enjoy a duty-free Heineken, then saunter into French territory and feast on a deliciously prepared Creole dinner accompanied by a glass of elegant burgundy. These enchanting cultures, sweeping beachscapes, volcanic craters, verdant forests, and flowering tropical foliage are just waiting for you to lace up those walking shoes, put one foot in front of the other, and go do some exploring!

Before the original publication of this guidebook, information on walking and hiking in the Virgins and Leewards was unobtainable until one reached the islands – even then it was rather sketchy. The purpose of the book is to aid in the planning of your trip, help you decide which walks appeal to you, alert you to any possible dangers, guide you to and through the walks, and add to the general enjoyment of your trip.

The Caribbean is one of the fastest-changing places in the world, and you may find hotels on beaches that were once secluded. Trails and paths may have become roads or no longer exist. If this should happen, please help future travelers by sending all updates to: Leonard Adkins, c/o Hunter Publishing, 130 Campus Drive, Edison, NJ 08818, or via e-mail to hunterpub@emi.net..

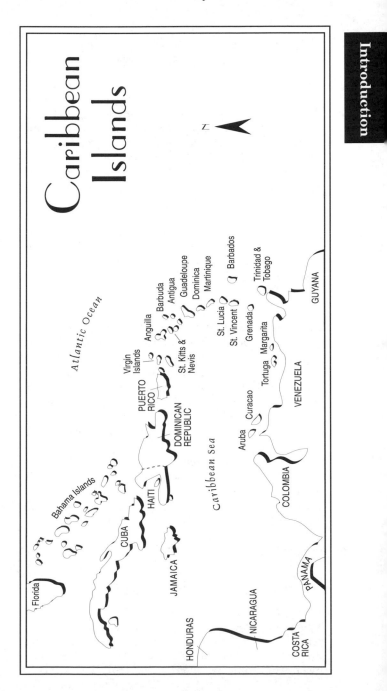

How To Use This Book

It is not within the scope of this guide to provide information on accommodations, shopping, or dining in the Caribbean. There are many books covering these subjects and you are strongly urged to obtain one or two (see *Suggested Readings* and *Field Guides*). In addition to the lodging, dining, and shopping advice, they contain many useful hints on what to pack, methods of transportation to the islands, and how to get the most for your money. They are also good for a capsule view of tourist attractions such as casinos, bus tours, aquariums, etc. Out of the many that are available, *Frommer's Guide to the Caribbean, Birnbaum's Caribbean*, and *Fodor's Caribbean* are probably the most comprehensive and informative.

Each chapter in this guidebook covers one island (or group of islands such as the US Virgin Islands) and includes a general description, a reference map, a short history section, important data, and the walks and hikes to be found there. The chapters start in the United States Virgin Islands and head south. The maps are intended to be used as a general guide only, showing the approximate locations of the walks and trails. Detailed trail maps are unnecessary as the islands are small and most of the hikes are short. Road maps, which are all that's really needed, may be obtained in bookstores or tourist offices once you reach the Caribbean. Some car rental agencies even provide them free of charge.

The Data Sections

Transportation to the Islands: Since fares, schedules and companies are continually changing, it is best to check with a travel agency for the most recent information. Experienced travelers will contact several agencies to learn which one can provide the most comprehensive services and lowest rates. It pays to shop around and even do some investigating on your own.

Entry: Most islands will grant entry to American and Canadian citizens upon presentation of a voter's registration card or a birth certificate. However, a passport is always the best form of I.D. when traveling to foreign lands and you are strongly urged to obtain and carry one with you at all times. Americans may apply for a passport through their local post office.

The Caribbean may be lax in checking for entry I.D., but you can be assured that officials will ask to see an ongoing or return transportation ticket and sufficient monetary funds to cover the expenses of your visit. Failure to meet either one of these requirements could result in the denial of entry. If you are arriving by cruise ship, all of these formalities should be taken care of by the ship's staff. Crew members of private yachts must check in with the customs and immigration officers immediately upon arrival.

Currency: American dollars are generally accepted throughout the Virgin and Leeward Islands, but it is almost always better to exchange a small amount for the local currency. Travelers' checks are the safest bet. ATMs are another option.

Tourist Information: The North American and the European address of the tourist bureau for each island is given in the text, along with the location of the tourist office on the island itself. While most tourist bureaus are geared toward providing general information on lodging, dining, and shopping, their literature will usually include a good overview of the landscape and daily life on the island.

Driving: You must present a valid driver's license to rent a vehicle on all of the Virgin and Leeward Islands. Some places require that a temporary local permit be obtained; many rental agencies will take care of this paperwork for you. Before you drive off, be sure to check which side of the road to drive on!

Language: The residents of the islands speak a wide variety of languages. It may be that more national languages and variations of these languages are spoken in this small corner of the world than in any other area of equal size. English, Spanish, French, Dutch, and sundry forms of these – Creole, Papiemento, French Patois, and even an Irish brogue – will be encountered on islands that are no more than a 15-minute flight from each other. But do not despair – English is spoken by enough people that you will be able to get by.

Walking and Hiking Guide Companies: Only companies that specialize or have a significant interest in walking and hiking tours are listed. When the services of a local guide are recommended, please heed this advice. They are only recommended when there is the possibility that you may become lost or are going to walk into a dangerous area. Tourist offices and the management of hotels can usually suggest additional qualified guides in the event you are unable to contact one of those in this book.

Camping Areas: Only official campgrounds are listed. The exceptions to this are the informal campsites on Martinique and Guadeloupe that have become accepted by the authorities over the years. Regulations for camping on beaches and in the forests vary from island to island and from time to time. In a response to what they perceived to be vagabonds and/or drug runners, many of the islands recently prohibited camping anywhere except at approved commercial campgrounds. In some places, such as the British Virgin Islands, this policy is vigorously enforced. The wisest and safest thing to do is to contact the tourist office or the civil authorities of the island for current policies.

Recommended Readings: Each island chapter has a short list of books, pamphlets, or newspapers that will lead to a greater understanding and enjoyment of the land and the people you are going to visit. In addition, be sure to look over the Suggested Readings and Field Guides list at the end of this guidebook. Many of these will provide a botanical, zoological, ecological, and historical understanding of the Caribbean as a whole. Others are field guides that should be carried with you to increase your awareness of your surroundings as you walk.

Interpreting the Terms Used

Ranging from easy strolls on the beaches to walking tours of historical districts to challenging mountain climbs of volcanic summits, the great variety of walks listed for each island makes it possible for anyone to enjoy the pleasures of exploring and discovering the Virgin and Leeward islands by foot.

The lengths of the walks are measured in time, not distance. Trails in Europe are gauged by this method, and it is actually a more accurate portrayal of the length and difficulty of an excursion. Depending on the terrain and its difficulty, it can take anywhere from 15 minutes to a full hour to cover one mile.

The average person can comfortably walk two to two and a half miles in one hour on a moderate grade, and this is what the time distances are based upon. Take one or two of the shorter, easier walks and compare the time it took you to complete them to the times given. This will give you a frame of reference to work with. For example, the stated walking time is 40 minutes, but you complete the walk in 30 minutes. Based on this, it should be fairly safe to assume that you will complete a two-hour hike in one hour and 30 minutes, a three-hour trip in about two hours and 15 minutes and so on. Be sure to remember that the stated walking times do not include any rest breaks.

The term **unimproved road** refers to a secondary road, often an unpaved and rutted road suitable only for walking or for a four-wheel-drive vehicle.

An *easy walk* will usually last no more than an hour and has little or no change in elevation.

A walk is rated as *moderate* when there is a gradual change in elevation or it lasts for more than an hour, or both.

When called a *hike*, the excursion can last anywhere from one to several hours. An *easy hike* is almost the same as a moderate walk – gradual changes in elevation, only more of them. (All of the walks and easy hikes should easily be within the range of anyone, even those who are not in the best of shape.)

A *moderate hike* involves a number of ascents and descents on rougher footing and may even include a couple of steep inclines.

A great amount of physical exertion will be needed to complete a *strenuous or ambitious hike*. A number of steep ascents and descents, often on rough, muddy, overgrown, or dangerous terrain, will be encountered on these treks. Strenuous hikes should only be undertaken by experienced hikers in good physical shape.

If the need for *mountaineering skills* is mentioned for a particular hike, it is best not to attempt it unless you have a working knowledge of rock climbing and the use of ropes. Even then, you should probably employ the services of a guide familiar with the area.

All *beach walks* may be considered easy. The walks pointed out in this guide are particularly enjoyable, but there are literally hundreds of other beaches deserving of your time. Those noted are highlighted because they are personal favorites, possess a high degree of historic or scenic value, or are secluded and uncrowded.

A *one-way* outing is just that – you walk in one direction, ending the hike at a different point from where you started. Most of the one-way excursions in this guide begin and end on driveable roads so that you can arrange a car shuttle of some kind. The exceptions are in areas where there are many inter-connecting trails, such as on St. John, Guadeloupe, and Martinique. It will be noted in the text if an excursion is a one-way walk or hike to connect with another trail or trails. At the connecting point, you decide either to walk the new route or to retrace your steps.

On a *round trip* you go to your destination and return via the same route.

A *circuit walk/hike* will take you on a circular route, returning to the starting point. There will be little, if any, rewalking of the same ground.

Precautions

Water: It cannot be emphasized enough – be sure to carry an ample supply of drinking water with you. Remember that you are in the tropics and will be exposed to the hot sun for long periods, which will increase your daily fluid intake considerably. Do not assume that it is safe to drink from flowing springs or crystal clear streams. The waterways of a number of the islands, such as Guadeloupe and Martinique, have been known to harbor a parasitic disease called bilharziasis. While bilharziasis has not been found on every island of the Caribbean, it is still a good idea to avoid swimming in any standing pools or slow-moving waters. Drink only bottled water or water from a treated public water system. It is even possible for this snail-borne parasite to enter the blood stream through the skin and, in some cases, it can cause death.

Snakes: There are snakes living on almost every island, but only Martinique has a poisonous one. Since the fer-de-lance lives and hides in the more remote areas, attacks and bites are rare. You should, however, always be on the lookout because the venom is extraordinarily potent and can cause death in a relatively short time.

The best defense against the fer-de-lance is to hike in a large group or tap the ground in front of you with a stick as you walk. The majority of attacks have occurred when the fer-de-lance is surprised and does not have the time or opportunity to escape.

Plants To Avoid: The small green apple of the manchineel tree is highly poisonous and should never be eaten. It can cause throat constrictions so severe as to be fatal. The sap from its trunk and branches, even the rain run-off from its leaves, may cause a painful rash. This tree is common through-out the Virgins and Leewards. Be sure to have someone point it out to you soon after your arrival.

Also, avoid the sap from the oleander. This poison is so strong that it can taint food cooked over a fire of oleander wood. Although you probably do not have the urge to do so, do not ingest the blossoms of the poinsettia. They, too, contain a highly toxic poison.

Insects: The two most common pests in the Virgins and Leewards, the mosquito and the sand flea, are more of a nuisance than a real problem. Neither is usually encountered in any great numbers, but some beaches or swampy areas have higher concen-trations than other places. For such areas, you should carry a bottle of repellent in your pack.

Sun: Protecting yourself from the concentrated rays of the tropical sun should be a major concern. Increasingly, the consensus in the medical profes-sion is that you should obtain the highest strength sun block lotion available and use it every day, even after you have acquired that long sought-after tan. Remember, a tan is nothing more than your body trying to protect itself from further damage by the sun.

Beach Walking: In the shallow waters of the shoreline there is the possibility of stepping on a sea urchin or sting ray. While the former usually hides in labyrinths of coral caves and will only cause se-vere pain, the latter buries itself underneath the sand (making it hard to detect) and will strike when stepped on, injecting a poison that can lead to serious illness. Also, avoid the coral – it is so sharp that barely touching it may cause a deep cut or gash.

Proper Clothing: Bikinis, swim suits, and light cover-ups may be fine for a beach stroll, but not for hikes to the higher elevations. Even though rain squalls may be short-lived, they will, many times, appear without warning. The mountains and hills are often 8°-10° cooler than the shoreline and the winds, of course, are stronger.

These factors are the perfect ingredients for developing a case of hypothermia. Just because you're in the tropics, don't think it can't happen – most cases occur at 50-60° temperatures. Therefore, always carry a windbreaker/rain jacket and long pants to put on if the need arises.

Unless you suffer from foot, ankle, or leg problems, there's definitely no need to invest in a pair of heavy-duty, mountaineering-type hiking boots for walking and hiking in the Caribbean. Sturdy, comfortable walking, running, or tennis shoes should suffice. When walking in arid places, remember that cactus needles can puncture the sole of a shoe!

Medical Care: The quality of medical care varies from very efficient to non-existent. The best advice is to join the International Association of Medical Assistance to Travelers (IAMAT). This organization furnishes information on which inoculations are required for travel to different parts of the world. A listing of English-speaking doctors and/or medical contacts in the Caribbean is also provided. The address and phone number is:

  ✍ IAMAT
    417 Center Street
    Lewiston, NY 14092
    ☎ 716-754-4883

As this is a nonprofit organization, it would be a nice gesture to include a donation with your request for information so that IAMAT may continue to provide this valuable service.

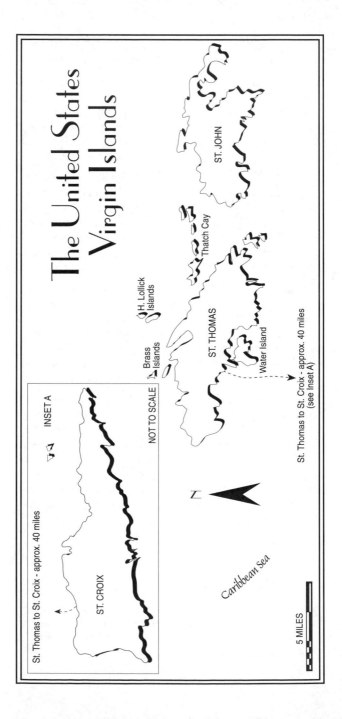

The United States Virgin Islands

The United States Virgin Islands (USVI) are, possibly, the most visited of the Caribbean Islands, lying about 1,100 miles southeast of Miami, Florida. It is estimated they receive at least two million visitors a year. About 50 islands make up the USVI, some large and others just rocks or coral that barely rise above sea level. Most visitors concentrate their efforts on the three largest islands, St. Croix, St. Thomas, and St. John.

The islands are in the direct path of the trade winds, which make the temperature and the weather superb year round. Temperatures average in the mid-80s and the sun shines nearly every day, with an occasional rain squall that almost never lasts more than a half-hour.

There are modern, high-rise hotels with world famous restaurants or bare site campgrounds with picnic tables to accommodate the visitor. No matter where you stay, a tropical wonderland is waiting to be discovered. The islands abound with bougainvillea, oleander, carissa, flamboyant, jasmine, and the territorial flower of the USVI, the ginger Thomas. Orchids of seemingly endless varieties cover each of the islands, as do the red, white, and

The towering century plant.

yellow frangipani. The century plant bloom, growing 10 to 20 feet high in the spring, is also a common sight.

The USVI are a good introduction to the many topographical features found throughout the Caribbean. As a general rule, the lower elevations receive substantially less rainfall than the highlands. Scrub brush and succulents, such as the Turk's cap cactus, are the dominant vegetation in these arid areas. As the elevation changes, so does the vegetation. In just a few hundred feet, the ground can change from sea grape-lined beach to a swampy mangrove thicket to cactus-covered, sandy soil. Higher up, you will discover rolling green meadows followed by hardwood forest. On the taller peaks of the islands, such as Bordeaux Mountain on St. John, a full display of dense, moist tropical rain forest vegetation will be encountered.

On St. John, water island rock – hardened volcanic rock from deep below the ocean –makes up a good amount of the shoreline and is evidence of the violent origins of the Caribbean chain of islands. Huge boulders, scattered at odd places on the hillsides, were literally thrown up from the depths of the earth.

The USVI also provide an introduction to the wildlife of the Caribbean. The mongoose, originally brought to the islands to control the rats that ate the sugarcane, can be seen scurrying through the underbrush. The fierce-looking but harmless iguana scampers away at the first sound of humans. Also rarely seen, but often heard, are the numerous tree frogs that serenade the islands with their nightly chirping. Hawks, pelicans, hummingbirds of radiant colors, soaring tropic birds, frigatebirds, and gulls fill the air, while yellowtail snapper, parrotfish, angelfish, and bluehead dart in and out of the multi-hued coral labyrinths undersea.

History

The Carib Indians greeted Columbus' crew with a barrage of arrows when the Europeans landed on St. Croix in 1493 in search of fresh water. Retreating, Columbus continued north through a maze of islands, dubbing them "Los Virgines," as their beauty and numbers reminded him of the story of St. Ursula and the 11,000 virgins.

For almost a century the Caribs remained the sole inhabitants of the islands. However, in the middle part of the 17th century, the Dutch and British began establishing plantations on St. Croix. In 1650 the Spanish returned to regain possession, but quickly lost it to the French. In less than three years, France leased St. Croix to the Knights of Malta (of Crusading fame). Disenchantment for the Knights came a decade later, and St. Croix was once again turned over to French rule.

While the French continued their interest in St. Croix, the Danish West India and Guinea Company took possession of St. Thomas. The town of Charlotte Amalie was established in 1672, and the rest of the island was divided into neatly parceled out plantations. In 1717, the company expanded to St. John and was joined by a few British settlers who arrived from Tortola in the British Virgin Islands. As on St. Thomas, the Danes turned St. John into a sugarcane-producing island.

Although extensive plantations thrived on St. John, the topography of St. Thomas was too rugged for large-scale agriculture. Lacking the prosperity of a large plantation society, St. Thomas gradually developed into the trade center of the Virgin Islands. Merchant ships, lured by the duty-free status established in the 1770s, began arriving in great numbers by the late 18th century. These, in turn, were followed by buccaneers and pirates, who were tantalized by the riches of the trading vessels and the numerous bays and coves of the islands where they could hide.

In 1733 Denmark purchased St. Croix from the French. However, all was not well on St. John. Tired of the harsh treatment at the hands of their masters, slaves on St. John rebelled against the plantation owners that same year. For six months the slaves ruled the island, slaughtering some of their former masters and destroying many of the plantation buildings. It finally took a company of French soldiers to return the island to its previous owners.

The plantations went through a prosperous period, but with the worldwide decline in cane sugar prices as well as the emancipation of the slaves in 1848, they slowly began to disappear. St. Croix diversified its crops and remained more of an agrarian society than the other two USVI, while tropical growth has now reclaimed much of the land on St. John.

In 1867, the United States first sought to purchase the Virgin Islands from Denmark. The negotiations failed, as did another attempt in 1902. Finally, in 1917, the US purchased all three islands as a defensive base for the Panama Canal.

While there are many reminders of its former owners – Danish architecture, French place names and English customs – the islands are now moving into mainstream American culture. Discos, fast food restaurants, and high-rise hotels are developing rapidly and, with each passing year, the USVI receives more cruise ships and tourists.

St. Croix has historic towns, rural sites, and rolling hills to attract the visitor, St. Thomas has some of the most beautiful beaches in the world and scores of duty-free shops, and St. John has the tropical serenity of Virgin Islands National Park.

Data

Transportation to the USVI: There are direct daily flights from North America to St. Thomas and St. Croix. European connections are usually made through Puerto Rico or Antigua. The USVI may also be reached by air from many of the other nearby islands, such as Sint Maarten, St. Kitts, and the British Virgin Islands. There are daily air and/or sea connections between all three of the largest islands. St. Thomas and, to a lesser degree, St. Croix are popular ports of call for cruise ships. There is no departure tax.

Entry: Proof of citizenship (passport, birth certificate or voter's registration card) is required of US and Canadian citizens. Other nationalities should follow whatever regulations are required by the US for their country.

Currency: The US dollar. Credit cards are readily accepted on St. Thomas, St. Croix, and St. John.

Tourist Information: The USVI have tourist information offices in major cities in the United States and Canada.

In the United States

✍ The USVI Division of Tourism
1270 Avenue of the Americas, Suite 2108
New York, NY 10020, ☎ 212-322-2222

✍ 2655 Le Jeune Road, Suite 907
Coral Gables, FL 33134, ☎ 305-422-7200

✍ 460 Wilshire Blvd., Suite 412
Los Angeles, CA 90010, ☎ 213-738-0138

In Canada

✍ USVI Division of Tourism
3300 Bloor Street, Suite 3120
Center Tower, Toronto, ONT M8X 2X3
☎ 416-233-1414

The US Virgin Islands

In Europe

🖎 **USVI Division of Tourism**
2 Cinnamon Row
Plantation Wharf, York Place
London, SW11 3TW
England, ☎ 0171-978-5262

Each island also has its own tourist information office. On St. John the office is right next to the Cruz Bay dock:

🖎 **St. John Tourist Information Office**
PO Box 200, Cruz Bay, St. John
United States Virgin Islands 00830
☎ 340-776-6450

St. Croix has two tourist information offices. One is in Christiansted, the other in Frederiksted. Both are located close to the forts of each city. Their mailing addresses are:

🖎 **St. Croix Tourist Information Office**
Frederiksted Custom House Building
Strand St., Frederiksted, St. Croix
United States Virgin Islands 00840
☎ 340-772-0357

🖎 PO Box 4538
Christiansted, St. Croix
United States Virgin Islands 00822
☎ 340-773-0495

On St. Thomas, the official tourism office is on Tolbod Gade, one block from the waterfront and next to Emancipation Gardens. The office provides a hospitality lounge where you may rest. If you've taken advantage of the duty-free shopping in Charlotte Amalie, it also provides a check-in service for packages/shopping bags.

🖎 **St. Thomas Tourist Information Office**
PO Box 6400
Charlotte Amalie, St. Thomas
United States Virgin Islands 00804
☎ 340-774-8784

Driving: Rental cars are available on all three islands. A valid driver's license is required. Mopeds may also be rented, and St. Thomas and St. Croix have bus service between major points.

You may be in the United States but, in a holdover from Danish ownership, driving is on the left!

Language: English.

Walking and Hiking Guide Companies: The National Park Service on St. John leads regularly scheduled, organized walking and hiking tours. Information on times, difficulty, etc. may be obtained at the visitors' center in Cruz Bay or by contacting:

✒ Superintendent, USVI National Park
PO Box 6310 Estate Nazareth
Charlotte Amalie, St. Thomas
United States Virgin Islands 00802
☎ 340-776-6201

For an individual hike or tour get in touch with the tourist office in Cruz Bay or the Maho Bay Campground. Either should be able to put you in contact with a qualified guide.

The St. Croix Environmental Association (SEA) works on many ecological concerns, such as programs to monitor sewage and other water pollution problems, promote recycling, and provide educational material and expert testimony on numerous issues. It is a very active and effective group, also sponsoring regularly scheduled natural history walks and hikes to numerous sites on the island. You may write to the nonprofit organization at:

✒ SEA
PO Box 3839
Christiansted, St. Croix
United Stated Virgin Islands 00820
☎ 340-773-1989

Much like SEA on St. Croix, the nonprofit Environmental Association of St Thomas-St. John (EAST) also promotes ecological awareness, encourages responsible legislation, and sponsors guided outings:

✍ EAST
PO Box 12379
Charlotte Amalie, St. Thomas
United States Virgin Islands 00801
☎ 340-772-7545

On either St. Croix or St. Thomas, the environmental associations or the tourist offices can put
you in contact with qualified escorts for an individual tour or hike.

Camping Areas: Established by the National Park
Service, Cinnamon Bay Campground on St. John
offers cottages and wall tents completely equipped
with beds, linen, stoves, and all cooking and eating
utensils. A few bare sites are also available for those
with their own tent and equipment.

➤ **Special Note:** This is an extremely
popular place and reservations must be
made almost a year in advance!

1. ✍ Cinnamon Bay Campground
PO Box 720, St. John
United States Virgin Islands 00831
☎ 340-776-6330

Maho Bay Camp is also on St. John. It offers completely equipped, multi-room tents, but there are no
bare sites.

➤ **Special Note:** This is another very
popular campground. Make reservations as early as possible.

2. ✍ Maho Bay Camp
PO Box 310, St. John
United States Virgin Islands 00831
☎ 340-776-6504

3. The Howard M. Walk Boy Scout Camp on St. Croix
will allow non-scouts to use their camp. Unfortunately, you cannot make arrangements until you
arrive on the island. Informal camping is also permitted on some of the beaches, such as the one at
4. Cramer Park. The authorities have no rigid rules

for pitching your tent; it depends upon the time and situation. Therefore, it is recommended that you have a back-up plan for accommodations.

Recommended Readings

📖 *A Guide to the Natural History of St. John* by Doris Jaden

📖 *St. John Backtime* by Ruth Hull Low and Rafael Valls

📖 *The Virgin Islands Alive* by H & D Greenberg

📖 *Romantic History of St. Croix* by Florence Lewisohn

📖 *Rape of the American Virgins* by Edward O'Neil

📖 *Don't Stop the Carnival* by Herman Wouk

📖 *Night of the Silent Drums* by John Lorenzo Anderson

📖 *Adventure Guide to the Virgin Islands* by Harry S. Pariser

📖 *Virgin Islands Birdlife* by S. and N. Scott

📖 *Inside American Paradise* by June W. Brown

📖 *Diving the Virgin Islands* by W. Lynn Seldon, Jr.

The US Virgin Islands

There are local newspapers on St. Croix and St. Thomas and these offer the best insight into daily life in the USVI. The *Avis* is printed on St. Croix, while St. Thomas has *The Daily News*.

The National Park Visitors' Center in Cruz Bay, St. John, has a good selection of books on the history, geology, flora, and fauna of St. John and the other islands. The Bookie in Christiansted and Trader Bob's Dockside Books in Gallows Bay, St. Croix keep well supplied with numerous natural and human history books and other guides to the USVI and the Caribbean.

Saint Croix

St. Croix, the largest island of the USVI, has a terrain much gentler than St. Thomas and St. John. The rolling fields have given the island a rich agricultural heritage and, as a result, the pace of life is more relaxed here than on St. Thomas. Cattle graze on the hillsides, goats scamper up the rocks, and fruit and vegetable gardens cover much of the island.

Fewer tourists are attracted to St. Croix than St. Thomas, which means its beaches and other attractions are less congested and better for undisturbed exploration. Scattered throughout the island are the remains of former vast plantations, the crumbling ruins now covered by purple blooms of the bougainvillea.

Although St. Croix does not receive enough precipitation to qualify as having a true rain forest, its northwestern section does have some rain forest-type vegetation such as giant kapok and mahogany trees; a vast variety of orchids and epiphytes live on these and other host trees. In contrast to the lush vegetation of the rain forest, cactus and desert-type plants thrive on the arid eastern point of the island.

Just north of St. Croix is Buck Island Reef National Monument. The island invites exploration on foot, while an underwater trail marks the beauty of the coral reef.

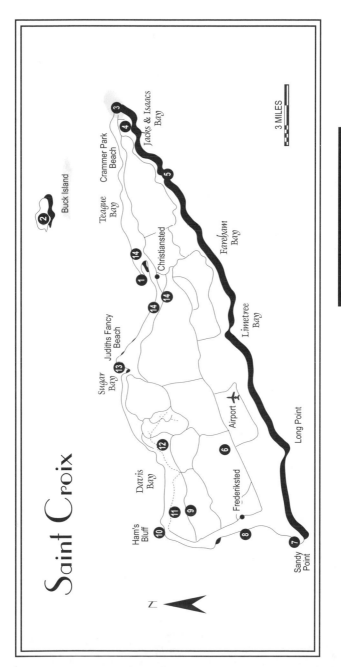

Saint Croix

N

Buck Island

Ham's Bluff

Davis Bay

Sugar Bay

Judiths Fancy Beach

Teague Bay

Crammer Park Beach

Jacks & Isaacs Bay

Christiansted

Fareham Bay

Limetree Bay

Long Point

Airport

Frederiksted

Sandy Point

3 MILES

Until recently, St. Croix was all but overlooked by walkers and hikers. But now, due to the influence of active environmental organizations and the local desire to protect and designate natural and scenic areas, the island is becoming increasingly popular as an outdoor destination.

1. A Walking Tour of Christiansted

Christiansted, the largest town on St. Croix, offers much for the walker. Begin your tour of the down-town district at Fort Christiansvaern. Built largely of yellow bricks used as ballast in ships sailing from Denmark, the fort was completed in 1749. Despite several alterations, the garrison is an excellent and well-preserved example of the military architecture the Danes employed in the New World. A pamphlet available on the fort's grounds will help explain its barracks, ammunition magazine, kitchen, dun-geons, and more.

From the fort, walk along D. Hamilton Jackson Park (named for a labor leader and judge) and pass by the Old Danish Customs House, which dates from 1751 and presently houses the National Park Service offices. Continue along the walkway to the Scale House, constructed in the mid-1800s to weigh and inspect all imports and exports. The Visitors' Center is now located in this building and is the best place to obtain detailed information on St. Croix. The Scale House is at the end of King Street, which you'll now follow, passing by a couple of short blocks of arcaded buildings – one of which is known as the Alexander Hamilton House. Local lore has it that he once worked as a clerk here.

Further along King Street is Government House. It was originally two separate buildings constructed in the 18th century, but they were joined together in the 1830s to become government offices. Be sure to check out the inner courtyard of small gardens and pools and the formal staircase leading to the second-story ballroom. Across the street from Government House is the Lord God of Saboth Lutheran Church, built in the 1740s. The Gothic Revival tower was added sometime in the 1830s. Walk one more block on King Street and make a right onto King Cross Street to arrive at Florence Williams Library which, like Fort Christiansvaern, is built of Danish sailing ship ballast.

Retrace your steps back to King Street, which you will cross, and continue to Company Street where you'll encounter the hustle and bustle of Christiansted's open-air Market Place. Walk along Company Street (heading back toward the fort) and stop in Apothecary Hall, a pharmacy of the 1700s and now a place of offices and shops. Beyond the hall is the US Post Office, housed in the former headquarters of the Danish West India and Guinea Company. Its courtyard was once a slave auction site. Across the street is Steeple Building, the original home of the Lord God of Saboth Lutheran Church and currently a notable museum with exhibits on numerous facets of Crucian history.

The last stop on the tour is the small but fascinating St. Croix Aquarium in the Caravelle Arcade – worth a stop, especially if you have children.

The walking tour comes to an end as you cross the street to return to the fort and its parking area.

2. The Buck Island Walk

Walking time: 2 hours to circumnavigate the island

This mile-long, 865-acre national monument lies off the northeastern coast of St. Croix and is a place not to be missed. Charter companies, most of them based in Christiansted, offer daily excursions to the island. They range from half-day trips in glass bottom boats to sailing yacht tours complete with cocktail lunches and guides for the underwater trails.

Buck Island has been a monument since the mid-20th century. It was once the site of much human activity, although it was nearly denuded in the 18th century as goats browsed on the artificially created meadows. The goats overgrazed the land, destroying much of the tropical vegetation. The goats and other human intrusions have now been eliminated and the land is returning, somewhat, to its natural state.

Most people come to Buck Island only to snorkel the marked underwater reef trail (which should be done; it takes about 45 minutes). This gives the island a solitude that makes for pleasurable exploring. Buck Island has white sand beaches, and a walk of the circumference will take no more than two hours. The interior of the island should also be explored, and there is a trail that goes through the re-emerging tropical vegetation to the top of the island. There are excellent views of Buck Island, St. Croix, and the string of sail and excursion boats crossing the azure-blue waters between the two islands. A number of charter companies stop here, and it may be the most accessible deserted island in the Caribbean. Do not pass up this opportunity.

Expect to spend a full day sailing to and from the island and exploring its reef, beaches, and vegetation.

3. The Cramer Park - Point Udall - Isaac Bay Walk

Walking time: 2 hours, round trip

To reach the easternmost point of the United States, take the East End Road (Route 82) to its second junction with Route 60. Continue eastward to Cramer Park and begin the walk here.

The beach has a picnic area, is lined all around with sea grapes, and the swimming is good in the calm waters. Continue east along the rutted and rough dirt road through an arid and windswept countryside. The road ends at Point Udall, the easternmost point of the United States. Cactus, other succulents, and numerous wildflowers grow in great numbers on this point overlooking the rich blue waters of the Caribbean Sea. Spend some time exploring this area and you will discover a dirt track dropping down to East End Bay on St. Croix's southern coast. For almost exclusive privacy, walk the sands to the west and follow an obvious trail up and over a small headland to Isaac Bay. This beach is so inaccessible and secluded that, on some days, it is used by those who enjoy bathing *au naturel*.

View from Point Udall.

4. The Goat Hills to Jack Bay Hike

Walking time: less than 2 hours, round trip

Just past Cramer Park (see Walk #3 for directions) is a walkable dirt road that climbs the dry slopes of Goat Hills. The high point of the area, Sugarloaf Hill (672 feet), may be reached by turning left onto the only road ascending off the dirt track. The summit affords grand views across the eastern portion of St. Croix, north to St. John, St. Thomas, and the British Virgin Islands, east to Point Udall, and south overlooking Isaac and Jack bays. Return to the main dirt road, bear left and descend to isolated Jack Bay, whose white sands and rolling surf will tempt you to linger for an hour or more.

(Beachcombers should walk eastward along the bay to cross over Isaac Point and arrive at Isaac Bay, see Walk #3.)

5. The South Side Beaches Walk

Walking time: 3 hours, round trip

Leading off the Southshore Road (Route 60) and the Southside Road (Route 62) are quite a number of dirt roads and tracks going down to the secluded and uncrowded beaches of the southern coast. If you are looking for a prolonged trek, it is possible to walk from Rod Bay, along Robin Bay, swing around to Great Bay and even walk around brackish Salt Pond for some quality bird watching. You should plan on at least three hours for this easy hike.

Further west along the southern coastline are numerous other undeveloped beaches, and some of the best ones include Spring Bay, Halfpenny Beach, and Manchenil Bay.

6. The Botanical Garden Walk

The St. George Village Botanical Garden is east of Frederiksted on Centerline Road (Route 70). (Some maps identify this as Queen Mary Highway.) The 17 acres of the garden are on the site of an old rum factory and workers' village.

Winding trails meander through areas of open countryside and landscaped plots ranging from cactus gardens to oleander and flamboyant trees in full bloom to the giant kapok trees of the rain forest. Since having to rebuild much of the gardens after the devastation of Hurricane Hugo in 1989, the emphasis has been on cultivating plants and trees native to St. Croix. On your walk you'll be exposed to many of these, such as Christmas orchid, naked wood, prickly pear cactus, San Bartolome tree, sea grape, lignum-vitae, and calabash trees.

Spaced around the gardens are the buildings of the 19th-century village. The blacksmith shop has been restored and even the gift shop is housed in one of the factory's reconstructed buildings. The structures that remain in ruins, such as the workers' quarters, have been stabilized and are now covered by creeping bougainvillea vines and other tropical growth.

The quiet, cool paths of the Botanical Garden can be a welcome relief from the sometimes noisy streets of Christiansted and the glare of the tropical sun. An hour or a full day can pass by quickly while enjoying the hibiscus, frangipani, poinsettia, shrubs, cactus, and trees that line the pathways. Business hours vary, so it's probably best to contact the tourist office for current information; there is a small admission fee.

As an excursion that combines the history of the Caribbean islands with the beauty of nature, this is a highly recommended walk.

7. The Sandy Point National Wildlife Refuge Walk

Follow Route 70 south from Frederiksted to where it makes a 90° left turn and heads east toward Christiansted. At this point you will want to continue straight on Route 661 to its 90° intersection with Route 66. Now, turn right onto a dirt road. Drive along this road, keeping left at the first intersection. Avoid another road just a few hundred yards later (this one coming in from the left) and in 0.9 mile you will arrive at a gate.

Established in 1984, the 398-acre refuge is usually open to the public only Saturdays and Sundays. (Regulations are subject to change; it might be a good idea to check with the St. Croix Environmental Association in Gallows Bay for the most up-to-date information.) If the gate is shut, it may mean the refuge area is closed to protect nesting turtles or for some other environmental reason. If this is the case, turn around and take another one of the walks listed for St. Croix, knowing that you are doing your part to protect a fragile world. However, if you find the gate open, continue to drive, passing along the shore of Westend Salt Pond, where you might see plovers plowing the water in search of a meal. Just beyond the pond is a dirt road to the left leading to a small parking area and a short trail out to the beach. You may leave you car here or continue along the dirt track and park on any of the other side roads.

The pristine beach at Sandy Point.

Now you can really explore on foot miles and miles of continuous, unspoiled beach with, usually, very few people around. Brown pelicans dive for food, terns share the airwaves with them, and ghost crabs scurry from their small holes to wet their bodies in the rolling surf.

Sandy Point National Wildlife Refuge is a grand place to spend a full day walking, swimming, relaxing and picnicking.

　　Be aware that vandalism and robberies have occurred here. It would be wise to go with a group of people.

8. A Walking Tour of Frederiksted

The walking tour of St. Croix's second principal city begins like the tour of Christiansted – in a fort. Fort Frederik, named in honor of King Frederik V of Denmark, was built during the latter half of the 18th century. Inside the fort are historical exhibits and an art gallery.

From the fort, walk to the foot of the pier, where you'll find the old customs house and the Division of Tourism's Visitor's Bureau. In the arcaded buildings along the waterfront (Strand Street) is Worldwide Calling. Here, you may place an international call and, if the Visitor's Bureau is closed, pick up many free brochures or purchase a book or two about St. Croix and the rest of the Caribbean. Further along Strand Street is Victoria House, dating from 1803 or earlier. Much of the house was burned during the uprisings of 1878, but the elaborate gingerbread trim you see was part of the original structure. Continue on Strand Street for another full block and make a left onto King Cross Street. In four short blocks you will come to St. Paul's Anglican Church. You have to admire the tenacity of this building as it has survived numerous hurricanes since its 1812 construction.

Taking Prince Street to the north, pass by the Old Danish School, which dates from the early 1800s. Across from this building is Frederiksted's Market Place, which has existed on this same spot since the city's earliest days. Diagonally across the street from the market is St. Patrick's Catholic Church. See if you can make out the inscription on its weather-worn entrance stone.

Following Prince Street from the church and making a left onto Lagoon Street will return you to the fort.

9. The Rain Forest Hike

Walking time: 2½ hours, one way

To reach this hike, follow Route 631 north out of Frederiksted to the intersection of Routes 63 and 76. Continue north on Route 63 and make a right turn onto Creque Dam Road (Route 58). Have your driver drop you off here and begin the walk.

Follow the road through the Sprat Hall Plantation and gain altitude as you enter the rain forest in approximately one mile. Technically, the area does not receive enough precipitation to be classified as a rain forest, yet it does have the look, feel, and much of the vegetation of a true rain forest. Soon, you'll pass by 150-foot Creque Dam, whose lake has now been drained. You are passing through the grounds of a private estate; please respect the owners' wishes by staying on the road. While keeping a sharp eye out for a darting mongoose or two, enjoy the yellow cedar, wild lilies, and other enchantments of the forest.

Continue on the road through the kapok, cocoa, monkey pistol, and turpentine trees and arrive at an intersection; keep to the right. Open meadows permit views onto central St. Croix as you bear right onto Annaly Road (Route 765) and descend. (The Scenic Road West Hike is to the left; see Walk #11.)

Gradually lose elevation and, three miles into the hike, keep left on Annaly Road when Route 763 comes in from the right. In a landscape almost reminiscent of rural Virginia –wooded mountain ridges rising above green fields dotted with cattle and swine – you will come to the end of your four-mile hike. Have your shuttle car pick you up at the intersection of Annaly Road and Mahogany Road (Route 76).

The Rain Forest Hike follows roads that are passable by car. However, they see very little traffic, are unimproved for the most part, and the forest is better explored on foot. The gradual changes in elevation make this a moderate hike.

10. The Ham's Bay and Bluff Hike

Walking time: 1½ hours, round trip

Ham's Bay is reached by following paved Route 63 past Creque Dam Road (see Walk #9 for directions) until it turns to dirt at the concrete pillars marking the beginning of the Scenic Road West Hike (see Walk #11). Your car may be left here.

Rock formations at Ham's Bay.

Walk east along the beach. Ham's Bay beach holds many surprises for those interested in shelling and watching tidal pool life caught among the interesting rock formations. The waters are also reported to have some of the best fishing around St. Croix.

To reach the lighthouse perched on the bluff, follow a paved road uphill to some fenced-off government property. Walk around the outside of the fence, cross a small footbridge and begin what one Crucian described as a "healthy climb" to the lighthouse. This spot offers good views of Annaly Bay and the Caribbean Sea.

The US Virgin Islands

11. The Scenic Road West Hike

Walking time: 5 hours, one way

This hike begins at the same point as the Ham's Bay and Bluff Hike (see Walk #10). The Scenic Road West (Route 78) is a dirt road that is passable by car, although four-wheel-drives are recommended to negotiate the rough terrain. You should encounter little traffic on the hike and will certainly experience more on foot than in a vehicle. Follow the dirt road gradually uphill from the concrete pillars, passing by ginger Thomas and tan-tan. The road becomes steeper and, in some places, is paved to improve grip for vehicles. Slight views to the north give you a hint of the terrain further on.

In one mile there are grandstand views into the deep cup of the rich, dark green Caledonia Valley and its surrounding ridgelines. The road now passes through private property (so please don't do any off-road wanderings) in a dense forest of mahogany, kapok, Spanish cedar, and turpentine trees. Giving color to the forest are the wild lilies and orchids. Thick vines, which begin growing on high branches, drape down to settle themselves on the damp soil of the rain forest floor. Be on the lookout for Christmas bush, which can cause a poison ivy-like rash. Stinging nettle is also abundant here.

In 2.5 miles you will have the opportunity to take a two- to three-hour, strenuous, but worthwhile side trip. At the top of the open ridgeline, go through a gate on your left, being sure to close it behind you. Make an immediate right and descend very, very steeply on a dirt road. About the time your knees feel ready to crumple, you'll see remnants of a sugar mill dating from 1796. Here, you'll bear right and head down to Black Rock Beach and Wills Bay. Both beaches are perfect for isolated sunbathing. Returning to the sugar mill, you can then descend through an experimental mahogany forest to the sandy strip of beach along Annaly Bay before returning to the Scenic Road West. If you have the time, take this side trip – many Crucians consider it the finest walk on their island.

Continuing along the main road, you will come to an intersection; stay to the left. (A right turn would lead to Creque Dam Road and Walk #9.) Continuing on you route, a rather new housing development will, sadly, break your solitude, but it does permit excellent views across much of the island.

After 5.6 miles of hiking along the Scenic Road West, there will be a deeply rutted road to the left. Five minutes on that road brings you to Bodkins Mill and an Olympian 360° view of Blue Mountain to the east, Davis Bay to the north, and the green rolling turf of the Carambola Golf Course to the south. Continue on the main road, descending by mahogany and teak trees. Vistas to the south open up as you come to the intersection with Route 69 and the end of this 7.5-mile hike.

Due to its length, isolation, and the changes in elevation, this hike is recommended only for those who are in good condition and are willing to devote a major portion of the day to the excursion. However, nowhere else on St. Croix is it possible to walk for so long without meeting many other people or seeing constant reminders of civilization. Do not underestimate the length of this hike.

12. The Scenic Road Central Hike

Walking time: 2½ hours, one way

This hike, which passes just below the two highest points on St. Croix, makes use of the middle section of the Scenic Road (Route 78). To reach it, take Route 631 north from Frederiksted to its intersection with Route 63. Take Route 63 north and you'll soon make a right onto Mahogany Road (Route 76). As Mahogany Road is one of the most scenic drives on St. Croix, enjoy the trip through the rain forest and turn left onto River Road (Route 69). Just past the Carambola Golf Course is the Scenic Road Central

Hike on the right. (To the left is the Scenic Road West Hike; see Walk #11.)

Begin this hike by ascending the dirt road (Route 78) on the eastern side of River Road. With occasional views out across the St. Croix acreage, you may also see indigo buntings flying around the branches of native rubber and sandbox trees. Higher above you there might be red-tailed hawks soaring on thermals rising from the valleys below. Orange-yellow passion fruit dots the otherwise

green foliage lining the road. Passing from a moist to a dry forest, the trek makes a hard swing to the left and descends. (The private road right climbs Blue Mountain.)

Bromeliads drape from the rocks and soon the road becomes paved as it weaves around several private homes and comes to an end at Canaan Road (Route 73).

The prickly trunk of the sandbox.

This is a good excursion for the adventurous. It does gain and lose quite a bit of elevation, and the maze of roads and paths near Blue Mountain can be confusing. If you should become disoriented, do not be alarmed. Simply follow one of the roads downhill and you will reach a paved highway within an hour or two. Do not let these cautions deter you from this hike. This trip showcases the great variety of scenic wonders on St. Croix.

13. The Salt River Bay Walk

Walking time: 45 minutes for the complete circuit

Dedicated in 1991, the Salt River Bay Historical Park and Ecological Preserve boasts the only documented landing of Christopher Columbus on what is now land owned by the United States. Artifacts found on the site date human habitation as far back as the second century A.D. Today, the estuary and its mangrove thickets provide habitat and nesting sites for migrating birds and several endangered species, including the peregrine falcon and roseate tern.

The bay may be reached by following Northside Road (Route 75) west from Christiansted for several miles. Make a right onto Route 751 and drive to the end, where you'll see the gate for Estate Judith Fancy. Even though this is private property, you'll be permitted access to the trailhead. Continue driving the maze of roads through the subdivision until you reach the final house. Park your car well off the pavement.

A clearly worn trail ascends several feet to an old dirt road on which you'll turn toward the water. The small knoll you are descending was named Cabo de las Flechas (Cape of the Arrows) in 1493 by Columbus after he met with a hostile welcome from the Amerindians living on the island. This is the first recorded conflict between peoples of the Old and the New Worlds.

Once you're on the shore, bear right to discover the tidal pools and driftwood along the multicolored boulders, known as "Easter Rocks" by some Crucians. After exploring, return to the dirt road and walk toward the mouth of the bay. Rounding the small spit of sand, be careful where you step. This is a nesting site for the endangered least tern. Continue on past the inner lagoon and take another dirt track to the left, which will return you to your starting point.

If you wish, continue beyond the second dirt track to explore a portion of the largest mangrove system re-

The US Virgin Islands

maining in the United States Virgin Islands. Lining
the eastern section of the bay, the area will doubt-
less wet your feet, but you might catch a glimpse of
a white tail deer.

14. Walks on Resort and Hotel Grounds

Several of the tourist accommodations on St. Croix
are situated on meticulously maintained grounds
and these areas should not be overlooked as good
opportunities for enjoyable walks.

   It is common courtesy to ask permission
before enjoying the grounds of any hotel
if you are not a registered guest.

The Gardens of Colony Cove are not large, but
are packed tightly with flowers, trees, vines, and
other plants. It is definitely worth it to take a walk
here, especially if you are new to the Caribbean.
Much of the vegetation is signed and you will learn
to identify such things as cashew trees, cattle
tongue, Surinam cherry trees, red ginger, ixora, and
firecracker. You'll soon be able to point out bougainvillea, hibiscus, frangipani, and bird of paradise to
other first-time visitors. Colony Cove is also involved in the environmental issues of St. Croix and,
as such, its Ecocenter has books and exhibits concerning Caribbean seashells and an interesting display about herbology on the island over the years.

The Buccaneer Hotel is on the rolling grounds of
a 17th-century sugar plantation. It includes a golf
course, three excellent beaches, a small exercise
area, a two-mile jogging trail, and some of the original plantation buildings.

The 24 acres of the **Nature Conservancy's Estate
Little Princess** has two former plantation great
houses, an environmental education center, and
several short paths leading to a fine white sand
beach. It does not, however, offer accommodations.

Saint Thomas

St. Thomas, the second largest Virgin, is the most visited of the three main islands. Charlotte Amalie, the capital of the USVI, is also the most frequented cruise ship port of call of any city in the Caribbean. It is not uncommon for as many as five giant cruise ships a day to arrive in the harbor, their passengers swarming the streets of the city in search of duty-free bargains.

Magens Bay, one of many azure-blue swimming spots on St. Thomas.

The island possesses arguably some of the most beautiful beaches in the world and, even though many are extremely crowded, others are secluded – sometimes not seeing more than two or three people a day.

The lowlands of the northern and southern coasts are separated by a rugged mountain ridgeline that runs east to west along the central portion of the island. In the mountains are the larger trees and lusher vegetation; along the coastline are the palms, cactus plants, sea grapes, and mangroves. Ginger Thomas, the showy official flower of the USVI, seems to grow everywhere, as does the trailing vio-

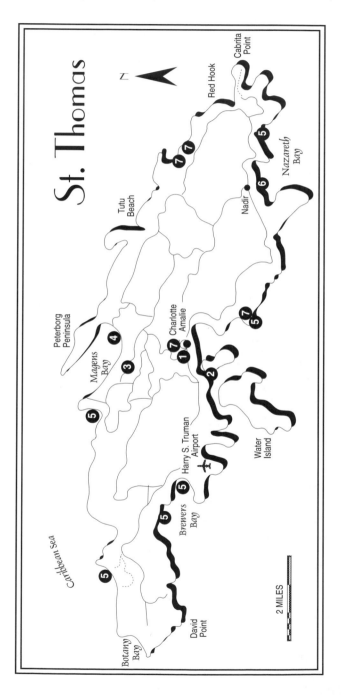

let, fuschia, orange, and pink blooms of the bougainvillea.

Special Walk: This walk along the mountain crest
should not be missed. Crown Mountain Road (Route
33) offers good views, the Mountain Top complex
(highest point on St. Thomas), and Fairchild Park, a
bit of tropical greenery and a rest spot. East on Route
40 is Drake's Seat, the famous view from which Sir
Francis Drake supposedly watched for boats sailing
between the USVI and the BVI. Drake's Seat has a
commanding view of Magens Bay, Peterborg Peninsula, and the eastern hills. Skyline Drive (part of
Route 40) has good views all around. This is a recommended walk, but remember that these are main
highways and have a lot of traffic. Exercise caution
while walking.

1. A Walking Tour of Charlotte Amalie

Walking time: 2 to 3 hours

The best place to begin is right on the waterfront.
The wide walkway is a good spot to stand and watch
sailboats and commercial ships working their way
through the busy harbor. Along the waterfront are
some shops, but the most interesting buys here are
freshly squeezed fruit juice or a coconut that will be
opened for you with a machete by one of many street
vendors.

Go west along the harbor to Nye Tvaer Gade, turn
right for one block, then make another right on
Kronprindsens Gade to arrive at the stately and impressive Catholic Cathedral. The doors and wood-
work are worth stopping at to take a closer look. If
you are feeling particularly energetic, ask directions
through the maze of small streets that go up the
steep side of Berg Hill to the Danish Consulate. This
building, which has an excellent view of the whole
harbor area, is a fine example of the Danish colonial
architecture of the 1800s that borrowed heavily from
the Greek Revival style.

From the consulate, return to the church and head east along Kronprindsens Gade to arrive at the open air market square. The large metal roof over the market place came from a 19th-century European railway station. This was the site of one of the busiest slave markets of the 18th century, but it now becomes a hive of activity on Saturday mornings when fresh fruit and vegetables arrive from gardens all over the island. The street you have been following becomes Dronningens Gade (locally known as Main Street) at the Market Square. Continue on it for a block to the three-storied Enid M. Baa Library, constructed in the mid-1800s as a private residence. Another block of walking and you will be at the home of French impressionist painter, Camille Pissaro. Pissaro was born on St. Thomas in 1830 and lived upstairs in this building (which is now the Tropicana Perfume Shop) before moving to Paris. He lived there until his death in 1903, remaining a Danish citizen in rememberance of his beloved Virgin Islands.

You are now in the heart of the shopping district. There are literally dozens of stores lining Main Street and stretching out into quaint alleys and squares. Anything from jewelry to electronics to tableware can be purchased duty free on St. Thomas. From Main Street, turn left onto Radets Gade for two blocks and come to Crystal Gade and the Synagogue of Berecha V'Shalom V'Gemilath Hasidim. It was built by Sephardic Jews in 1833 on the site of several previously destroyed structures and is reputed to be the second oldest synagogue in the New World. Sand on the floor is symbolic of the Jews' flight from Jerusalem.

Continue east on Crystal Gade for one block to the St. Thomas Reformed Church which, like the Danish Consulate, was constructed in the 1800s and makes use of the Greek Revival style of architecture. Proceed on Crystal Gade for one block, turn right onto Garden Street and in a half-block climb the stairs to Kongens Gade.

Near the top of the steps is Hotel 1829. Originally built as a mansion for a sea captain, the hotel opens up to a flower-draped courtyard that has become a favorite local lunch spot. Just beyond the hotel are the 99 Steps, the remnants of many such step "streets" that used to criss-cross the hillsides of Charlotte Amalie. At the top is Crown House, erected in the mid-1700s as a residence for Danish government officials. Also home to two past governors, the stately manor is now a private residence. Not far from Crown House, along Lille Taarne Gade, is a building of ironwork trim and yellow ballast brick. Once a parsonage, it is now a small restaurant and hotel. Beyond this are the grounds of Blackbeard's Castle Hotel.

Go back down the 99 Steps, turn left, and walk for a block to arrive at the three-story masonry Government House. This neo-classical building was built in 1867 and is now the residence of the governor of the Virgin Islands. Visitors are allowed on the first and second floors, which contain murals and other noteworthy artwork. Eastward a few steps on Kongens Gade you'll pass Moron House, built in the late 1800s, and the Lieutenant Governor's Office, dating from the mid-1800s. Next to this is Knud Hanson Alley, which you may use to tour Seven Arches Museum, the restored 18th-century home of a Danish Craftsman.

Return to Government House, go down the stairs to Norre Gade, and take a right to the Frederick Lutheran Church, constructed in the early 19th century. Next to the church is the Jacob Lind House. Also built in the early 19th century, this two-story structure has served as a private residence, school, retirement home, post office, and parish house.

Turn left onto Tolbod Gade and reach the US Post Office, which has wall murals by Stephen Dohanes, cover artist for the *Saturday Evening Post*. Across the street is the Grand Hotel. It was originally built as a three-story Greek Revival structure in 1840, but the third floor was lost to hurricane and fire. It now contains offices and shops. Cross the street and walk through Emancipation Gardens, which commemorate the freeing of the slaves in 1848. The pavilion is the site of occasional concerts and other outdoor entertainment. Beyond the gardens, take a tour of Fort Christian. Built in the 1660s, it is believed to be the oldest structure in Charlotte Amalie. The fort now houses a small museum with good displays of Arawak and Carib artifacts. Across the street from the fort is the Legislative Building, constructed as barracks by the Danes. This Italian Renaissance building is presently home to the Virgin Islands Senate. (The public is permitted to observe legislative sessions.)

The walking tour of Charlotte Amalie ends back on the waterfront.

2. The Hassel Island Walk

Walking time: just under 2 hours, round trip

Hassel Island, one mile long and part of the National Park system, lies just off the coast in St. Thomas Harbor. It has a couple of good beaches, and the interior features the ruins of Fort Cowell and its associated batteries. Since few people ever visit here, you should find it pleasantly uncrowded.

Hassel Island can be reached only by boat. You should be able to hire one in Charlotte Amalie. Better yet, strike up a conversation with the skipper of a private yacht and have yourself invited on a trip over to the island.

3. The Botanical Gardens Walk

Smaller than other gardens, the Estate Saint Peter Greathouse Botanical Gardens is still well worth a visit. Situated on the grounds of a plantation dating back to the 1800s, the gardens are, in part, traversed by an elevated walkway, permitting you to stroll by the hundreds of identified tropical plants.

The plantation's greathouse has been painstakingly rebuilt, using stonework to accent the traditional Caribbean architecture. Attached to it is an observation platform providing a remarkable view of more than 20 islands surrounding St. Thomas, all of which are identified on plaques. This is a great spot to orient yourself among the myriad islands that make up the Virgin Islands. A fee is charged for admission to the gardens.

4. The Magens Bay Beach Walk

Take Route 35 north out of Charlotte Amalie to its end at Magens Bay. Although this is an extremely popular and often crowded beach, it would be a mistake not to walk along what *National Geographic* has determined to be "one of the 10 most beautiful beaches in the world." The emerald-green waters, surrounded by sea grape and palm trees, make this a highly recommended walk.

Fishing nets drying in the sun at Magens Bay beach.

At one end of the beach be sure to visit the more than 125 species in an arboretum designed in 1908. Having fallen into disrepair, it is once again open to the pubic, thanks to the efforts of the Rotary Club of Charlotte Amalie.

5. Beach Walks

On an island famous for its fun in the sun and sand, Magens Bay is obviously not the only beach worthy of your walking attentions. Brewers Bay beach, close to the University of the Virgin Islands, is known as the place to go beachcombing for thousands of small seashells. Further west is Perseverance Bay, a short hike from the road. Also only accessible by foot – a walk of half a mile – is Stumpy Bay on the northwestern coast. Hull Bay, next door to Magens Bay, is shaded by palms and beckons snorkelers with its offshore reef. If you would have suntanning companions, head to either Secret Harbour or Morningstar beach. Both have resorts and hotels adjacent that provide plenty of bodies to watch as you stroll along.

6. The Benner Bay Salt Pond at Compass Point Walk

Walking time: 30 minutes, round trip

Like wetlands, salt ponds and mangroves are some of the most important ecological systems in the world. The shallow ponds produce an extraordinary amount of organic material, providing nutrients to millions of small aquatic creatures. With the movement of the tides, these nutrients and creatures move back and forth between the pond and the mangroves lining the seashore. Thus begins the first link in the food chain which reaches far out into the oceans.

Thanks to the efforts of volunteers from the Rotary Club of St. Thomas-East, one of these areas is now easily accessible to the public. Benner Bay Salt Pond is reached by taking Route 38 east from Charlotte Amalie. Make a right onto Route 32 at the Fort Mylner Shopping Center. When you pass the junction with Route 30, begin looking for the right turn to Benner Bay and Compass Point. This is an ever-changing part of the island and nature can sometimes overtake the best efforts by volunteers to keep the trail system in good shape. Ask about current conditions at the visitor center in Charlotte Amalie before starting out on a hike.

The trail begins by passing through an area where native plants have been tagged and identified, some with additional information as to their function in the natural world. Continuing, reach a raised boardwalk permitting you to walk over the surface of the salt pond and out to two blinds. From inside these, you may unobtrusively observe life in the shallow waters. The walkway will also bring you by mangroves which, in this area, includes all three types – red, white, and black. The underwater roots of the trees are covered by algae, sponges, tunicates, and barnacles, which give nourishment to immature fish, such as snappers, groupers, and grunts. They will grow to adulthood safe within the twisted roots, before venturing out into the oceans.

➤ Allow more time if you want to study this unique area.

7. Walks on Resort and Hotel Grounds

Many of the hotels are set on extensive properties with beautiful gardens and manicured grounds.

➤ If you are not a registered guest of a hotel, it is common courtesy to ask permission before beginning your walk.

The US Virgin Islands

Bluebeard's Castle sits on a bluff with good views of Charlotte Amalie Harbor and surrounded by 20 acres of tropical gardens. **Point Pleasant Hotel**, which has won accolades for its environmentally sensitive development, is a complex whose grounds include viewpoints overlooking Water Bay, abundant birdlife, and trails winding through interesting rock settings, century plants, and flowering trees. **Frenchman's Reef Beach Resort**, near Charlotte Amalie, and **Stouffer Grand Beach Resort**, on the eastern coast, both offer free guided tours of their extensive gardens.

Saint John

St. John is the smallest, the least populated, and the least developed of the three main Virgins. And, as the United States Virgin Islands National Park covers about 55% of the island, it will remain so for many years to come.

The national park makes St. John the nature lover's walking paradise of the USVI. Marked and maintained trails wind their way along the coastline by mangrove thickets, onto pebbled beaches, and out to rocky overlooks. Other trails go into the mountains through the rich vegetation of moist and dry tropical forests and up to summits for rewarding views of the Caribbean Sea, the USVI, and the nearby BVI.

With nearly 10,000 acres to explore, it is almost impossible to feel crowded on St. John. On many trails, and a few of the beaches, you can go for days without seeing anyone. The sea grape, kapok trees, century plants, cactus, and calabash trees are quickly reclaiming the land that had once been cleared for sugar and cotton plantations and livestock grazing. The overgrown ruins of bygone days can now be explored via a number of trails.

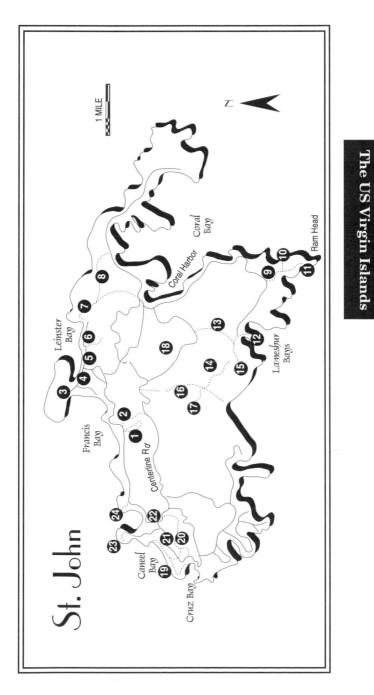

St. John

The US Virgin Islands

1 MILE

Francis Bay

Leinster Bay

Centerline Rd

Caneel Bay

Cruz Bay

Coral Harbor

Coral Bay

Lameshur Bays

Ram Head

Much of the island is returning to its natural state, and walkers on St. John will discover a land that closely resembles the way many Caribbean islands may have appeared when Columbus first arrived in the New World.

➤ **Note:** The numerical designations below pertain only to this guide and will be different than those shown on the National Park map. The National Park Service leads interesting and informative organized guided hikes and walks throughout the island. Be sure to join one of these while on St. John. Information on times, difficulty, etc. may be obtained at the visitor center in Cruz Bay. Also be aware that during wetter periods trail conditions can change quickly with the rapid growth of vegetation. Check with park rangers about current conditions.

1. The Cinnamon Bay Nature Trail

Walking time: 1 hour, for the complete circuit

To reach this easy, self-guided circuit trail, take the Northshore Road from Cruz Bay out to the Cinnamon Bay Campground. The nature trail is across the road from the campground. There are signs along this route marking the vegetation and historical points as it passes through a former sugar factory site.

2. The Cinnamon Bay Trail

Walking time: 1 hour, one way

This hike begins at almost the same point as the Cinnamon Bay Nature Trail (see Walk #1). Making use of an old plantation road, the trail works its way up the heavily forested mountainside to Centerline

Road. It can be made easier by walking downhill from Centerline Road to Northshore Road.

3. The Francis Bay Trail

Walking time: 30 minutes, round trip

This very short, easy walk is reached by following Northshore Road past Maho Bay beach and turning left toward Mary Creek. The trail begins at the end of Mary Creek Road. (Also at the end of Maho Bay beach is a short trail that winds along the hillside to Maho Bay Camp.)

Heading toward the beach, it passes through a dry, scrubby woodland and by the Francis Bay Estate House. The brackish pond and mangrove swamps form a good bird-watching area, and the beach makes for some pleasant walking.

4. The Annaberg School Walk

Walking time: 15 minutes, round trip

Just before turning left onto Mary Creek Road (see Walk # 3), look for the Annaberg School Walk trailhead on your left. Be careful as there is really no good spot to park your car. A short trail of only 0.2 mile rises as it reaches the ruins of one of the oldest public schools in the Caribbean. Stabilized by volunteer help from the St. John Historical Society, the site also permits a pleasant view of Leinster Bay, Mary Point, and Tortola in the British Virgin Islands.

5. The Annaberg Sugar Mill Ruins Walk

Walking Time: 30 minutes, complete trip

Instead of turning left onto Mary Creek Road (see Walk #3), turn right onto Leinster Bay Road and follow it to the end. This is a showplace of the National

Park. Park Service personnel lead guided tours of the ruins on a regular basis. Inquire at the visitor center in Cruz Bay for dates and times.

A series of steps and wooden boardwalks ascends from the parking area through mangrove forest and dry vegetation to a paved trail, which leads the walker around the ruins of an 18th-century sugar plantation.

Along the way you will see the windmill tower, the slaves' quarters, and the great vats that were used to turn sugarcane into brown sugar. Ruins of the still are attached to the outside of a factory building. The construction of the buildings is a combination of ballast brick (from early sailing vessels), stone, and coral from the bay. This mixture of building materials can be found throughout the islands of the Caribbean. The ruins offer a good view of Tortola and Jost Van Dyke across the waters of Sir Francis Drake Passage.

The old windmill tower at Annaberg Sugar Mill ruins.

Because what you learn here will add in-depth background to many of your other island excursions throughout the Caribbean, this walk is highly recommended.

6. The Leinster Bay Road Walk

Walking time: 45 minutes, round trip

This can be taken in conjunction with the Annaberg Sugar Mill Ruins Walk (see Walk #5). Just continue to walk the unimproved road along the bay. The roadbed dates back to when the Danes controlled the island and leads all the way to Waterlemon Bay, an excellent swimming and snorkeling area. Be careful if you do go swimming; the coral can cause deep cuts and, in this bay, it is sometimes only two to three feet below the surface.

7. The Johnny Horn Trail

Walking time: 2 hours, one way
(including use of the Leinster Bay Road Walk to reach the trailhead)

To reach this trail, follow the Leinster Bay Road Walk (see Walk #6) all the way to Waterlemon Bay. The Johnny Horn Trail heads uphill on a pathway behind the beach. In 0.3 mile, once on the ridgeline, a short side trail to the left leads to an old school site on Leinster Point. From here, there is a beautiful view of sailboats darting back and forth in the waters of Sir Francis Drake Passage. Across the passage are Tortola, Great Thatch, and Little Thatch in the BVI.

Back on the Johnny Horn Trail, another trail, about 0.7 mile from Waterlemon Bay Beach, comes in from the left (see Walk #8). Continue straight on the Johnny Horn Trail, going up and down a number of ridges on an old road, to its end at the Emmaus Moravian Church and Coral Bay.

Due to the number of short, but steep ascents and descents, this is classified as a moderate hike.

The US Virgin Islands

8. The Brown Bay Trail

Walking time: 1½ hours, one way

This rough trail leaves the Johnny Horn Trail (see Walk #7) about 0.7 mile east of Waterlemon Bay. The thorn brush and numerous ups and downs of the unmaintained trail make it only for the adventurous. However, those who do hike it will be rewarded by walking along isolated Brown Bay and with good views of Hurricane Hole. The trail ends at the East End Road, east of Coral Bay settlement.

Although the Brown Bay Trail is only 1.2 miles, its difficulty is reflected in the walking time given above.

9. The Salt Pond Bay Trail

Walking time: 25 minutes, round trip

This easy, gently graded trail to the bay takes off from the parking lot 3.9 miles south of Coral Bay on the paved highway. The cactus-lined pathway provides access to Salt Pond Bay (excellent swimming, snorkeling, and walking in splendid isolation), Drunk Bay (see Walk #10), and Ram Head trails (see Walk #11).

10. The Drunk Bay Trail

Walking time: 30 minutes, round trip (not including the time taken to reach beginning of the trail via the Salt Pond Bay Trail)

Here is another short, easy trail that begins on the southern end of the beach in Salt Pond Bay (see Walk #9). The trail turns east and follows the shore of a small salt pond that is still used by some island residents to harvest salt. Continuing through the cactus and scrub brush, the trail comes to a coral rubble beach in Drunk Bay. The coral and pounding surf are impressive, but swimming here is very hazardous.

11. The Ram Head Trail

Walking time: 1½ hours, round trip (not including the time taken to reach beginning of the trail via the Salt Pond Bay Trail)

Despite two ascents and descents, this is an enjoyable and easily traversed trail. It also begins on the southern end of Salt Pond Bay (see Walk #9) and gently rises over a small ridge. Whereas the trails on the northern shore and those through the mountains go through lush, moist tropical forest, this is the dry side of the island and the Ram Head Trail is lined with Turk's cap cacti and century plants.

Dropping from the ridge, the trail comes to a small blue pebble beach. It is worth the time spent exploring the rocks, rubble, and coral of this unusual beach. The trail now switches back over an easy grade and finally reaches Ram Head, a cliff 200 feet above the crashing surf. This cacti-covered point has superb views of Salt Pond Bay, Bordeaux Mountain, the British Virgin Islands and, on good days, St. Croix may be seen in the haze of the horizon. Be careful along the edge of the cliffs as footing is not stable in some places. Feral goats and burros live here and they can often be seen scrambling among the rocks and underbrush.

12. The Yawzi Point Trail

Walking time: 40 minutes, round trip

The short Yawzi Point Trail begins at the head of the peninsula between Greater and Little Lameshur bays on the Little Lameshur Bay Road, which is connected to the paved road leading to Salt Pond Bay (see Walk #9). Lameshur Bay is a good walking and swimming spot and is deserted for much of the day. The scrub-lined path leads to small secluded coves along the coastline that offer interesting explorations of small tidal pools.

The Yawzi Point Trail may also be reached by the Lameshur Bay (see Walk #14) or Bordeaux Mountain (see Walk #13) trails.

13. The Bordeaux Mountain Trail

Walking time: 1 hour, one way (if descending)

This old carriage road leads from the unpaved Bordeaux Mountain Road down to Lameshur Bay. To reach the beginning of the trail, follow Centerline Road out of Cruz Bay for about 5.5 miles to its intersection with unpaved Bordeaux Mountain Road. Bear right onto the latter for 1.7 miles to reach the Bordeaux Mountain Trail. (Bordeaux Mountain Road is an excellent walk in itself; see Walk #18.)

In its 1,000-foot drop to the bay, this trail passes by kapok trees, century plants, ginger Thomas, and other abundant wildflowers. It intersects with the Lameshur Bay Trail (see Walk #14) in one mile. It is a good idea to check with the Park Service on current conditions before using this trail.

> Keep in mind that the 1,000-foot change in elevation takes place in only 1.2 miles. This will especially affect you if you plan to ascend the Bordeaux Mountain Trail from Lameshur Bay to the Bordeaux Mountain Road as you return to your car.

14. The Lameshur Bay Trail

Walking time: 2 hours, round trip

Another trail that makes use of an old road, this one serves to link the Reef Bay Trail (see Walk #16) and Lameshur Bay. Although it makes a couple of ascents and descents through the open, arid forestland, these are small changes in elevation and the pathway is relatively easy. There are also a couple of nice views of Reef Bay along the way.

15. The Europa Bay Trail

Walking time: 30 minutes, round trip (not including the time taken to reach the start of the trail via the Lameshur Bay Trail)

This short trail is accessible only from the Lameshur Bay Trail (see Walk #14). On its way down to the coral rubble beach in Europa Bay, the path skirts the edge of a small salt pond that sometimes proves to be a good bird watching area.

16. The Reef Bay Trail

Walking time: 1½ hours, one way

This trail begins a short distance west of the Bordeaux Mountain Road, or one mile east of the Cinnamon Bay Trail, on Centerline Road. This is the showpiece trail of the Virgin Islands National Park. In fact, National Park Service personnel lead guided hikes here on a regular basis. Inquire at the visitor's center in Cruz Bay for dates and times.

Even if you don't take a guided hike, you will still know what you are seeing along the way. As the trail drops from the ridgeline along the mountainside of dense tropical forest to the scrub brush of Reef Bay, there are signs identifying the vegetation and wildlife. Some give information on the ruins of the sugar plantation and communities that once existed, but are now being reclaimed by nature. Along the way it has a junction with the Lameshur Bay Trail (see Walk #14). The Reef Bay Trail will bring you past mango trees, broom palm, bay rum trees, century plants, lime trees, cacti and, during the rainy season, more wildflowers than you could possibly count. Also be on the lookout for hermit crabs and hummingbirds. Be sure to take the side trail to the petroglyphs (see Walk #17). The trail ends at Reef Bay Beach, which has a few picnic tables and pit toilets.

Remember, to reach a road once you finish the Reef Bay Trail you must 1) return the way you came, 2) use the Lameshur Bay Trail to meet a car in Lameshur Bay or 3) access the Bordeaux Mountain Trail (see Walk #13) to go back up to the main ridgeline of the island.

⇶ A highly recommended walk. Due to the number of signs, ruins, and scenic wonders along the way, it might be wise to spend more than the 90 minutes it takes to walk this trail.

17. The Petroglyph Trail

Walking time: 20 minutes, round trip (plus the time to reach the start of the trail via the Reef Bay or Lameshur Bay trails)

This is a short, easy path leading to the pools of a small waterfall and the rock drawings. It is accessible from the Reef Bay Trail (see Walk #16) about 1.5 miles down from Centerline Road. It is also near the point where the Lameshur Bay Trail (see Walk #14) intersects the Reef Bay Trail.

The Petroglyph Trail arrives at a cool, shaded spot overlooking the waterfall and the drawings. There is still some debate as to the origin of the rock carvings. Some credit them to the descendants of the Arawak Indians, others attribute them to the Caribs, while still others speculate they were made by pre-Columbian Africans or African slaves. No matter who made the drawings, this is a great place for a pleasant rest and a swim.

18. The Bordeaux Mountain Road Walk

Walking time: 2 hours, one way

Although this is just an unpaved public road, the lack of traffic makes it a very pleasant walk. Bordeaux Mountain Road is about 5.5 miles east of Cruz Bay on Centerline Road. At the intersection of Centerline Road and Bordeaux Mountain Road there is a superb view of Bordeaux Mountain, Coral Bay, Black Rock Hill and, across the sea, Norman Island in the British Virgin Islands.

The road is relatively easy walking with short ascents and descents until its final, more strenuous climb to the summit of the mountain. From the peak, the road passes by Bordeaux Mountain Trail (see Walk #13), more or less deteriorates into a jeep trail, and steeply drops down to the paved road in Coral Harbor.

This walk is through the pleasant, shaded moist tropical forest and is probably the best place to observe this type of vegetation without soon dropping down out of the mountains and into the drier scrub brush of the lowlands. A highly recommended walk and a truly enjoyable one. Remember that this is on an unpaved road in the forest, so be prepared for muddy walking and rain puddles in the wet season and volumes of dust during the many dry months.

➤ This is such a good walk that, even if you don't want to walk all of the way to Coral Harbor, it is suggested you at least walk some distance on Bordeaux Mountain Road. Don't miss this one!

19. The Lind Point Trail

Walking time: 45 minutes, one way

The Lind Point Trail begins at the visitor's center in Cruz Bay. The pathway climbs through open scrub brush on its way to Lind Point, which is reached in

15 minutes. From here is a view across Pillsbury Sound back to St. Thomas. The trail then drops, passes by a trail to Salomon Beach, and comes to an end at Honeymoon Beach in Caneel Bay Plantation.

20. The Caneel Hill Trail

Walking time: 1½ hours, one way

This somewhat strenuous hike begins on North-shore Road, opposite the road leading to Caneel Bay.

The first steep ascent through woodlands leads to Margaret Hill and intersects the Water Catchment Trail (see Walk #22) about half-way to the summit. From Margaret Hill, the trail descends, only to rise again and offer a view from Caneel Hill. From here the trail drops quickly and intersects the Caneel Hill Spur Trail (see Walk #21) before arriving in Cruz Bay.

21. The Caneel Hill Spur Trail

Walking time: 20 minutes (from the road to the trail's intersection with the Caneel Hill Trail)

This trail has two sections and may be reached by following Northshore Road just a short distance from Cruz Bay. The trail leaves the road at a spot that overlooks Caneel and Cruz bays. To the west of the road the path leads to its intersection with the Lind Point Trail (see Walk #19) in 20 minutes. To the east, it ascends to intersect the Caneel Hill Trail (see Walk #20), also in 20 minutes. It joins the Caneel Hill Trail about half-way to the summit.

22. The Water Catchment Trail
Walking time: 30 minutes, one way

This wooded trail begins off Centerline Road, about a mile east of Cruz Bay, and descends for one mile to Northshore Road. The Water Catchment Trail is a good introduction to the forests of St. John. Near Centerline Road is a dense, moist tropical forest. As the trail descends, the trees become smaller, the vines and flowers become fewer and, by the time the Northshore Road is reached, you are walking through the dry forest vegetation of the lowlands.

> If the Water Catchment Trail is followed in the direction described, the walking is all downhill! There is no other walk so short and so easy that will give such a good overview of the different changes in vegetation.

23. The Caneel Bay Plantation Grounds Walk

Caneel Bay Plantation is situated on 175 meticulously manicured and landscaped acres. The resort is one of the plushest in the Caribbean and visitors may enjoy the grounds if permission is obtained first. In fact, guided walking tours are held on a regular basis. Inquire at the office for dates and times.

The 40-minute round trip Turtle Point Trail is also on the grounds of Caneel Bay Plantation and leads to a viewpoint overlooking the numerous cays that lie off the northwest coast of St. John.

24. The Peace Hill Walk

Walking time: 20 minutes, round trip

This is such a short trail that it almost does not qualify as a walk. However, the view from the hill is so superb that it should not be overlooked, especially because it takes so little effort to reach it.

Take Northshore Road from Cruz Bay, go past Caneel Bay Plantation, and the parking lot and trail will soon appear on your left, just past Hawksnest Bay. Peace Hill overlooks the bay, Trunk Bay, St. Thomas, numerous small islands off its northern coast, and even offers glimpses of the British Virgin Islands across Sir Francis Drake Channel.

The "Christ Of The Caribbean" statue that had stood on this hill for 20 years was destroyed by Hurricane Marilyn in September, 1995. This is a popular stop for the tour operators of St. John. Even though the statue is no longer there, this spot offers fantastic views.

The British Virgin Islands

The British Virgin Islands (BVI) comprise 50 to 60 islands. Tortola, the largest, is 21 square miles, while others, such as Round Rock, are no more a few yards of volcanic material just above the sea. The BVI have a population of about 12,000, 10,000 of whom live on Tortola, leaving the other islands sparsely populated or completely uninhabited.

Most of the islands are volcanic in origin and are the result of molten lava cooling as it rose from the depths of the sea. Anegada is one of the rare exceptions. It was not formed by volcanic action, but is actually a large coral formation rising less than 30 feet above sea level.

Vegetation ranges from lush, vine-covered trees and other rain forest-type vegetation on Sage Mountain, Tortola, and Gorda Peak on Virgin Gorda to the arid scrub land on Anegada. In addition to tropical fruit such as mangoes, bananas, and avocadoes, the islands boast a wide variety of flowers. Oleander, bougainvillea, flamboyant, exotic frangipani, and hibiscus, with its many colors, grow on almost all of the islands. The towering 20-foot bloom of the century plant can be seen thrusting toward the sky, high above the lower vegetation. There are 154 species of birds in the BVI. American kestral, smooth-billed ani, pearly-eyed thrasher, gray kingbird, and numerous terns, herons, and egrets may be found here. Brown pelicans, frigatebirds, and brown boobies fly high above, while on the ground slither iguanas, geckos, and a host of land crabs, most often hidden by lush growth.

Perhaps more than the vegetation and fauna, the wonderful isolation is the reason to come to the BVI. Many of the smaller islands are hard to reach, yet

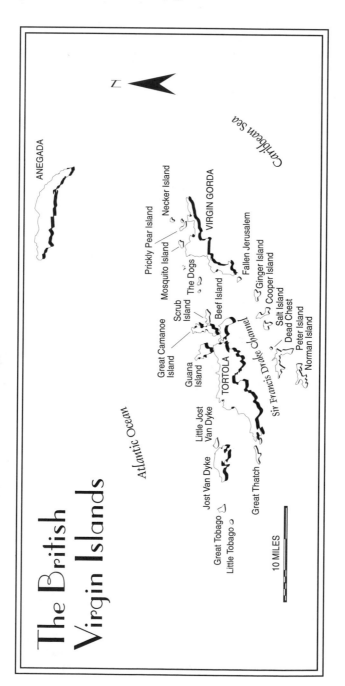

have beautiful palm-lined coral sand beaches just waiting to be visited. It is possible to spend full days exploring the shores and low-lying ridges of these islands without seeing another person. Even on the populated islands there is an abundance of secluded spots. Tortola, Jost Van Dyke, and Virgin Gorda all have beaches that are rarely visited.

The National Parks Trust has become very active in protecting the unique and fragile areas of the islands. As a result, more and more trails and footpaths are being developed. While these pathways open up new areas to explore, they also make it easier for the trust to monitor and manage the areas. Along with privately managed pathways, there are now trails on Tortola, Virgin Gorda, Sandy Cay, Mosquito Island, and Guana Island.

Commercialism is slow in coming and the government and people keep close watch on the development of tourist attractions. The emphasis is on quality and not quantity. They realize that the lure of these islands is their uncrowded feel and unharried pace of life.

History

There is little archaeological evidence of them, but the Ciboney Indians are thought to have been the first inhabitants of the BVI, occupying them as early as 300 BC. As on most Caribbean islands, the first peoples to leave behind more evidence of their existence were the Arawak Indians, who arrived at least 600 years before Columbus. They were, however, completely gone by the time Columbus arrived, having been killed or driven off by the cannibalistic Carib Indians.

In 1493, Columbus named the islands "Los Virgines," their numbers reminding him of the 11,000 martyred virgins of St. Ursula. Although the Spanish had claim to the islands, they never established a

permanent settlement. The absence of a government and the great variety of hidden bays and coves
made the islands perfect hideouts for the pirates of
the 17th century. Many ships, laden with goods
from the New World, were waylaid in these waters
and their treasures secreted on the islands.

In 1648, the Dutch established a colony on Tortola,
but were soon driven off by the English, who developed large sugar and cotton plantations based on
slave labor. With the arrival of the pacifistic Quaker
settlers, the attitude toward slavery began to
change. In 1798, the first law giving some rights to
slaves was passed and, in 1834, they were given
their freedom. Discouraged by the world-wide drop
in sugarcane prices and the growing resentment of
the slaves, many of the white settlers left the BVI.
As a result, much of the land came to be owned by
the black population.

The islands have had a stormy history. Numerous
riots and demonstrations in the first half of the 20th
century led to the creation of a constitution in 1966,
which granted a large degree of self-rule. Today the
BVI are considered a territory of the United Kingdom, with a governor acting as the representative of
the queen. The political and social situation is now
stable and, in fact, the BVI enjoy one of the lowest
crime rates in all of the Caribbean.

Special Walks: A number of the walks in this section are listed as reachable only by private or chartered boat. This means that there are no scheduled
air or sea services to these islands. Many of the hotels, campgrounds, and charter companies can arrange transportation to these islands for you.
Alternatively, strike up a conversation with the
skipper of one of the private yachts and get yourself
invited to take a sail. Do not let this little matter of
transportation stop you from visiting these islands.
Much of the charm and enjoyment of the BVI is to
spend the day walking and exploring an island that
you have all to yourself.

Data

Transportation to the British Virgin Islands:
There are no direct flights from the U.S., Canada, or
Europe to any of the islands. Once in the Caribbean,
however, there are a number of ways to get to the
BVI. There are flights to Tortola from Puerto Rico
and the USVI. It is even possible to fly to Tortola
from Anguilla, Sint Maarten, St. Kitts, and Antigua.
Fly BVI, a small, but most accommodating airline,
can arrange charter flights to just about anywhere
in the Caribbean.

Jost Van Dyke, Tortola, and Virgin Gorda may be
reached by ferry from the USVI. Ferries also ply the
waters between Jost Van Dyke, Tortola, Peter Island, and Virgin Gorda.

A departure tax is imposed upon leaving the BVI.

Entry: A passport, birth certificate, or voter's registration card and an ongoing or return airline ticket
are all that are required of American or Canadian
citizens. All others must posses a valid passport and
an ongoing or return ticket.

Currency: Interestingly, the national currency is
the U.S. dollar. Credit cards, rare just a few years
ago, are now more widely accepted.

Tourist Information:

 ✍ **In the United States**
  British Virgin Islands Tourist Board
  370 Lexington Ave., Suite 313
  New York, NY 10017
  ☎ 212-696-0400

 ✍ British Virgin Islands Tourist Board
  1686 Union Street
  San Francisco, CA 94123
  ☎ 415-775-0344

The British Virgin Islands

✍ **In Europe**
British Virgin Islands Tourist Board
110 St. Martin's Lane
London WC2N 4DY
England, ☎ 0171-240-4159

The BVI Tourist Board is located in the Social Security Building near the waterfront in Road Town, Tortola:

✍ British Virgin Islands Tourist Board
Waterfront Street, PO Box 134
Road Town, Tortola
British Virgin Islands
☎ 284-494-3134

Driving: Rental cars are available on Tortola and Virgin Gorda. (The other islands are so small that you won't really need a car.) A temporary driver's license is required and may be obtained through the rental agency for a fee and with proof of a valid driver's license. Drive on the left!

Language: English.

Walking and Hiking Guides: As this book went to press, the National Parks Trust was in the process of recruiting a Forester to conduct tours at the Sage Mountain National Park. The trust may also be able to recommend a competent guide for other places in the BVI.

✍ The National Parks Trust
P O Box 860
Road Town, Tortola
British Virgin Islands
☎ 284-494-3904

Camping Areas: On Tortola, Brewers Bay Campground offers prepared camping sites. These include a floored 9' x 14' or 10' x 20' tent with beds, linen, stove, and all cooking and eating utensils. It also has a few bare sites for those with their own equipment. The rates are about one-third of the cost of a prepared site on St. John in the U.S. Virgin Islands. There is also scheduled taxi service to Road Town from the campground.

✍ Brewers Bay Campground
PO Box 185, Road Town, Tortola
British Virgin Islands
☎ 284-494-3463

Tula's N&N Campground in Little Harbor, Jost Van Dyke, also offers prepared and bare sites. The rates are a little higher than Brewers Bay, but still substantially lower than those in the USVI.

✍ Tula's N&N Campground
c/o Lorna Johnson, A-12 Estate Tutu
St. Thomas
United States Virgin Islands 00802
☎ 284-495-9566

White Bay Campground, also on Jost Van Dyke, is by far the most rustic of the campgrounds here. It offers equipped and bare tent sites as well as cabins.

✍ White Bay Campground
General Delivery, West End P O
Tortola, British Virgin Islands
☎ 284-495-9312

You may rent furnished sites or bring your own equipment to Anegada.

✍ Anegada Beach Campground
PO Box 2710
Anegada, British Virgin Islands
☎ 284-495-9466

Camping is forbidden anywhere else on the BVI and this policy is strictly enforced.

Recommended Readings

📖 *Our Virgin Island* by Robb White

📖 *Letters From The Virgin Islands: Life and Manners of The West Indies* by John J. Abraham

📖 *Conquest of Eden* by Michael Paiewonsky

The British Virgin Islands

📖 *Tales of Tortola and the British Virgin Islands* by Florence Lewisohn

📖 *Concise History of the BVI* by Vernon Pickering

The *Island Sun* and the *BVI Beacon*, both weekly newspapers, are published in Road Town and are available throughout the islands. Both report local news and are a good way to catch a glimpse of island life. Copies may be obtained by writing:

✍ c/o the newspaper you wish to receive
Road Town
Tortola, British Virgin Islands

Despite their names, the Sunny Caribbee Spice Company (on Main Street) and Pusser's Pub and Company Store (on Waterfront Drive) are the best places in Road Town, Tortola, to obtain books on the BVI. The Craft Shop in the shopping center next to the yacht harbor on Virgin Gorda also carries a few books of interest.

Tortola

Tortola, the largest and most populated of the BVI, is the usual point of entry for visitors to the BVI. Road Town, on the south coast, is the administrative capital of the islands.

The southern coast of Tortola is characterized by dry scrub land, and frangipani, tamarind, and loblolly grow well here. Most of the shipping and trading of the islands is done on this side of Tortola, while the northern coast hosts miles of secluded white sand beaches, mango and banana trees, and groves of sea grapes and manchineel trees. The higher elevations of Mt. Sage and the ridgeline of the middle of the island trap more moisture than the coast and, as a result, the vegetation is much thicker. While not receiving enough rainfall to be

technically called a rain forest, the center of the island possesses many plants commonly found there –
philodendron, mahogany trees, ferns, and orchids.

1. The Sage Mountain National Park Trails

Established in 1964 to preserve and protect Tortola's
remaining woodlands and its bordering watersheds,
the 92-acre Sage Mountain National Park is reached
by taking the main highway (Joe's Hill Road) northwest out of Road Town to Leonard's. Here you'll
make a left onto Ridge Road, which is followed to the
left-hand turnoff leading to a parking area and the
park entrance.

An entrance route through mammee apple trees and
heliconia delivers you to numerous easy-to-
moderate trails winding their way through the remnants of the rain forest-type vegetation that used to
cover much of the Virgin Islands. All of the trails are
well defined and maintained, and they interconnect.
Some are even signed to identify vegetation, such as
manalkara, mountain guava, and white cedar trees.
An observation tower and other points permit views
over much of Tortola and out across the Caribbean
Sea to Jost Van Dyke and its outlying islands.

The park is a pleasant place for a picnic (on tables
along the trails) and a spot to spend the day walking
around the sides and to the summit of Sage Mountain, which offers good views of the surrounding islands and the Sir Francis Drake Channel. At an
elevation of over 1,700 feet, Mt. Sage is the highest
point in the BVI. Elephant ears and ferns line the
pathways, while kapok and mahogany trees tower
above.

> ➤ As new trails are being developed, you
> should stop at the National Parks Trust
> headquarters in Road Town for current
> information and to pick up the Sage
> Mountain brochure, which provides
> natural history information.

The British Virgin Islands

2. The Brewers Bay Beach Walk

Brewers Bay is on the north coast of Tortola and is reached by taking Great Mountain Road out of Road Town, bearing left on Ridge Road, and then turning right to descend the steep road to Brewers Bay. The bay has been referred to as the most beautiful in all of the BVI. The white sands are often deserted, the surf is gentle and the snorkeling is good. Palm trees provide a shady resting spot, while the bar at Brewers Bay Campground is a welcoming watering hole. The operators of the campground may be able to arrange for guided hiking tours to other places on the islands for you.

3. The Windmill Ruin at Mount Healthy National Park Walk

Walking time: 15 minutes, one way. Moderately steep.

The windmill tower in Mount Healthy National Park.

Along the road dropping down to Brewers Bay (see Walk #2), there is a short and somewhat steep route up to the ruins of an 18th-century plantation. Established by the National Parks Trust in 1983, the one-acre site on Mount Healthy contains the restored tower of a windmill (the only one on Tortola) that was used to crush sugarcane for molasses and rum. There are good views from here back down to the palms and surf of Brewers Bay. A short, three-minute trail also winds around the sparse vegetation of the park.

4. The Sopers Hole - Smugglers Cove Hike

Walking time: 1 hour, one way

Drive the main highway westward from Road Town all the way to the end of its pavement at the ferry dock in Sopers Hole. Begin the walk by taking the rough road uphill to the right, passing by cactus and other dry land vegetation as the route swings around Steele Point. The unimproved road, providing views of Great Thatch and Jost Van Dyke, leads to secluded beaches along Smugglers Cove. The uncrowded sands are delightful and perfect for beachcombing, and the coral reefs not far from shore make it worthwhile to bring snorkeling gear.

➤ This hike could be extended by combining it with the Long Bay Beach Hike (see Walk #5).

5. The Long Bay Beach Hike

Walking time: the combined excursions (see note below) would take about 2-3 hours to hike, one way

Long Bay may be reached by following the highway westward from Road Town. Turn right onto Zion Hill Road and in 0.5 mile turn left to Long Bay. This mile-long, white sand beach is nearly deserted. The only development is a few guest houses and the Long Bay Hotel, whose bar and restaurant might be a welcome respite from the tropical sun.

➤ The hike may be extended by continuing southwest on the road in Belmont Estates, around Belmont Pond, and joining up with the Sopers Hole – Smugglers Cove Hike (see Walk #4).

The British Virgin Islands

6. The Ridge Road Hike

Walking time: 3 hours, for the complete circuit

The Ridge Road runs along the crest of Tortola in an easterly direction toward Westly Will. Although it is a popular scenic tourist drive with turnouts to enjoy the views, it is better experienced on foot. Traffic is usually light, but remember that you are walking on one of the main highways of the island.

For an exhilarating start, begin this outing near the police station in Road Town. Walk the road that heads out of town in Huntman's Gut (Great Mountain Road). You should take this portion of the hike only if you are feeling energetic, since it gains over a thousand feet of elevation in a little less than a mile. If you don't wish to walk up, drive out of town and begin walking to the right at the intersection on top of the ridge. Areas of dense vegetation alternate with excellent views of the Caribbean Sea, the Sir Francis Drake Channel, and the surrounding islands. Because of the way the sunlight plays on the water and the distant lands, the views will take on a different feel and look depending on what time of day it is. Continue on the Ridge Road for two miles and, just past Wesley Will, turn right downhill on Belle Vue Road. The descent, as sharp and steep as the ascent, brings you to the main road along Road Bay. Turn right along the waterfront for 1.5 miles and arrive back in Road Town. Recommended.

7. The Elizabeth Beach Walk

The Elizabeth Beach Resort – four or five cottages with marvelous views out across the sea – has recently extended the road past its grounds, permitting motorized access to Elizabeth Beach. On many days you may be the only person on the powdery white sand, surrounded by tropical greenery.

8. The Long Bay Beach Walk

Long Bay is located on Beef Island, connected to Tortola by a bridge spanning the narrow channel off the east coast of Tortola. Until 1966, those flying into the airport on Beef Island had to ferry across the waters to reach Tortola. To get to Long Bay from the east end of Tortola, take the first road to the left after crossing the bridge. In just a few hundred yards is a small road going off to the right; since this road is usually gated, park here (without blocking either road) and walk 0.2 mile through cacti and century plants to horseshoe-shaped Long Bay Beach. Overlooking Great and Little Camanoe Islands and Marina Cay, the beach is a great place to be when the first rays of a rising sun coat the water and sands with a pinkish-gold hue. Terns nest near the salt pond behind the bay, while tropic birds may be seen soaring above the sea grape and manchineel trees.

9. The Buck Island Walk

Buck Island is off the southeastern coast of Tortola and can be reached only by private yacht. The island is deserted and has an excellent sand beach for walking and shelling. The interior of this low lying land is open scrub country and, if you do a little exploring, you may find the remains of the grassy runway that served as Tortola's only airport.

Guana Island

Guana Island, at 850 acres, is the sixth largest of the BVI. It is named for an iguana-shaped rock formation on its northwestern coast and is just off the northern coast of Tortola. The island is now privately owned, although it was inhabited in the 18th century by Quakers who raised cotton and vegetable crops as well as a small amount of livestock. The present-day owners' interest in conservation has led them to establish Guana Island as a true nature preserve and wildlife sanctuary. Closed to the public for several weeks each year, the resort hosts conferences in which some of the world's most distinguished naturalists, botanists, biologists, and other scientists gather to study the island's unique natural history. It is proclaimed by these scientists to have the "richest fauna known for an island its size anywhere in the West Indies and possibly in the world." Guana Island has a long-term program to restore and protect native flora and fauna. The success of this program may be measured by the re-establishment of myriad plants and the return of the Caribbean roseate flamingo, the land turtle, and the Anegada iguana. The Anegada iguana *(Iguana pinguis)* was once found throughout the BVI and Puerto Rico, but now lives only on Anegada and Guana Island. It is massive compared to its more common relative, the *Iguana iguana*. It weighs in at more than 70 pounds and can attain lengths of more than six feet. You'll also find numerous other varieties of lizards, in addition to turtles, frogs, snakes, and bats.

A first-class resort built on some of the original Quaker structures, Guana Island's acreage is never crowded due to the fact that there are rooms for only 30 guests at a time. This insures visitors receive the best that the island has to offer – seven secluded beaches, small land and watersports facilities, meals of fresh seafood and island-baked breads, the individual attentions of the staff, and the run of the island via more than 20 trails snaking out to its most hidden recesses. Only registered guests are permitted on the island. For more information contact:

✍ Guana Island Reservations Office
10 Timber Trail
Rye, New York 10580
☎ 914-967-6050
www.guana.com

10. Guana Island Trails

With more than 20 interconnecting trails reaching to nearly every ridge, ghut and far-off point, it is possible to spend days exploring the island. Many of the trails have no established treadway and are little more than routes marked by yellow, blue, or red ties around trees or small arrows painted on rocks. While these may not be as easily traversed as groomed trails, they do give you a feeling of exploring on your own, yet with the safety of markings showing the way. All are rated moderate to strenuous. Most people begin their hikes from the main resort area, following trails named for the places they lead. Some of the most popular are listed below.

The Long Point Trail passes by side routes to Crab Cove (possibly the best diving and snorkeling spot around the island) and the coral cobblestone beach of Muskmelon Bay. This is the dry side of a dry island, yet the vegetation, such as century plants and bromeliads draping themselves on the cactus, grows to large proportions.

A rugged hike with loose and rocky footing is the trail down the water drainage of aptly-named **Palm Ghut**. Descending the ravine and passing by hundreds, maybe thousands, of fan palms, the trail eventually emerges onto North Beach. One ravine over from Palm Ghut is **Grand Ghut**, where you can walk through some of oldest-growth forest in the BVI.

The pathway to the **Big Cave** is not to be undertaken lightly. There are confusing trail intersections, steep climbs over loose rocks and boulders, scratching and entangling vegetation, and biting insects. Once there, though, you may have a chance to observe two species of bats hanging upside down in their natural habitat. The Antillean fruit bat has a wingspan of almost 18 inches, but no tail, while the much rarer cave bat, an omnivore, is one of the few animals in the world with bicuspid canines.

The Summit Trail is the one most often used to ascend from the main resort area to the highest point on the island, Guana Peak. At 806 feet above sea level, the peak provides a 360° view of the surrounding islands – Tortola to the south, Jost Van Dyke in the west, Great Camanoe to the immediate east with Virgin Gorda further out across the waters.

The well-built **Dove Trail** presents the best possibility of sighting the bridled quail dove which, using Guana as its main habitat, is making a comeback from near-extinction.

Plan on spending the better part of the day if you want to go the isolated beach at **Monkey Point**. Probably the longest excursion you can do in a more-or-less straight line on the island, the hike brings you by a stand of some of the largest members in the bromeliad family, the *Bromelia pinguin*.

A spectacular view from Guana Peak.

Virgin Gorda

Columbus named the island "Fat Virgin" because its profile reminded him of a heavy woman lying on her back. The southern portion of Virgin Gorda is a low lying land, attaining a height of only 447 feet on Cow Hill. Among the scrub brush and century plants are giant boulders that came to rest here after volcanic activity ceased centuries ago. Virgin Gorda Peak, the "stomach" of the fat virgin, rises in the center of the island to over 1,300 feet. The greenest and lushest vegetation of the island can be found here. The peninsula to the east of Gorda Peak forms the legs of the virgin and is much lower in elevation. On the low ridges, the vegetation is a mixture of that found in the scrub country and in the mountain region. This eastern peninsula is accessible only by boat, but offers some excellent, isolated walking places.

Virgin Gorda is only eight square miles, which means most of the island is within a few hours walk. The seldom-driven roads should not be overlooked, however, for they can provide enjoyable walks, going past sparsely populated hamlets and out to such pleasant points as Little Dix Bay, Gun Creek, and Pond Bay.

11. The Little Fort Area Walk

Just 0.5 mile south of the Virgin Gorda Yacht Harbor is a National Parks Trust Reserve. There are no trails through this 36-acre wildlife sanctuary but, if you walk carefully in the boulder-strewn area, you should be able to discover the disappearing remains of the old fort. This is a very easy walk just down the road from the harbor and is a quiet place to escape the activity of the marina.

12. The Spring Bay Walk

Another National Parks Trust area, this palm-lined, coral sand beach is reached by taking the main road south out of The Valley. Follow this road toward The Baths to a sign pointing the way to Spring Bay. A short trail leads from the parking area down to a boulder-strewn beach. This is a recommended walk made even more enjoyable if you walk the road all the way from The Valley to Spring Bay.

13. The Baths and Devils Bay Walk

Walking time: 45 minutes, for the complete circuit

The Baths is the showplace of Virgin Gorda and one of the main reasons people visit the island. Huge granite rocks and boulders lay scattered along the beach and partially submerged in the tropical waters. The boulders form caves and grottos, some filled with water, some open to the sun, and still others almost as dark as an underground cavern. The pathways among these natural arches lead through an eerie and enchanted place.

The Baths may be reached by continuing on the road past Spring Bay (see Walk #12) to the turn-around. A short, descending pathway, first through cactus, then lusher vegetation, and finally lined by palms, leads from the parking lot to the beach.

After you've taken a dip and explored the beach for a while, look for the sign directing you southward along the Devil's Bay Trail – one of the most fun excursions in all of the Caribbean. Those who are familiar with hiking the Appalachian Trail in North America will soon know why this trail has been referred to by some as the "Mahoosic Notch of the Caribbean." The route leads you over giant boulders – some-

The Baths.

times aided by ladders or rope holds, sometimes not – into narrow passageways, through waist-deep pools, into the heart of The Baths, and eventually out to Devil's Bay. This bay is enclosed by even more boulders, which make for some interesting snorkeling.

A 15-minute ascending pathway runs from Devil's Bay through open organ pipe cactus and scrub brush country, then back to The Baths turnaround parking area.

> ⚡ Allow much more time than the walking allotment given so that you may fully enjoy this most unique area. A very fun and highly recommended walk; don't miss this one!

14. The Copper Mine Point Hike

Walking time: 1 hour, 15 minutes, one way

It is possible to drive all of the way to Copper Point, but to really get a feel for Virgin Gorda, its topography and its flora, walk the main road southward from the Yacht Harbor for about 0.5 mile. Make a left to turn east over the ridge from Fort Point and continue to the eastern shore and the site of an old copper mine. At this point there is no land between Virgin Gorda and Africa. Because of this, the waves are larger and more spectacular than on the western shore.

On Copper Mine Point are the remains of an 18th-century copper mine; the chimney and a couple of walls of the boiler house are still standing. There is speculation that this mine was originally worked by Carib Indians, who used the copper for trade. Later, Spaniards went into the mine hoping to find gold, but were eventually disillusioned and moved westward in the New World, continuing their search. Around 1850, miners from Cornwall arrived, but they too soon lost interest in this mine. It is said that some of the shafts extend out below the sea.

The British Virgin Islands

View of Virgin Gorda from Copper Mine Point.

🌩 *Be careful in this area as there may be hidden mine openings.*

15. Virgin Gorda Peak National Park Trails

Walking time: 1½ hours, making use of both trails and a short portion of the main road to form a circuit hike

Everything above 1,000 feet on Virgin Gorda is considered a part of this 265-acre national park established in 1974. Two official, maintained, and connecting trails wind their way through the forest of indigenous and exotic plants and up to the summit of Gorda Peak. These may be reached by taking the main road out of The Valley and heading toward North Sound. About three miles from The Valley you will be on the side of Gorda Peak and the marked trails begin here. You can obtain a brochure (from the National Parks Trust in Tortola or the Virgin Gorda warden at The Baths) which offers wonderful tidbits of information on the plants and animals you are likely to see on the Gorda Peak trails.

There are designated picnic areas along both of the trails as they ascend. At an elevation of over 1,300 feet, the summit has an observation point with views over most of Virgin Gorda, out to North Sound and the small Dog Islands, and, on clear days, there is a good view to the west of Sage Mountain on Tortola.

➤ **Note:** A number of other unofficial and unmaintained trails rise from different points below the summit to connect with the National Parks Trust trails as alternative ways of reaching Gorda Peak. One of these is the old road, which used to connect Little Dix Bay with North Sound and, as such, is nicely graded. This route makes for a pleasant and easy ascent. Remember, if taking any of these alternative routes, that they are unmaintained and that you may have to inquire locally as to where they begin.

All of the trails on the mountain can be rated moderate and, even if you followed every one of them, you could still get back to The Valley in time for the evening meal. Check with the Olde Yard Inn as their information sheet is actually the best available trail map of Virgin Gorda Peak. The restaurant is also a good choice for dinner.

16. Biras Creek Resort Trails

Situated on the 140-acre northeastern peninsula of Virgin Gorda, the first class Biras Creek Resort offers a top-notch system of marked and maintained pathways meandering into the furthest reaches of its property. The resort and its trails are accessible only by boat.

➤ Although the trails are open to both guests and the general pubic, it is common courtesy to ask permission first and wise to check on trail conditions.

If you don't have a boat, make a lunch or dinner reservation – you'll be glad you did –and they will send a launch to pick you up at the jetty in Gun Creek. In addition to the trails, which are designated by letters of the alphabet, the resort offers guided walks of its extensive gardens on a regular basis.

Trail A is really just an easy, short trail taking you from the estate's road system through a pleasantly shaded wood of turpentine trees, locally known as tourist trees because their skin is always red and peeling. Diddle-doe cactus will accompany you as the route connects with Trail B.

If you have a limited amount of time, **Trail B** is probably the best choice; it passes through a great variety of environments and vegetation along a route of only moderate ascents. Leaving Trail A to rise onto a low ridgeline, the route enters a garden of Turk's cap and diddle-doe cactus, agave, and aloe. The succulents are so numerous and eye pleasing that you might think they have been planted intentionally. Continuing along the ridge there are views of the Atlantic, the Caribbean, and out across North Sound. Descending, the trail skirts a small mangrove area before coming to Biras Creek's private beach on Deep Bay. Birders need to be on the lookout as the pathway swings back toward the main resort area, following the edge of the salt water lake. You're almost sure to spot herons and egrets, with the slight possibility of sighting a clapper rail or an elusive sora. A few yards after the lake you'll return to the starting point of the walk. *Walking time: 30 minutes, full circuit.*

Trail C, which shares some of its length with Trail F (as well as hummingbirds and bananaquits), connects the main resort area with the marina and service center. *Walking time: 20 minutes, one way. (You may return to the main resort area via the service road –an easy walk of 10 minutes.)*

Ascending the dry, scrub brush-covered ridge on the opposite side of the valley from Trail B, **Trail D** winds its way up to views overlooking the complete resort area and its three surrounding bodies of salt-water. You'll pass through small thickets of frangipani, which is well suited for arid soils such as this. Descending via small switchbacks, the trail comes to an end, conveniently, near the beach bar at Deep Bay. The main resort area is a short 10-minute walk away. *Walking time: 1 hour, full circuit.*

An amusing sign along the trail.

Trail E connects Biras Creek Resort with the Bitter End Yacht Club and Resort. Running more or less along the shore with little change in elevation, the trail could be used to identify tropical flowers such as the yellow alamanda or the exotically-shaped spider lily. An easy walk. *Walking time: 1 hour, 10 minutes, round trip.*

A view along Trail F.

The longest and probably the most scenic outing, **Trail F** starts just beyond the last cottage in Berchers Bay. This coral cobblestone beach has such a variety of coral that you should bring along a guide book to make positive identifications. As you ascend the arid hillside, the vegetation never grows to any size, so you will have good views . Looking out to the east, remember that the ocean is unbroken by any land between here and Africa. Accompanied by dozens of hermit crabs, you'll be amazed at the size of the organ pipe cactus as you top the first portion of the ridgeline. A trail bears left 100 feet to a grandstand view of South Sound and Copper Mine Point. Continuing the ascent along the main trail, you'll soon reach the summit of the more than 400-foot knob. Scramble up the rocks for a 360° view of Virgin Gorda and its surrounding islands. The trail now winds its way down the northern slope of the mountain, intersecting Trail C and returning to its starting point. *Walking time: 1½ hours, complete circuit.*

Mosquito Island

17. The Mosquito Island Walk

Mosquito Island is just off the coast of Virgin Gorda in North Sound and is owned by Drake's Anchorage Resort Inn. You should obtain permission before exploring this island. On the southeast side is a shoreline trail along the gentle surf. A path on the north side leads to the top of the hill with good views of North Sound to the east and the Seal Dogs to the west. Not only is this a highly recommended walk, but Drake's Anchorage is also a suggested spot for lunch or dinner. ☎ 284-494-2254.

Anegada

18. The Walk on Anegada

Anegada is the second largest of the British Virgin Islands and lies directly north of Virgin Gorda. It contains 15 square miles and may be reached by air from Tortola. Unlike most Caribbean islands, which are of volcanic origin, Anegada is a coral atoll, and its highest point is less than 30 feet above sea level. Being at such a low elevation it receives little rainfall, so only dry land vegetation, such as loblolly and tamarind, grows well here. There are no mongooses on this flat island; the rock iguana is found only here and on Guana Island, but nowhere else in the world.

The ground is so level and the vegetation so open that you could walk just about anywhere. Since the population is less than 200, you should be able to wander around without worrying about elbow room. Western Anegada has the Flamingo Pond Bird Sanctuary, a salt pond and mangrove area that is home to waterfowl, a variety of herons, terns, osprey, and snowy plovers. Also in this area, the National Parks Trust has imported a flock of flamingos from Bermuda in hopes of re-establishing this bird, once found in great numbers throughout the BVI.

The one real settlement on Anegada is called just that, The Settlement, and has the only few feet of paved road on the island. Further east is another salt pond, Budruck Pond.

19. The North Side of Anegada Beaches Hike

This is it. If you want miles of unbroken white sand beaches you won't find anything better than the north coast of Anegada. With almost no inhabitants and absolutely no hotels on this coastline, the coral sand stretches unbroken for almost 20 miles! Foaming waves call you from one bay to the next, each with a name to remember: Cow Wreck Bay, Bones Bay, Windlass Bight, and Soldiers Wash. Imagine walking all day long with the tropical sun above, the white sand beneath and the clear blue water beside you and possibly not seeing another human being the whole time you are walking. Occasionally, an osprey may fly overhead; you are almost guaranteed to meet one or more of the hundreds of feral goats, donkeys, or cows.

Nowhere else in this part of the Caribbean can you walk so long on such an undeveloped, pristine shoreline for as long as on the north coast of Anegada.

> *Special Note: This isolation brings some responsibilities your way. There are no hotels or other places to obtain fresh water; bring plenty with you. Also, there is very little shade along this coast. Be sure to bring cover-ups to protect you from the sun. The area has no clutter, so please take extra care to carry out any trash you may have with you.*

Be sure to leave explicit instructions as to where you wish to be picked up. A road parallels the coast from the island's western end to Windlass Bight, but from there it is several miles to the only other road touching the coast at Loblolly Bay.

Jost Van Dyke

20. The Great Harbor to the High Point at Little Harbor Hike

Walking time: 1½ hours, one way

Jost Van Dyke lies west of Tortola and is reached by ferry from Tortola or the U.S. Virgin Islands. It has only three square miles and 150 people. Therefore, it is a good place to leave the car behind and let your feet do the exploring.

Walk the main road from Great Harbor up and over several knobs and hillocks for approximately two miles to descend into Little Harbor (where a couple of small bars could help alleviate your thirst). Continue along the road, making a moderately quick ascent to the top of the rise. Here is a small dirt road, which you now follow uphill to the left. Near the ridgeline the road ends and a narrow pathway can be followed to a viewpoint.

This is an easy hike and the effort is rewarded with good views of East End Harbor, Garner Bay, Little Jost Van Dyke, and small Sandy Cay lying in the foreground, with the mountains of Tortola thrusting up in the distance. A highly recommended hike.

➤ **Note:** From the viewpoint at the top of the ridge is an undefined pathway which rises to the main crest of the mountains and continues most of the way to West End. Be forewarned, however, that this trail is used very little other than by goats; be prepared to spend the better part of the day negotiating your way over, under, around, and through scratchy and knarled branches. Only for the most adventurous.

The British Virgin Islands

21. The White Bay Beach Hike

Walking time: 2 hours, 20 minutes, round trip

White Bay is reached by walking westward from Great Harbor along the shore lined with sea grape. At the end of the small settlement, ascend the rise, following the dirt road amid cactus and century plant blooms. Avoid the road going up to the left and continue to the top of the rise for a view of your destination – White Bay. Descend and make a hard switchback to begin walking along the beach (respect the rights of private residents).

With the green of St. John and St. Thomas rising above the blue across the Caribbean Sea, you'll soon go by the tents of White Bay Campground, partially hidden by the scruffy vegetation. A short pathway beyond the campground will bring you out to the far reaches of the bay and a small restaurant.

Verdant hills slope gently to the sand at White Bay.

Sandy Cay

22. The Sandy Cay Beach and Trail Walk

Walking time: 30 minutes, round trip

Sandy Cay lies just east of Jost Van Dyke and can be reached only by private or chartered boat. This is a popular picnic and lunch spot with the yachts that cruise these waters, yet it is often possible to spend a whole afternoon on the island without running into anyone else.

The trail leaves the beach and passes through a stand of palm trees before coming back out to the shoreline and more white sand. From this second small beach the trail rises and follows the edge of the low cliffs above crashing surf. The pathway now turns inland and cuts across the island through a swampy area of palms before returning to the starting point. A very pleasant and highly recommended walk.

Norman Island

23. The Norman Island Hike

Walking time: 1 hour, 20 minutes, round trip

Norman Island is south of Tortola and can be reached only by private or chartered boat. It is most famous for the caves just south of Treasure Point, a couple of which are large enough to be explored by small dinghies. Local lore holds it to be the location of Robert Louis Stevenson's *Treasure Island* and, to be sure, Stevenson did sail the waters around the island.

The island is deserted, and the best point to begin a walk is on the beach of its largest bay, The Bight. Along with the scrub brush here are a number of small ruins and other signs of former habitation. A good walk for the adventurous is to climb the small ridge behind the bay and walk east along the ridge through overgrown vegetation for just over a mile. There is no official trail here, but small pathways are evident and can be followed. In about 40 minutes you will come to the secluded white sands of Money Bay. Return by the same route.

Peter Island

24. The Peter Island Hike

Walking time: 3 hours, round trip

Peter Island lies about five miles directly south of Road Town, Tortola. The island is owned by the Peter Island Hotel and Yacht Harbor; the few roads see little traffic. The Peter Island Ferry makes several runs daily from Tortola. It is possible to arrive early, enjoy a full day of exploring, swimming and snorkeling, yet still make it back to Tortola early in the evening.

A pleasant excursion is to walk the road east from the resort and down to the white sand beach of Sprat Bay for a quick dip in the palm-lined cove. Back on the road, ascend the low ridge, looking east to admire the surf crashing onto the shore of Big Reef Bay. Continue walking south, dropping off the ridge, unitl you come to White Bay. This quiet, white sand beach has a gently rolling surf. The waves can be seen lapping the shore for miles to the east and west. A recommended hike.

Cooper Island

25. The Cooper Island Hike

Walking time: 1 hour, 20 minutes, round trip

Cooper Island may be reached only by chartered or private yacht. The island has very few inhabitants. A very good hike can be had by following the short trail that leads up the ridge from the Cooper Island Beach Club. The trail follows the ridgeline and has views across to Tortola, Salt Island, Ginger Island, and Virgin Gorda.

The British Virgin Islands

Sint Maarten/ Saint Martin

With over 30 beaches surrounding the island, the emphasis here is on the surf, sun, and sand. These beaches are as varied as they are numerous. Some are ringed by limestone cliffs indented with caves to explore, while others have palm trees swaying in the soft tradewinds. On Sint Maarten/Saint Martin you can have the luxury of stepping out of your hotel door and onto the beach, or you can freely explore an isolated, nearly-deserted cove. The island even gives you the possibility of doing your exploring and discovering *au naturel*, as there are a few beaches that the official tourist guide describes as "clothing-optional."

Dominating the scenery at about 1,400 feet in elevation is Pic Paradis, the highest point on the island. Although not quite high enough to capture the moisture needed for a rain forest, the summit is lush and green. Major points of the island can be seen from the top.

The coastline is rugged, with hidden bays and coves. Along the southern coast, the land rises steeply from the ocean, but the northern coast slopes more gently down to the sea. Much of the French side of the island is open, rolling countryside, while the Dutch side is dominated by two large salt ponds that, in previous times, were major sources of income for the inhabitants. Philipsburg, the capital of Sint Maarten, occupies a narrow strip of land between one of the salt ponds and Great Bay. The town is a booming shopping center, whose Dutch roots are reflected in the architecture of its oldest buildings.

Although recent high-rise condominium, hotel, casino, and shopping development has destroyed much of its cultural heritage and natural land features, the island still retains a unique attractiveness. One of its more pleasant aspects is that you can be immersed in the Caribbean Dutch culture of Philipsburg at one moment and, after only a short drive, you can feast on some of the most delicious French and Creole cooking found anywhere. Both sides of the island are equally charming and the residents appear genuinely happy to see you. (Almost 70% of the population is employed in some aspect of the tourist trade.)

Note: In the text that follows, Sint Maarten refers to the Dutch side of the island and Saint Martin to the French side.

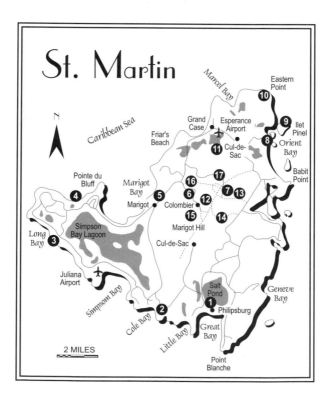

History

Sailing by the island on the feast day of Saint Martin de Tours in 1493, Columbus named the island San Martino after the saint. For more than a century the land remained in the hands of the Carib Indians, with only an occasional buccaneer ship using the isolated bays and coves as hiding spots. Around 1624, the French and Dutch began to settle the island and in 1631 a fort was established by the Dutch near Philipsburg. The Spanish, however, decided to reclaim the land and, two years later, drove the Dutch off. In a famous month-long battle in 1644, Peter Stuyvesant (who was wounded in the fighting) and the Dutch attacked the Spaniards at Fort Amsterdam. Even though the effort failed, Spain apparently lost interest in the island and abandoned it in 1648.

The year the Spanish left, the French and Dutch returned and divided the island – 16 square miles to the Dutch and 21 square miles to the French. For the next two centuries there were occasional clashes between the two nations for complete control of the island, but in 1869 a final agreement was reached honoring the original boundaries set in 1648. The two-nation island has existed peacefully ever since.

Sint Maarten, with Saba and Sint Eustatius, is part of the Netherlands Antilles, and the inhabitants enjoy much the same rights and privileges as their countrymen on the European continent.

Saint Martin, along with St. Barthélemy and Guadeloupe, is a department of France and its French citizens have voting representation in the French government.

Around 1960, Sint Maarten/Saint Martin was discovered by tourists in search of duty-free bargains. Since that time the hotels, shops, and restaurants have proliferated and now provide major income to the island. Between overnight hotel guests and

Sint Maarten/St. Martin

cruise ship passengers, the island sees more than one million visitors a year.

Data

Transportation to Sint Maarten/Saint Martin:
There are direct daily flights between North America and Sint Maarten. European-based airlines also have direct flights on a scheduled basis. Within the Caribbean, Sint Maarten is connected by air to a number of neighboring islands, such as Anguilla, Puerto Rico, Saba, St. Barthélemy, Guadeloupe, Sint Eustatius, St. Kitts, and Antigua.

A departure tax is imposed upon leaving the island.

Philipsburg, the capital of Sint Maarten, is a favorite cruise ship port of call, with Marigot on the French side gaining popularity.

Entry: If entering on the French side, Americans and Canadians need only proof of citizenship (passport, voter's registration card, or birth certificate) and possession of an ongoing or return airline ticket. All others will need a valid passport in addition to the required ongoing or return ticket.

Entering via the Dutch side, all foreigners (except American) need a valid passport and an ongoing or return ticket. Americans need only the required transportation ticket and proof of identity.

Currency: On the Dutch side, the national currency is the Netherlands Antilles florin (guilder). In Saint Martin, the French side of the island, it is the franc.

This island presents a unique situation in deciding which currency to exchange for your dollars. It may be wise to change just enough money to get you by for a few days and then exchange again if it becomes necessary. American dollars are almost universally accepted. Most establishments give close to the exchange rate that could be obtained at a bank. (Some even give discounts when payment is made in U.S. dollars!) Credit cards are accepted by most businesses.

As a general rule, banks in Sint Maarten are open Monday to Friday, 8:00 A.M. to 3:00 P.M., with a couple of them offering Saturday service.

Saint Martin banks are usually open from 8:30 A.M. to 1:30 P.M. and re-open from 2:00 P.M. to 4:00 P.M., Monday to Friday. They are closed Saturday and Sunday.

Tourist Information:

✍ **In the United States**
Sint Maarten Tourist Office
675 3rd Avenue, Suite 1806
New York, NY 10017
☎ 212-953-2084

✍ **In Canada**
Sint Maarten Information Office
243 Ellerslie Ave.
Willowdale, Toronto
Ontario, M2N 1Y5
☎ 416-223-3501

✍ **In Europe**
Minister Plenipotentiary of the
    Netherlands Antilles
Badhuisweg 173-175
2597 JP
'S-Gravenhage, The Netherlands
☎ 070-351-2811

On Sint Maarten the Tourist Office has a small welcome center in Cyrus Wathey Square, next to the pier on the waterfront. The executive office is located at:

✍ Sint Maarten Tourist Bureau
Imperial Building
W Nisbeth Road 23
Philipsburg, Sint Maarten, N.A.
☎ 5995-22337

Sint Maarten/St. Martin

For information specifically about the French part of the island write:

✍ **In the United States**
St. Martin Office of Tourism
10 East 21st Street, Suite 600
New York, NY 10010
☎ 212-529-8484

✍ **In Canada**
French Government Tourist Office
1981 McGill College Ave., Suite 490
Montreal, Quebec H3A 2W9
☎ 514-288-4264

✍ **In Europe**
French Government Tourist Office
178 Piccadilly, London W12 OAL
England, ☎ 0171-493-9232

In Marigot, Saint Martin, the Visitor's Bureau is housed in a small building next to the pier:

✍ Office du Tourisme
Port de Marigot
Marigot, Saint Martin 97150
French West Indies
☎ 590-87-53-21

Driving: Mopeds and rental cars are available in Philipsburg and Marigot. A valid driver's license is required.

There are public buses to major points on the island.

Language: The official language of Sint Maarten is Dutch; in Saint Martin it is French. The common spoken language of the entire island, however, is English.

Walking and Hiking Guide Companies: A relatively young organization, Action Nature, has taken upon itself the task of building trails throughout the least developed portions of the island. In conjunction with the Heritage Foundation of Sint Maarten, the group holds outings on a scheduled basis that are well-attended by locals. Action Nature has also trained a group of knowledgeable guides for visitors who wish to go on individual hikes and tours. That organization, known as the Association des Guides Randonneurs Professionnels de St. Martin, may be contacted through the French Tourist Office in Marigot.

Camping Areas: There are no official campgrounds on Sint Maarten/Saint Martin, but the Association des Guides Randonneurs Professionnels de St. Martin will arrange to take you on overnight backpacking trips.

Recommended Readings

📖   *St. Maarten, Saba and St. Eustatius* by Dr. J. Hartog

📖   *The French in the West Indies* by W. A. Roberts

📖   *Netherlands Windward Islands* by S. J. Kruythoff

📖   *Islands to the Windward: St. Martin, St. Barts, Anguilla, Saba, and Statia* by Brian Dyde (out of print)

Walks

1. A Walking Tour of Philipsburg

Philipsburg is second only to Charlotte Amalie, St. Thomas in the Virgin Islands as a major shopping center. Shops lining Front and Back streets are filled with everything from fine china and linens to first class French wines and delicious Dutch cheeses.

Begin walking on the pier in Great Bay. In the square (now known as Cyrus Wathey Square, but

Sint Maarten/St. Martin

still called De Ruyterplein by many locals) is the
Tourist Office – the best place to obtain information. At the head of De Ruyterplein is the Court
House. Built in 1793, it was destroyed by a hurricane and rebuilt in 1825. Through the years it has
served as a commander's home, jail, fire station,
town hall, and post office. Incidentally, postage
stamps from Sint Maarten are often colorful and
are highly prized by philatelists.

Turn right on Front Street and enter the frenzied
world of duty-free shopping. Every store offers
something of interest, but keep careful watch on
prices – many items are cheaper in your home town.
Nestled among all of this commercialism is the Roman Catholic Church, two blocks from the pier.

Continue on Front Street, passing by more shops,
the hospital, and a bank or two where you may exchange money. Near the banks is Pasanggrahan
Royal Inn, built around what was originally a government guest house. Come to the head of town,
where you'll see impressive Buncamper House, an
excellent example of an upper class island home.
Turn left and walk for one block, then turn left
again onto Back Street. This narrow road is not as
crowded as Front Street; the shops here are a little
more low key and are tucked between residential
homes. Continue on this quieter street for six
blocks, turn left onto St. Jansteeg Groene, then
right onto Front Street and on to the Methodist
Church. As you continue through town on Front
Street, the shops become fewer and are inter-
spersed with homes laced with the gingerbread fret-
work that is so common in the Netherlands Antilles.
Your walking tour comes to an end when you reach
the foot of Front Street.

2. The Cole Bay to Cay Bay Hike

Walking time: 1 hour, 45 minutes, round trip

Drive the main highway westward out of Philipsburg and go uphill. At the "T" intersection make a

left turn. Ascend Cole Bay Hill, where there are magnificent views over the sea. Continue on and turn left onto the road for Cay Bay.

This hike follows a trail that is actually a horse path, and will lead you onto the shore of Cole Bay. From the bay, the route rises until it arrives at a viewpoint overlooking Great Bay and Little Bay. Following switchbacks, it then gently drops to the secluded beach in Cay Bay. Cay Bay Beach is one of the less visited spots on the island and both swimming and exploring can be done in relative isolation.

3. The Cupecoy Bay and Long Beach Walk

From Philipsburg, drive the highway past the airport and, soon after Sapphire Beach Club, take the road to the left. You will arrive at some stone markers that indicate the paths down to the beach. Walk one of these and come out onto a most interesting beach. The dominant features are rugged sandstone cliffs that rise sharply from the sand and contain a number of small caves waiting to be explored. Continue eastward and you will come soon to Long Bay – also ringed by sandstone cliffs. The two beaches together make for about an hour's worth of walking. Incidentally, *au naturel* bathing is accepted on both beaches. Because of the unique cliffs, this is a recommended beach walk.

4. The Baie Rouge Beach Walk

Drive toward Sandy Ground out of Marigot, Saint Martin. Go through Sandy Ground, along Baie Nettie, and then begin looking for signs to Baie Rouge Beach.

Almost two miles of white sand stretch out along some of the most gentle surf on the island. On the eastern end is Pointe Du Bluff and "Devil's Hole," a curious formation of eroded coral. Although not officially designated as such, Baie Rouge Beach is a topless bathing area.

5. A Walking Tour of Marigot

Walking time: 1 hour, for the complete circuit

Begin your walking exploration of the major city of French Saint Martin at the Market Square on the waterfront. As with all of the marketplaces in the Caribbean, the busiest and most colorful time to visit is on Saturday morning.

After visiting the Tourist Office next to the pier – the best place to obtain detailed information – go one block to begin walking along Rue de Liberté. You are now in the heart of the duty-free shopping center of Marigot. (Best buys here are French perfumes, fashions, and wines.) In one block is the post office. As in Sint Maarten, the colorful stamps of French Saint Martin make good souvenirs and collector's items. Turn left onto rue de Président Kennedy, which is lined with numerous restaurants and cafés. Lunch or dinner is certain to be delicious in any of these establishments since most specialize in French or Creole cooking. Turn back toward the main part of town on rue Charles de Gaulle and, in one block, pass by the Mairie (City Hall).

Continue on rue Charles de Gaulle, turn left at Waterloo Alley and then right on Rue Maurasse. Cross rue de la République and follow a narrow alley for one block, turn right, then left, and then another quick left on rue de l'Hôpital. Walk uphill to the parking area for the fort. Take a tour of renovated Fort de Marigot and enjoy the view of the city, the bay, and the flat island of Anguilla lying five miles away across the waters of the channel. From here it is a easy matter to return to the waterfront, ending your exploration of this bit of France in the New World.

6. The Road to Colombier Walk

Walking time: 45 minutes, one way

Take the main road north out of Marigot and, just past the turnoff for Friars Bay, turn right onto the road to Colombier. There is no place to park your car, so arrange to be dropped off here and picked up at the ending point of the walk.

This outing follows the paved road through the vegetation-rich countryside. While it is a main road for this part of the island, traffic is relatively light and walking is pleasant. The bucolic scenery is dotted with cattle and goats grazing in small meadows; oleander, hibiscus, and bougainvillea line the road and gardens grow a wide variety of tropical vegetables. The road dead-ends just as the land begins to rise toward the hill country of Saint Martin. (It is possible to continue walking from here on a pathway to the heights of the mountains – see Walk #15.)

A short distance before the dead-end is La Rhumerie, an excellent restaurant, which makes for a perfect resting spot at the conclusion of the walk. Specializing in Creole cooking, the restaurant has expansive windows, which allow the cool country breezes in and afford restful views of numerous hummingbirds flitting in and out of nearby bushes.

➤ This is a highly recommended, peaceful, and enjoyable stroll through the countryside. In fact, it's such nice country that if you don't have time to take the walk, you should at least drive some of the road to Colombier.

7. The Pic Paradis Hike

Walking time: 1 hour, 20 minutes, round trip

Driving from Marigot, continue past the road to Colombier (see Walk #6) and, just after the sign for St. Louis, turn right onto the road to Pic Paradis. Continue until you reach an intersection with the gate of a private residence on your right. You'll know you are in the right place if you see two large concrete urns covered by vegetation flanking the gate. The track to Pic Paradis is on the left and can be driven (most safely by a four-wheel-drive vehicle). It is more enjoyable, however, to make the climb on foot, so park here and begin walking.

As the road rises, the vegetation becomes thicker and lusher. Saint Martin receives little rainfall, but what does fall lands on Pic Paradis, so this walk will show you more mosses and ferns than others. Follow the road to a dirt parking area near the summit. At approximately 1,400 feet, this is the highest point on the entire island. To the right is the radio tower and excellent views of Marigot and the bay. To the left is a short trail and views of Philipsburg, Salt Pond, Great Bay, and even of Oyster Bay and the eastern shore of the island. To the south you should be able to make out Ile Fourchue, St. Barts, Saba, Statia, St. Kitts and, on a clear day, Nevis. Don't miss this wonderful view!

Because this is a hike up the mountainside, it is classified as a moderately strenuous excursion.

An overview of Philipsburg from Pic Paradis.

8. The Cul-de-Sac to Baie Orientale Hike

Walking time: 2 hours, one way
Marked by red and white blazes

Drive the main road north out of Marigot, through Grand Case and take the first left. Follow this road all the way to its end. In the not-too-distant past, Cul-de-Sac and Baie Orientale were undeveloped and two of the least visited beaches. Today, however, the area has become a watersports, sunbathing, and partying haven, lined with hotels and restaurants. Do not let this deter you, for the sun, sand, and surf may still be enjoyed as you walk south to the end of Baie Orientale and the official naturist beach.

9. The Ilet Pinel Hike

Walking time: a little over an hour to go around the circumference of Ilet Pinel

Across the water from Cul-de-Sac (see Walk #8) is the small island of Ilet Pinel. This is a popular picnic and swimming spot and can be reached only by boat. A number of small companies operating from here will be happy to make round-trip arrangements.

Ilet Pinel is only half a mile square, but it makes for great explorations. The beach on the side facing Saint Martin has beautiful white sand and gently rolling surf. Climb the small knoll behind it and watch wild goats grazing on the scrub brush and cactus. Be careful of prickly pear cactus needles, which have been known to go through the sole of a shoe.

On the northern shore the waves come crashing in with tremendous fury on the boulders and gravel of the sea grape-lined shore. (Swimming would be dangerous here.) Explorations along the coast reveal interesting rock caves and formations.

Since Ilet Pinel may be one of the most accessible uninhabited islands in the Caribbean (although the main beach does attract a lot of bathers), this is a recommended excursion.

Sint Maarten/St. Martin

The Trail System of Saint Martin

Walks #10 to #17 exist due to one man's vision and the dedicated efforts of many others. Apprehensive that development would soon rob Saint Martin of its few remaining open spaces, Eric DuBois Millot of Marigot conceived the trail system as a way of introducing people to these areas and making them aware of what would be lost if all of Saint Martin were heavily developed. His efforts and ideas must have struck a chord, because numerous members of the organization he founded, **Action Nature**, have devoted countless hours of volunteer labor to building an excellent system of trails that has opened the interior to exploration. Traversing terrain that most visitors (and many island residents) never see, the pathways bring you into a world much different than that of the beaches, the towns, or the country roads.

Action Nature's primary goal and emphasis may be preservation and protection, but the group must also be admired for the work and dedication it brings to building and maintaining the trail system. But vegetation grows quickly and rampantly, often overtaking the best of trail markings and maintenance. Therefore, you may find yourself on poorly defined trails. If you are uneasy with this, obtain the services of an Action Nature-trained guide – a member of the Association des Guides Randonneurs Professionnels de St. Martin – for any of the walks listed below. See Walking and Hiking Guide Companies above for more information.

10. The Cul-de-Sac to Cactus Natural Park to Anse Marcel Hike

Walking time: 3 hours, one way
Marked by red and white blazes.

If you want some isolated walking instead of the crowded beaches of Cul-de-Sac and Baie Orientale (see Walk #8 for driving directions), this is the hike for you. Instead of walking southward in Cul-de-Sac, turn to the north and follow the dirt road which swings around to Eastern Point. From the road's end, you're pretty much on your own as you walk the open countryside above the blue waters of the Baie des Petites Cayes and the Caribbean Sea. Rounding the Pointe des Froussards, you'll pass through an area crowded so heavily with succulents that some residents have dubbed it Cactus Natural Park.

Follow the lay of the land. The hike will eventually lead you to the marina in Anse Marcel and the end of the hike. This outing is on fairly level terrain, but prepare for high temperatures and unrelenting sun.

➤ If you can't make arrangements to be picked up in Anse Marcel, you can easily walk the lightly-traveled road from Anse Marcel back to Cul-de-Sac (30 minutes).

11. Sentier Ravine Careta

Walking time: 3 hours, for the complete circuit
Marked by blue and purple blazes

Reach the beginning of this hike by driving northward from Marigot on the main road. Just after passing the Espérance-Grand Case Airport, look for the small sign on your right indicating the road that leads to the trailhead.

The circuit trail encircles the main crest of Mont Careta. Entering the Ravine Careta, the route first traverses the lower slopes of Mont O'Reilly before crossing the ravine to follow the contours on the

Sint Maarten/St. Martin

western side. With Pic Paradis and Montagne France looming above, it then swings around the mountain to begin its descent back to the starting point.

➤➤ Since this hike passes through private property you should check with the Tourist Office in Marigot first so that they may obtain proper permission for you.

12. Sentier des Crêtes

Walking time: expect to devote a major portion of the day to this strenuous, but highly recommended hike

The showpiece of the trail system, the Sentier des Crêtes is also its longest route, following the main crest of the mountains from the northeastern corner of Saint Martin to its southwestern area. Since it is such a long hike through an area that is little traveled, it is strongly suggested you obtain the services of a guide. This will also eliminate the need for someone to drop you off at the beginning of the trail and pick you up at its end.

The northeastern trailhead may be reached by driving the main road from Marigot, continuing past the turnoff for Cul-de-Sac and looking for the parking area of the scenic pullout overlooking Baie Orientale. The hike, marked by red and blue blazes, begins immediately across the main road (look for the wooden trail sign) and ascends a secondary road to Petit Fond before gaining the crest of the ridgeline on an old mule trail. The hike works its way toward the Pic Paradis road, which it meets after about two miles. You may decide to take the short side trip on your left to the summit and enjoy the view (see Walk #7).

To stay on the Sentier des Crêtes, continue to the right on the Pic Paradis to a dead-end. Leave the pavement along the side of the parabolic dish antenna and enter a world that is most unexpected on such a dry island. The route, now marked with red and green blazes, is bounded by giant elephant ear leaves and old-growth gommier trees. Almost taking on the feel of a rain forest, the branches of the trees are adorned with bromeliads and other epiphytes, some of which send their long tentacle roots to the ground. Making a series of twists and turns (which can be confusing if you don't have a guide), the trail crosses the Sentier Grand-Fond (see Walk #14) and climbs to the highest point of the route, Mount Flag-staff.

Even though you are on the highest point of the trip, it is not all downhill from here. Continue on the un-dulating ridgeline, passing two side routes to Colom-bier and an occasional good view across the eastern portion of the island, before coming to an unpaved road and then to the road in Concordia Pass. You may end your hike here or continue along the Sen-tier des Crêtes. The trail does proceed for 30 minutes or so to the summit of St. Peter Hill but, as there is not a driveable road on that peak, you would have to retrace your steps back to Concordia Pass. (Action Nature has plans to extend the trail to the main road near Cole Bay via Sentry Hill.)

13. Sentier Source Moho

Walking time: 1½ hours, one way, to the intersection with Sentier des Crêtes
Marked by pink and green blazes

From the village of Orléans this enjoyable trail rises through Moho Gut (or the Ravine du Paradis) to in-tersect the Sentier des Crêtes (see Walk #12) on the southwestern side of Pic Paradis. Watch closely for Arawak petrogylphs on a stone near an old well. About an hour into the trip, you'll be able to refresh yourself at the Moho Spring, which is surrounded by cedar, avocado, and cacao trees.

Sint Maarten/St. Martin

14. Sentier Grand-Fond

Walking time: 2 hours, one way, to the Sentier des Crêtes junction

Like the Sentier Source Moho, the Sentier Grand-Fond starts in the village of Orléans. This one, however, gradually ascends the Grand-Fond Valley to intersect the Sentier des Crêtes (see walk #12) just north of Mont Flagstaff.

> *Note: Mother nature has done a grand job of reclaiming the Sentier Grand-Fond pathway; it is now next to impossible to negotiate or follow. Not a recommended outing.*

15. The Colombier Valley to Hill's Top Circuit Hike

Walking time: 1 hour, 45 minutes, for the circuit Marked by pink and yellow blazes

Entering the remote village of Colombier (see Walk #6), you'll see a phone booth and a trail sign on the right. Park your car here and take the orange and blue marked route that winds around houses and yards growing pineapples, sugarcane, gombos, pidgeon peas, papayas, cassava, and other root crops. Coming to a "T" junction, turn right and start ascending on the path, soon to arrive at a view over the peaceful Colombier Valley.

Rising along the easily-followed trail, reach the ridgeline and a mountain pass, where you'll intersect the Sentier des Crêtes (see Walk #12). (To the right it is possible to follow that route for approximately 40 minutes to Concordia Pass.) Bear left (following red and green markers) along the old stone walls and negotiate the ups and downs of two small hills.

At the next intersection, leave the Sentier des Crêtes and descend left along the orange and green marked path, passing by an old well, and returning to the village of Colombier. A moderate hike.

16. Lotterie Valley Trail

Walking time: 1 hour, one way
Marked by yellow and green blazes

Descending from the parabolic dish antenna on Pic Paradis (see Hike #12 for directions to this point), this moderate walk passes by the ruins of the 18th-century Paradis sugarcane factory and crosses the Two Boilers Route (Hike #17) near the Two Boilers well. Continuing to the Lotterie Farm – now a country club – the route then makes use of an unpaved road referred to locally as the Large Mango tree Road. The hike comes to an end as it emerges onto the Colombier Road near the Main Road that leads around the island.

17. The Two Boilers Route

Walking Time: 45 minutes, complete circuit
Marked by yellow and blue blazes

Beginning near the summit of Pic Paradis (Hike #7), the Two Boilers Route descends to cross over the Lotterie Valley Trail near the well of the Two Boilers. It continues along a nice ridge overlooking the Colombier Valley before coming to the island's main ridgeline, which provides a sweeping vista of the eastern portion of Sint Maarten/St. Martin and out across the Caribbean to French St. Barth. Turning left to follow the red and green blazes of the Sentier des Crêtes (Hike #12), the route goes by a parabolic dish antenna, emerges onto pavement, and returns to the starting point.

Sint Maarten/St. Martin

Anguilla

J ust five miles north of St. Martin, Anguilla, like
St. Barth, is ringed by beaches – over 30 of them.
The island's main attraction is walking on the
sparkling coral sand. However, in contrast to the
nearby islands, many of the beaches here are lightly
developed or uninhabited. For splendid, isolated
walking on crescent-shaped, white sand beaches,
Anguilla can't be beat.

The highest point on the island is only 213 feet. Composed mostly of tertiary limestone, Anguilla receives
little rainfall, making the landscape stark and bare
when compared to its more mountainous neighbors.
While there are a few beaches lined with palm and
manchineel trees, most of the vegetation is low lying
scrub brush. There are several small islands around
Anguilla that are often visited by charter boats, and
each deserves some exploration. Anguilla, due to its
flat topography and uncrowded roads, has become
increasingly popular with people who come over
from St. Martin for a day of easy exploration and
surfside walking.

History

Recent archaeological evidence, backed by carbon
dating, shows that Anguilla was inhabited from as
early as 1600 to 1300 B.C. Not much is known about
these preceramic people. Later Amerindian inhabitants referred to their island as "Malliouhana."

Probably not actually seen by Columbus, the island
was named Anguilla (Spanish for "eel") by early
travelers to the New World because its low lying,
twisting landscape reminded them of an eel swimming in the water. The British, who arrived in 1650,

were attacked twice by the French in battles for domination. Britain, however, has always remained in possession of the island.

Because of the poor soil and low rainfall, the island was unsuited for the large-scale production of sugar that shaped societies on most Caribbean islands; Anguillan settlers made their living by raising livestock and harvesting salt from the island's numerous ponds. They also became excellent sailors and fishermen. Even today, Anguillans are recognized as some of the most expert seamen in the world.

Although Anguilla was part of a British colony that included St. Kitts and Nevis, it came under the local rule of St. Kitts. Tired of neglectful outside management and lack of control over its daily affairs, Anguilla declared itself independent in 1967. For two years this question of independence created heated arguments throughout the Caribbean. Eventually, in 1969, Great Britain landed troops on the island to "keep the peace." This resulted in what most Anguillans had wanted all along – a separate colony. In 1976 a constitution provided for a ministerial government and elected representatives. Formal separation from St. Kitts occurred in 1980; a new constitution in 1982 set up Anguilla as a British Dependent Territory with a governor who presides over an Executive Council. The House of Assembly oversees legislative matters.

At one time, Anguilla went unnoticed by tourists, attracting fewer than 1,000 visitors a year. This quickly changed in the 1980s as droves of daytrippers from St. Martin came to enjoy the secluded beaches. Hotels, villas, upscale resorts, and guest cottages, whose numbers could have been counted on one hand 30 years ago, are multiplying. Overnight visitors can come and enjoy the peaceful charms of an island that is 16 miles long and three miles wide, yet has fewer than 10,000 inhabitants.

Anguilla

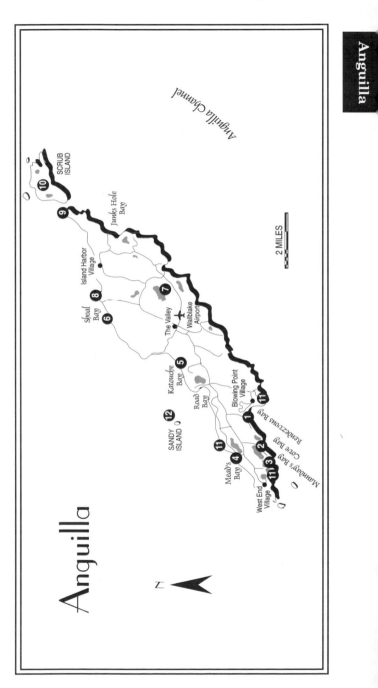

Data

Transportation to Anguilla: There are no direct flights from North America or Europe. The closest jet airports are Sint Maarten, Antigua, and Puerto Rico. Anguilla is also connected by regular scheduled flights with St. Kitts and St. Thomas.

Frequent ferries make the run across from Marigot, St. Martin to Blowing Point, Anguilla in about 20 minutes. Various companies operate these daily ferries, so it is possible to choose the time of day you wish to go. Check at the piers in Marigot and Blowing Point for schedules.

A departure tax is imposed when leaving Anguilla.

Entry: Canadian and American citizens need proof of identity. While a passport would be best, a photo ID card (such as a driver's license), along with a birth certificate (with raised seal), or voter's registration card will gain you entry. Citizens of the EEC need a valid passport. All visitors must possess an ongoing or return transportation ticket.

Currency: Anguilla is a dual-currency island. Everyone, even government offices, accepts both U.S. and East Caribbean dollars and, unless you request otherwise, your change will be returned in whichever currency you paid with. Remember to determine if the price quoted for an item is in East Caribbean dollars or American dollars.

Credit cards are not as universally accepted as on some other islands, although they are gaining more usage as time goes on.

For the most part, banking hours are 8:00 A.M. to 3:00 P.M., Monday through Thursday and 8:00 A.M. to 5:00 P.M. on Friday.

Tourist Information:

✍ **In the United States**
Anguilla Tourism Information Office
c/o Medhurst & Associates, Inc.
1208 Washington Drive
Centerport, NY 11721
☎ 512-425-0900

✍ **In Europe**
Anguilla Tourist Board
Windotel, 3 Epirus Road
London 3W6 7UJ
England, ☎ 0171-938-4793

The Tourist Office on Anguilla is located in the small administrative village of The Valley:

✍ Anguilla Department of Tourism
The Valley, Anguilla
British West Indies
☎ 264-497-2759

Driving: Mopeds and cars may be rented at various places throughout the island. A local driver's license is required and may be obtained upon payment of a fee and showing a valid foreign driver's license at the airport or any car rental agency. Drive on the left!

Language: English.

Walking and Hiking Guide Companies: There are none, but, with most walks centering on the beaches, open countryside, or on outlying islands only reachable by boat, a guide is unnecessary. Taxis can provide more than adequate driving tours of the island.

Camping Areas: With miles and miles of isolated beaches, it should be a simple matter to set up a tent and enjoy your stay. Unfortunately, camping is prohibited throughout the island. But, since this official attitude seems to change from time to time, contact the Department of Tourism or the Chief Minister's Office for current information.

Recommended Readings

📖 *Islands to the Windward: St. Martin, St. Barts, Anguilla, Saba, and Statia* by Brian Dyde (out of print)

Anguilla's weekly newspaper, *The Light*, provides insight into the daily lives of islanders.

Walks

1. The Rendezvous Bay Beach Walk

On Anguilla's southern coast, Rendezvous Bay is generally considered one of the most beautiful beaches and is renowned for the great variety of shells hidden in the sand. Although several resort complexes will be encountered on the 1.5-mile walk, they are removed from each other and, for the most part, do not intrude on the tranquility found here.

2. The Cove Bay Beach Walk

With no developments, Cove Bay is one of the quietest and most pristine beach walks to be taken on the southern coast. The urge to slip into the warm, placid water of the Caribbean Sea and loll about within the cool shadows cast by towering palm trees may bring your walk to a temporary halt. Once you have walked the full length of the beach, it is possible to do a bit of bird watching as you return to your car via the dirt road skirting the edge of Cove Pond.

Anguilla's tranquil shores.

3. The Maunday's Bay Beach Walk

Half moon-shaped Maunday's Bay has a popular beach and is home to Cap Juluca, one of the most exclusive (and expensive) resorts. A few restaurants and watering holes make it possible for you (if you have enough money with you!) to slake the thirst or hunger pangs that arise from walking the mile-long strip of developed white sand.

> ↪ **Note:** For those who can never get enough surf, sand, and sun, combine the above three walks into one long excursion for nearly a full day's worth of glorious tropical beachcombing.

4. The Mead's Bay Beach Walk

Just about a mile long, the beach at Mead's Bay has somehow managed to achieve an almost-perfect balance of development and serenity. With only a few tasteful resorts and a couple of dining spots (most of which are set well back from the sands), it is possible to walk along the beach enjoying the sun and surf with only minor distractions. On Anguilla's north-western coast, Mead's Bay is the perfect place to bob up and down in the slowly curling waves as a golden sun slips into a darkening Atlantic Ocean. After sunset, the sand, having been exposed to the sun all day, provides a warm viewing platform from which to gaze up at Ursa Major, Ursa Minor, Orion, and other constellations making their ritual journey across the night sky.

5. The Katouche Valley Hike

Walking time: 1 hour, round trip

On a dry island predominantly covered with scrub brush and small trees, a hike through Katouche Valley is a pleasant and surprising journey. Here, on your way to a most interesting cave, you'll find an unexpected forest of large trees, many of them decorated with hanging roots and gray-green foliage of numerous bromeliads, or air plants.

The beginning of the hike is reached by taking the road out of The Valley to the water tower on Crocus Hill. From the tower, you will descend via a winding (and maybe potholed) route, passing through the Masara Resort. Since this is private property, stop and ask – if the resort office is open – for permission to proceed. Begin the walk after parking your car at the end of the road at Katouche Bay.

About one-third of the way along the beach, which is not very long, you need to turn left onto an un-marked, but still noticeable pathway. Leaving the waves behind, you may be startled by the sudden flapping of wings when numerous turtle doves, the national bird of Anguilla, leave their perches, alarmed by your presence. Pass by a small brackish pond often inhabited by ducks, plovers, and a king-fisher or two. Those big holes in the mud are made by large land crabs, known for eating just about anything.

Fifteen minutes into the hike the ground rises steeply for a few hundred yards and then levels as stovepipe cactus and hummingbirds become more prevalent. Another 15 minutes and you'll arrive at your destination, Cavannagh Cave. Walk into this high, wide cave to discover small stalactites and many flying bats. A large tree grows from the center of the cave, the top branches escaping the near darkness by growing through a hole in the roof.

> Because of the unexpected vegetation in the valley and the chance to explore Cavannagh Cave, this is the most highly recommended outing on Anguilla.

6. The Copper Hole Walk

Walking time: 30 minutes, round trip

Like Thunder Hole in Maine's Acadia National Park, Copper Hole was formed after hundreds of years of bombardment by wind, waves, and salt spray. The rock and coral shoreline is inhabited by several species of lizards, while brown pelicans are often seen winging their way through the sky.

To find your way to Copper Hole, drive the main road from The Valley toward Crocus Bay, but be watching for the old hospital, where you'll make a right turn. In another 0.7 mile, bear right again to descend into a valley of grazing livestock. From the four-way intersection (where you will continue straight), proceed for another 0.4 mile and leave your car close to the geodesic dome house. As you walk along the deteriorating roadbed, you'll soon hear the sound of waves rushing into the blow hole. Within a few minutes, the road will end and you'll walk several more yards to the interesting rock formations of Copper Hole and the thunderous sounds they produce.

7. The 'Round Caul's Pond Hike

Walking time: 2 hours, for the complete circuit

Identified on tourist maps as a bird sanctuary, Caul's Pond is certainly not one of the easiest places to find. Driving from The Valley, take the road toward Shoal Bay. In less than two miles the road separates, the left fork continuing to Shoal Bay. You want to follow the right fork, paying close attention to the car's odometer. After 0.9 mile, turn right onto a nondescript dirt road (which is across the main highway from a small concrete factory). Pay close attention to these directions because, if you inquire locally, you'll soon find that many Anguillans haven't been to Caul's Pond and that quite a number have never even heard of it.

Once you find it, the correct dirt track leads to the northern side of the pond in 0.6 mile. Leave the car and begin walking on easy, flat ground, taking care not to brush against the prickly needles of the Turk's cap cactus growing in great profusion on the pond's western edge. Early morning walkers will be able to watch dozens of black-necked stilts take wing from their roosts. Great white herons, egrets, and belted kingfishers often troll the shallow water, attracted by the pond's abundant aquatic life.

An ancient Greek myth is the basis for a modern-day term and tells of the origin of kingfishers. Halcyone, who was the daughter of the King of the Winds, became distraught upon learning of the death of her husband at sea. Wishing to join her mate, she cast herself into the ocean. She did not die, but rather, with the gods taking pity on her, she and her husband's spirit were turned into kingfishers — birds capable of calming turbulent waters. From this old tale comes our phrase "halcyon days," used to describe peaceful and quiet times.

There is no real trail around Caul's Pond. Once you round the western point, thick vegetation may force you through oozing mud along the water's edge. The southern and eastern sides of the pond are also crowded with abundant (and prickly) growth. When one faint trail you are following becomes too over-grown, abandon it and search for a better way through the small forest. Sometimes you'll be walking on convoluted rock formations, other times pushing your way through native Anguillan frangipani. There is no danger of getting lost; it is easy to keep the pond within sight.

A recommended hike because of the variety of bird-life and the pond's wonderful feeling of isolation. However, because you have to make your way through thick vegetation along the pond's southern and eastern shores, the full excursion should be undertaken only by the adventurous.

8. The Shoal Bay East Beach Walk

Nearly two miles long, Shoal Bay East is considered by many visitors and residents to be the prettiest beach on the island. The white sands, curved almost in the shape of the number seven, are often deserted and contain a rich bounty for shell hunters. Sea grape and coconut palms provide shade, while several bars can furnish you with liquid refreshment.

9. The Windward Point Walk

The eastern end of Anguilla is uninhabited, wind-swept, desolate, and dry, which means it has all of the right conditions for a quiet and contemplative outing. You may drive to the beginning of this walk by taking the road eastward out of Island Harbor Village and turning south as the road bears right. Soon, you will turn left onto a dirt road identified by a sign marking Junks Hole Bay. Once on this track you'll be driving through sea grape. Keep left when the right fork veers to Junks Hole Bay in 0.7 mile. Continue through sea grape, frangipani, and cactus. Stay to the left for an additional 1.9 miles, soon coming to the end of the road and the start of your foot explorations.

With such sparse vegetation, you may wander just about anywhere you wish. The shoreline has numerous contorted rock formations that are constantly pounded by waves churned up by the meeting of the Atlantic Ocean and the Caribbean Sea at the island's eastern-most spot, Windward Point. Inland a bit, you can pick your way through the Turk's cap cactus and other succulents to a small knoll overlooking Scrub Island and out across the Caribbean Sea to St. Martin, St. Barth, and Saba.

Turk's Cap cactus along the Windward Point walk.

10. The Scrub Island Walk

Inhabited only by goats and located within yards of Anguilla's Windward Point, two-mile-long Scrub Island may only be reached by private or chartered boat. (Do not attempt to swim across the channel from Anguilla or you may get a free trip to the Virgin Islands!) Several companies specialize in arranging day sail, snorkeling, picnicking, and diving trips to the island and may be contacted through the tourist office.

You could easily spend a day here, walking along the white sand beach on the island's western shore, discovering the remains of a once-posh tourist resort, finding an abandoned airplane next to an old dirt airstrip, or winding your way through one of the most luxurious natural frangipani gardens to be found anywhere.

Frangipani, a small tree less than 15 feet in height with a pleasantly scented white or pinkish flower, is well suited for places like Scrub Island. Its soft branches hold water for long periods of time, helping the plant to survive arid conditions and the dry season. In fact, to conserve water and energy, the leaves drop off as the rainy season comes to an end. In a perfect example of nature's cooperation between plants and animals, frangipani caterpillars (whose large yellow and black bodies make them easy to spot) begin to feast on the frangipani's leaves just as the dry season begins. The leaves, which would fall off the plant anyway, provide the nourishment caterpillars need to pupate and undergo metamorphosis into hawk moths.

11. Walks on Hotel and Resort Grounds

In 1976, Anguilla hosted fewer than 1,500 tourists. Today, the island's annual visitors total close to 100,000. This growth has been accompanied by a corresponding increase of hotels, resorts, and villas – a number of which have grounds worth a stroll.

Carimar Beach Club's gardens are not extensive, but are well tended and contain a wide variety of tropical foliage, such as hibiscus, allamanda, firecracker, anthurium, frangipani, oleander, and spider lily. If not busy, the staff has been known to help visitors identify the dozens of different blossoms. **Cap Juluca** has two beaches and nearly 200 acres of landscaped gardens. **Malliouhana's** 25 acres thrust out between two beaches of white sand. **Rendezvous Bay Hotel** is surrounded by 60 acres of coconut palms and other Caribbean greenery.

➤ Remember, if you are not a registered guest, it is common courtesy to ask permission before enjoying the grounds of any hotel.

12. Off-Shore Islands and Cays

Within close proximity of Anguilla are numerous islands and cays worthy of your walking attentions. Charter companies, who may be contacted through the tourist office, can make arrangements for round-trip excursions to any of them.

Just two miles northwest of Anguilla, **Sandy Island** is visited on a regular basis for all-day swims and sea-side picnics. Surrounded by the turquoise sea and only 650 feet long, this is probably the perfect desert island. The land is uninhabited, palms are blown gently by the ever-present tradewinds, sea birds hover lazily overhead, and the surf rolls in softly and serenely.

The Prickly Pear Cays, two small islands, are six to seven miles out from Road Bay. The most popular spot for visitors is the expanse of white sand enclosed by coral reefs on Prickly Pear East.

Further out is **Dog Island**, whose Great Bay has an excellent beach perfect for some very private bathing. Bailys Cove offers labyrinths of coral and hundreds of iridescent fish, which make the snorkeling some of the best in the islands. Dog Island was inhabited at one time and, on your ramblings, you may discover the remains of an old runway and the rock walls that stretch from one side of the island to the other, reminders that farming this rough land was a challenge indeed.

St. Barthélemy

(St. Barth or St. Barts)

With over 20 beaches around the island, the emphasis here, as with Sint Maarten/St. Martin, is on the joys of white sand and tropical sun. Also known as St. Barth or St. Barts, St. Barthélemy lies 15 miles southeast of St. Martin and is decidedly French. The inhabitants are mostly descendants of early Norman and Breton settlers and much of that culture is still alive here. It is not uncommon, in fact, to see both men and women dressed in traditional French costume.

As on St. Martin, one has the choice of walking on a beach filled with tourists and lined by large hotels, or of exploring an isolated and deserted bay fringed by palm trees and tropical flowers. Most of the island is a landscape that is rugged yet relatively low in elevation. The small hills of volcanic origin overlook deep valleys checker-boarded by the green squares of family-owned gardens and fields. A lack of rainfall, coupled with the rough terrain, has prevented St. Barth from developing any large agricultural crops. As a result, much of the island is sparsely inhabited and the landscape in many places appears as it did when the first settlers arrived.

The tourist industry is only now discovering St. Barth, so it could still be classified as unspoiled. The hotels, for the most part, are small and unobtrusive, and the locals, like their French counterparts on the European mainland, are a warm and friendly people –once you are able to make it past their somewhat feisty exterior. Night life is almost non-existent and what does exist, is low key.

There are no large mountains to climb, so all walking on the island is easy to moderate. St. Barth is not for those seeking fast-paced thrills or long challenging mountain hikes, but if you are looking for relaxed walking and a kind of atmosphere that is quickly disappearing in the Caribbean, then a visit to St. Barth is for you.

History

St. Barth was claimed for the Spanish by Columbus in 1493, and named after his brother Bartholomew. The island remained uninhabited by Europeans until the mid-1600s (although the Carib Indians lived there), when the first French settlers from St. Kitts arrived. In the late 17th century, settlers from the coasts of Normandy and Brittany arrived in large numbers and the Caribs departed.

For the next 100 years the population survived by working the sea and the rocky soil of the island. In 1784, St. Barth was given to Sweden for trading rights in that country. The Swedes renamed the capital Gustavia and many of their buildings are still in use today. The new owners declared St. Barth a free port and, as a result, trade flourished. On the heels of the legitimate trade, contraband and smuggling also prospered. Unfortunately for St. Barth, the invention of the steamboat, which permitted shipping between Europe and the New World to take a more direct route, made St. Thomas the preferred trading port. This loss of commerce, coupled with hurricanes, earthquakes, and devastating fires, induced many residents to emigrate to other islands.

France regained title in 1878; St. Barth has been under French rule ever since. Today, along with St. Martin and Guadeloupe, the island is an overseas department of France, and the inhabitants enjoy the same rights, privileges, and responsibilities as those living in France.

Once the almost exclusive playground of the rich, St. Barth is opening up to more and more tourists, who search out the duty-free shops and the pleasures of Caribbean beaches. This island of only 5,000 inhabitants plays host to more than 120,000 visitors annually.

Data

Transportation to St. Barth: There are no direct flights from the U.S. to St. Barth. There are, however, air connections with St. Thomas, Sint Maarten, and Guadeloupe and each of those islands may be reached from the United States. Canada, on a somewhat limited basis, does have direct flights and, of course, being a part of France, the island has direct air connections with the homeland.

Ferry services run on a scheduled basis from Philipsburg, Sint Maarten. A number of charter companies based in Philipsburg also make Gustavia, St. Barth, a frequent destination.

Entry: Americans and Canadians will need some proof of citizenship (passport or birth certificate) and possession of an ongoing or return airline ticket. EEC citizens need their national identity card.

Currency: The national currency is the French franc, although U.S. dollars are widely accepted in shops and hotels. If you wish to exchange money, most banks are open from 8:00 A.M. to 3:30 P.M. or 4:00 P.M. with a two-hour lunch "siesta" from noon to 2:00 P.M.

Tourist Information:

✍ **In the United States**
French West Indies Tourist Board
610 5th Ave.
New York, NY 10020
☎ 212-757-1125

✍ **In Canada**
French Government Tourist Office
1981 McGill College Ave., Suite 490
Montreal, Quebec H3A 2W9
☎ 514-288-4264

✍ **In Europe**
French Government Tourist Office
178 Piccadilly, London W1Z OAL
England, ☎ 0171-493-9232

Information may be obtained on St. Barth at the
Tourist Office in the Quai Général de Gaulle next to
the pier in Gustavia:

✍ Office Municipale du Tourisme
Gustavia, St. Barthélemy
French West Indies
☎ 590-27-87-27

Driving: Rental cars are available in Gustavia and
at the airport. Something to remember is that St.
Barth contains under 10 square miles. This means
that just about anywhere you wish to go will be
within reasonable hiking distance. Hitchhiking is
widely accepted and practiced.

Language: French, no doubt about it. Unless you
speak fluent French, bring your phrase book and be
ready to communicate with a lot of sign language.
Some of the larger hotels do have an employee who
speaks English, and a few of the taxi drivers can
carry on rudimentary conversations in English.

Walking and Hiking Guide Companies: At
present there are none. From time to time, one of
the residents will lead visitors on guided walks. Ask
the Tourist Office or a hotel to suggest someone for
you.

Camping Areas: There are no official campgrounds and no camping of any kind is permitted.

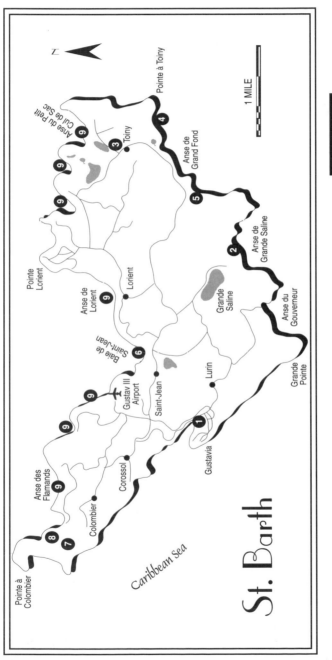

Recommended Readings

📖 *The French in the West Indies* by W. A. Roberts

📖 *The History of St. Barthélemy* by Georges Bourdin

📖 *Islands to the Windward: St. Martin, St. Barts, Anguilla, Saba, and Statia* by Brian Dyde (out of print)

Walks

1. A Walking Tour of Gustavia

Walking time: 1 hour, one way

Begin this walk on the waterfront as you watch the customs guards darting their motorboat in and out among visiting yachts in the busy harbor. Walk uphill toward the large, shingled clock tower that can be seen from anywhere in town. From the manicured garden courtyard there is a view that takes in all of Gustavia and the harbor.

On your way back into the main part of town, turn onto rue de l'Eglise to reach the Catholic Church, built in 1822 and refurbished in 1842. The Spanish-looking façade, with its numerous pilasters and two-statue nooks, seems a bit out of place in a town more or less dominated by Swedish architecture. One block away on rue Gambetta is the 1855 Anglican Church, constructed of local stone and bricks imported from France. Continue into the shopping district, working your way past numerous small shops and restaurants. The best duty-free bargains on St. Barth are French perfumes, wines, and fashions. If you have worked up an appetite, almost any restaurant will serve you a delicious meal.

This is truly one of the joys of the French islands – it seems that every cook in every restaurant, no matter how small or large, is a master chef. It is next to impossible to find an unsatisfying meal.

Near the small open air market is the Town Hall, whose base and foundation is lavastone held together with a volcanic sand and limestone mortar. Once the governor's house, it now serves as administrative offices. Continue walking on the narrow main road that ascends the hillside on the far end of town. Finding the winding, cactus-lined pathway, work your way up to the site of Fort Gustav. Constructed in the late 1700s by the Swedes, most of the fort is now in ruins, but the knoll you're standing on offers views over Gustavia, the harbor, and the western coast of St. Barth.

2. The Anse de Grande Saline Walk

To reach this grand, undeveloped strip of soft sand along St. Barts southern coast, drive from Gustavia to Lurin, keeping left at the intersection of a road which descends on the right to Anse du Gouverneur (also a nice, but shorter beach walk). Dropping off the ridgeline, make a right and leave your vehicle in the car park at La Grande Saline. While walking along the five-minute pathway to the beach, you can admire the rugged and rocky slopes of Morne Rouge.

Once on the shore you may decide to join others who are sunbathing *sans* clothing. Though technically banned, the enforcement of the ordinance against total nudity on beaches is very lax. However, be aware that arrests have been made from time to time. At the eastern end of the beach it's possible to climb up rocks along the lower slopes of Morne Rouge for an elevated view of your surroundings and out across the Caribbean Sea.

St. Barts

3. The Lorient to Grand Fond Hike

Walking time: 2½ to 3 hours, one way

This is one of the most enjoyable countryside outings that can be taken. Although it follows the main
road around the eastern section of St. Barth, traffic
is so light that this should pose no problem or de-
tract from the scenery along the way. Take the main
road past the airport to the little village of Lorient
and begin the hike here – after stopping to examine
the ceramic tile-covered graves in the cemetery. If
you are on St. Barth on All Saints Day, be sure to
make a pilgrimage here, for this is the day that
graves are restored and repainted and multitudes
of fresh flowers are placed on top. In the evening
and all through the night, the cemetery is illumi-
nated by hundreds of candles, casting shadows on
those who have come to honor their departed loved
ones.

Follow the road to the east. With the hills in the
background, your trek will always keep you close to
the shore. (Just about anytime you wish, you can
take a refreshing dip in the ocean.) The hike will
also take you by the small village of Grand Cul-de-
Sac, where there will be at least one good restaurant or watering spot. The dominant feature of the
hike, however, is the peace and serenity that you
will feel as you pass through this gentle country.
Beyond Toiny, snaking coral rock walls encircle cattle and goats grazing in green pastures. Trim red-
tiled country homes dot the landscape and the residents tend to slow you down with neighborly conversation and helpful suggestions. The hike ends
along the windy and rocky coastline of Grand Fond.

If you have not had enough walking, continue along
the same road and return to Lorient in about an
hour. This additional trip makes a long ascent over
the steep ridgeline separating the northern and
southern coasts.

A highly recommended, moderate hike. This is such
a beautiful landscape that it is strongly urged that

you drive through this area if you don't have the time to take the hike. You won't regret it.

4. The Anse Toiny to Pointe à Toiny Walk

Walking time: 50 minutes, round trip

As the main road from Grand Cul-de-Sac drops onto the southern coast and swings westward toward Grand Fond, a small dirt road, almost hidden by vegetation, veers off to the left and descends to deserted Anse Toiny. The road is heavily rutted, so leave your car near its beginning and walk onto the curving white sands. With usually no more than two or three people around and only scrub brush for vegetation, you should have no trouble working on your tan – just be sure to bring cover-ups to escape the sun.

For those who like to make their own way, it is possible to continue eastward, walking off the beach and ascending the open country to Pointe à Toiny and a commanding view of the waves washing onto Anse Toiny and Anse de Grand Fond.

5. The Chemin Douanier

Walking time: 2 hours, round trip

The longest and most enjoyable trail hike to be taken on St. Barth, the Chemin Douanier is accessed by leaving your car at the small parking area on the very western end of Anse de Grand Fond and walking westward on the coral cobblestone beach. At the far end of the beach is an obvious pathway that leads to the cliffs.

With only minor ups and downs, this grand coastline hike overlooks the sea. At some places – such as the "Washing Machine," which you come across after just 10 minutes on the trail – the waves come in as impressive breakers causing thunderous booms. On other spots, the sea washes gently onto the coast, the resulting foam sparkling in the sunshine and covering the flat rock beds like a satin blanket.

The trail, through open country of cactus and scrub brush, hugs the lower slopes of Morne Rouge, whose heights could be climbed if you don't mind picking your own way on unsure footing. After about an hour's worth of walking the terrain becomes steeper and the pathway will begin to fade; retrace your steps to your car.

A very highly recommended and isolated moderate hike. Remember to bring cover-ups or sunscreen as the entire route is exposed to the sun.

View from Chemin Douanier.

6. The Plage St.-Jean Walk

Plage St.-Jean is probably the most popular beach on the island. It is reached by driving past the airport north of Gustavia. The picture-perfect, crescent-shaped bay has white sand and calm waters, as well as a number of hotels close by and even a few seaside cafés for lunch or a cool, refreshing drink.

Don't expect to have quiet hours of beachcombing here. Plage St.-Jean is usually saturated with locals and tourists alike coming here in large numbers to look at, and be seen by, each other.

7. The Anse de Colombier Trail

Walking time: 40 minutes, round trip

A marked route to a hidden, but popular beach, the Anse de Colombier Trail is accessed at the end of the paved road in Colombier on St. Barth's northwest corner. Before beginning the walk, take a few moments at the viewing platform to enjoy the scene spread out before you. On the far horizon sits Sint Maarten, with Ile Fourchue lying in front. Closer to St. Barth, stretching in a line to the northeast, are small parcels of green surrounded by a sea of blue – Ile Chevreau, Ile Fregate, and Ile Toc Vers. Below you and a bit to the left is the golden horseshoe of Anse de Colombier.

From the platform, walk along the road for a few feet to make a right onto a descending footpath. As this route can be rather steep and is bounded by tall stove pipe cactus, be careful what you grab for if you begin to slip. The numerous varieties of this cactus are known by many different names throughout the Caribbean – organ pipe, diddle doe, dildo, datu, night-blooming cereus and, no doubt, other names. No matter its moniker, the rows of densely packed spines will exact a heavy toll upon any flesh that touches it.

In less than 30 minutes of walking, the beach is reached and you can laze away the day watching pelicans and boobies diving into the sea and emerging with their afternoon meals. Or, you could be adventurous and follow the old dirt road and open country out to St. Barth's northwestern tip for even better views of Sint Maarten and Ile Fourchue. A moderate walk.

8. Sentier des Pêcheurs

Walking time: 40 minutes, round trip

Also providing access to the Anse de Colombier, the most popular walking route on St. Barth is Sentier des Pêcheurs, which begins at the end of the paved road in Flamands. Going under a couple of small overhangs, the trail is a pleasant coastline walk with only gradual changes in elevation. About 15 minutes into the walk, you could take a steep descending side trail to tidal pools that are home to a rich variety of sea life – urchin, anemone, crab, and more. From the side trail, it is only five more minutes of walking before Anse de Colombier is reached. A moderate walk.

> **Note:** If you are able to arrange a car shuttle, a most enjoyable outing would be to descend to Anse de Colombier via Walk #7 and then be picked up in Flamands after having walked out on Walk #8.

9. The North Shore Beach Walks

Take the main road out of Gustavia toward the airport. From here, it doesn't matter which way you go since you will run into wonderfully clean, uncrowded beaches in either direction.

To the west are Anse des Cayes, Anse des Lezards, and Anse de Flamands, with a full-service hotel and the prettiest beach on St. Barth. To the east are Anse de Lorient, Anse de Marigot, Anse de Grand Cul-de-Sac, and Anse de Petit Cul-de-Sac. Every one of these beaches deserves some of your walking time.

A Special Walk. Off the northwestern coast of St. Barth is the desert island of Ile Fourchue. There is no fresh water here and it is inhabited only by wild goats, so you will probably be alone on this unique and wonderful place. Ile Fourchue resembles a moonscape in that there are no trees, only rocks and large boulders scattered among the Turk's cap cactus and scrub brush. The inner bay contains a small beach from which you can begin your explorations. Rising quickly from the sea, the land reaches rocky, precipitous heights overlooking pounding surf. The waves come in with such force and rage that the spray is sometimes hurled 300 feet into the air.

There are five peaks on Ile Fourchue and they are all interconnected by high ridges. Each has a different view; one has crashing surf, another looks toward Sint Maarten, and yet another makes the coastline of St. Barth appear as if it were less than a mile away.

For those who can appreciate the stark landscape, this is a highly recommended trip. A full day could easily be spent exploring the island and watching the antics of the wild goats.

> ⟩⟩ **A few special notes about Ile Four-chue:** The island can be reached only by private or charted boat. Inquire in Gustavia about chartering one or hitching a ride on one of the cruising yachts.

>> *There is no fresh water on the island, so be sure to bring plenty with you. Since only cactus and scrub brush grow here, be prepared for constant glaring sunshine. Also remember that the needles of the cactus can go right through the sole of a shoe – be careful where you step. One final, important note – Ile Fourchue is a private island and, as such, you need to check with the Office du Tourisme in Gustavia about gaining permission to visit it.*

Saba

S aba, "The Unspoiled Queen of the Caribbean," lives up to her tourist bureau-inspired name. Saba has escaped the commercialism and destruction of natural beauty that has accompanied the rise in tourism on many other islands of the Caribbean. This five-square-mile island has but one small, naturally occurring beach and just a handful of guest accommodations, the largest consisting of only about 10 rooms.

Until recently all of Saba was a nation of walkers and hikers. Fifty years ago there were no cars or roads. Handcarved steps set in the mountainsides connected one village to another. Over 200 steps climbed the steep slope of the island from Fort Bay to The Bottom. Over 900 steps crossed the mountain to connect the capital city with the village of Windwardside, 1,100 feet higher in elevation. A total of 1,064 steps lead to the summit of Mt. Scenery, the highest point on the island at 2,854 feet. Other steps and mountain trails wound their way around the island.

"The Road" on Saba was built in the same manner as the trails and steps. The nine-mile road was cut through the mountains and the stones were laid by hand. Foreign experts had decided that the steep and rugged terrain of Saba prevented such a road from ever being built. One of the inhabitants, Josephus Lambert Hassell, disagreed and did something about it. Hassell had no formal training as a road builder. So, armed with only a correspondence course in engineering, he designed and oversaw the 20-year construction project of connecting the two ends of the island by road. Its completion brought about a decline in the use of the steps and pathways. Many fell into disrepair, and some even began to disappear. Today, though, due partly to the increased tourist awareness of walking and hiking and a desire to preserve island heritage, the Saba Conservation Foundation, in conjunction with many individual citizens, does an excellent job keeping the steps in good repair and maintaining, marking, and signing the routes. It is now possible once again to walk through the varied vegetation and terrain of the Unspoiled Queen.

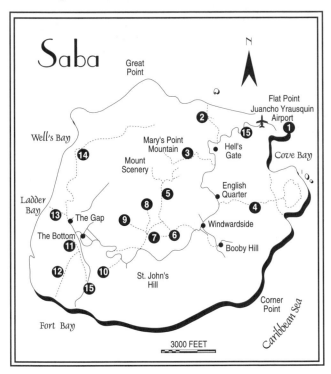

The mountainous terrain of Saba insures an abundant rainfall and the lush vegetation that accompanies it at the higher elevations. At a lower level, the rain forest gives way to scrub brush and below that are open fields and meadows. On your ramblings you may even encounter some of the hundreds of wild goats that still roam the island. Coconut trees, giant elephant ears, mango trees, cashews, mahogany, bananas, and a wide variety of orchids are just a part of the plant life to be seen.

The 1,200 inhabitants of Saba are, undoubtedly, the friendliest people in the Caribbean. Almost everyone will know that you are a visitor, when and how you arrived, and where you are staying. It is next to impossible to walk the road without someone engaging you in conversation or a driver inquiring if you need a ride. They are genuinely interested in you and wish to share the pleasures of their island. Don't be surprised as you walk along the narrow streets if you are invited into a living room to take a look at the delicate handmade lacework the women do on imported Belgian linen. They will be happy just to talk with you as you sip some Saba Spice. This drink, which varies from home to home, is made from fennel, cloves, cinnamon, and rum. It seems that almost every household has a small garden plot to grow these spices.

Saba

History

Sint Maarten, Sint Eustatius and Saba comprise the Dutch-owned Netherlands Antilles in the Leeward Islands. Along with Curaçao and Bonaire in the Windward Islands, they are constitutionally on the same level as the Dutch homeland. Although dependent on Holland for much of its economic life, Saba controls its own day-to-day affairs.

Columbus first sighted the island in 1493. For the next 150 years it was used as a rendezvous for Scandinavian pirates. The land changed hands among the French, English, Spanish, and Dutch 12 times before Holland took final possession in 1812. It is because of the English missionaries that English is so widely spoken on Saba today.

Early settlers depended on the sugar and rum industry until the mid-1800s when the sugar market declined worldwide. It was then that the male population went out to sea and developed into highly skilled fishermen and seamen. This expertise continues to this day, and they are recognized as some of the finest sailors in the world.

The Dutch influence is seen in the architecture. The homes are small and, as in the Netherlands, staircases are steep and narrow. Any large furniture used on the top floor must be hoisted through windows. When viewed from the mountains above, the red roofs, neat white exteriors, and gingerbread trim of each home make the villages look as if they had been transplanted from a Dutch fairy tale.

#

Transportation to Saba: There are no direct flights from the U.S., Canada, or Europe. However, all have direct flights to Sint Maarten, where there are frequent air connections to the island. Saba is also connected to Statia by air.

A ferry runs between Sint Maarten and Saba on a scheduled (but not daily) basis.

There is no customs; Saba is a free port. A departure tax is imposed.

Entry: Although a passport is best, a birth certificate or even a voter's registration card will do for American or Canadian citizens. All others must have a valid passport. As with all Caribbean islands, the visitor must possess a return or ongoing airline ticket.

Currency: The Netherlands Antilles florin (guilder) is the national currency. American dollars are accepted, but if you wish to exchange money, Barclay's Bank is open Monday to Friday from 8:30 A.M. to 2:00 P.M. and the Commercial Bank's business hours are Monday to Friday from 8:30 A.M. to 4 P.M.

Tourist Information:

✍ In the United States
Classic Communications International
Gail Knopfler, PO Box 6322
Boca Raton, FL 33427
☎ 561-394-8580

✍ In Europe
Minister Plenipotentiary of the
    Netherlands Antilles
Badhuisweg 173-175
2597 JP
'S-Gravenhage, The Netherlands
☎ 070-351-2811

✍ In Saba
Glenn Holm, Saba Tourist Bureau
PO Box 527, Windwardside, Saba
Netherlands Antilles
☎ 5995-62231
Mr. Holm is friendly and very helpful.
Ask anyone in Windwardside to point
his office out to you. It is close to the
post office and Sea Saba.

Driving: Rental cars are available and no special permits are required. Hitchhiking is widely accepted and practiced.

Language: The official language is Dutch, but English is universally spoken.

Walking and Hiking Guide Companies: With the increased popularity of walking and hiking on Saba, a number of people have begun to lead individuals and groups on a formal and informal basis. There are two who stand out and are recommended most often by those who have walked with them. Native Saban James Johnson has pioneered many routes off the usual beaten tourist paths and his wit, humor, and vast knowledge of the local use of plants for medicinal purposes is renowned. Tom van't Hoff, chairman of the Saba Conservation Foundation, is well versed in both the local and scientific names of a large percentage of Saba's foliage and fauna. Both guides are most easily contacted through the tourist bureau or next door at the Conservation Foundation's trail shop.

Camping Areas: In a departure from most of the other Caribbean islands, Saba actually welcomes campers and has four designated camping areas known as the Down Gut, Gray Bush, Mary Point and The Flat. These are primitive sites with no real amentities, but tents and related gear may be rented from the Conservation Foundation's trail shop in Windwardside.

Recommended Readings

📖 *History of Saba* by Dr. J. Hartog

📖 *Saban Lore – Tales From My Grandmother's Pipe* by Will Johnson

📖 *Islands to the Windward: St. Martin, St. Barts, Anguilla, Saba, and Statia* by Brian Dyde (out of print)

📖 *Saban Cottages: A Book of Watercolors* by Heleen Cornet

The Saba Herald, the island's semi-regularly published newspaper (in English), offers many insights into present-day Saba.

Walks

1. The Flat Point Boiling House Track
Walking time: 20 minutes, round trip

This walk can be reached by turning right (as you come from Hell's Gate) off the main highway onto the Cove Bay Road, which is just a few yards before the airport parking lot. The walk begins on the left at a right-hand turn in the road.

Following white marks painted on rocks, this excursion is an easy walk down to the sea. Be careful descending the steep and sometimes slippery volcanic rock formations for the last 10 to 15 feet of the walk. A grand abundance of life at the tide line remains in small pools along the rocky shore.

Volcanic rocks on the Flat Point Boiling House Track.

Check on current conditions before walking along the shore. When the surf is up, waves could be crashing forcefully onto the coast here.

An easy walk. If you are fascinated by the aquatic life – such as anemone, urchin, and hundreds of brightly colored fish – expect to spend quite a bit of time exploring the natural aquariums created by the waves amid the rock crevices.

2. The Sulphur Mine Track

Walking time: 45 minutes, round trip

As you are driving from Windwardside toward the airport, look for the church in Hell's Gate. Turn onto the second road to the left after the church. The Sulphur Mine Track begins on the concrete steps at the end of this road. About two-thirds of the way down, the footpath disappears, but just continue down through open countryside to the site of an old mine, inactive since the beginning of the century.

In addition to the airport and Pirate Cliffs on Saba, Sint Maarten and St. Barth can be seen across the dark blue waters of the Caribbean Sea. Bring binoculars as tropic birds, American kestrels, and magnificent frigatebirds may be seen riding the airwaves, while sooty and rutty terns use Green Island – just off Saba's coast – as a nesting ground from April to June.

3. The Sandy Cruz Track
Walking time: 1 hour, round trip

This enjoyable hike heads into the lushness of Saba's secondary rain forest. It begins at the end of the road that is the first possible left you can take in Hell's Gate as you drive from Windwardside. The path first ascends through open, cultivated fields, providing pleasant views. Becoming a bit more level, it abruptly enters a forest of tree ferns, wild begonias, mountain palms, and trumpetwood trees. In days gone by, the extremely buoyant trumpetwood was used to fashion sea-going rafts. Be prepared to dine on delicious raspberries, found throughout the year on Saba.

The trail continues once it emerges into another field with views onto the Cave of Rum Bay and Torrens Point, although it is advised that you end the walk here. An easy hike.

Special Hike: One of the best hikes on all of Saba begins where the Sandy Cruz Track comes to an official end. Although it may seem like a simple matter of just continuing along the obvious footpath, the treadway will soon disappear, possibly leaving you stranded and disoriented in a rugged and isolated area. But once you have obtained the services of a guide, it is this irregular terrain and seclusion that makes the hike so worthwhile. On this three-hour excursion you'll be climbing in and out of deep ravines, sliding over slippery rocks, and crossing ridgelines crowded with mahogany trees, heliconias, and mountain palms festooned with all manner of bromeliads and epiphytes before emerging from the tropical growth near Troy and The Bottom.

If you have the time to do the complete trek, don't miss it. But do not attempt it without a guide – several people have become lost while hiking here.

4. The Old Booby Hill Hike

Walking time: 2 hours, 15 minutes, round trip

In English Quarter, take the concrete footway to the right of the Agricultural Center. Follow the route out through more or less open country, watching for the remains of the Spring Bay Flat Boiling House along the way. Just before the final ascent to Old Booby Hill, tracks will lead left to Spring Bay and right to Cove Gut Bay, but it's suggested you hire a guide before attempting these. Be aware that there are manchineel trees at the head of Cove Gut Bay.

Once you reach the summit of Old Booby Hill, spend some time observing the nesting tropical birds, enjoying the view of Statia and St. Kitts to the east, and playing among the large lava boulders. A recommended hike.

5. The Mount Scenery Steps

Walking time: 2½ hours, round trip

Possibly the best and certainly the most unusual hike on the island. The path begins in Windwardside at the road sign marked "Mt. Scenery - 1,064 steps." It can also be reached a little higher up by driving to the end of the Mountain Road from Windwardside, where the steps of the trail begin. This saves about 15 minutes of uphill walking, but you miss a lot of interesting vegetation.

If you are observant as you climb you can feast on a host of tropical delicacies. Remaining from earlier agricultural days are guava, banana, avocado, and lemon. Raspberries, coco plums, and delicious surinam cherries grow naturally. You could even add a bit of spice to your evening meal by picking the cilantro growing out of cracks in the steps.

About a third of the way up, the open views are blocked by the elephant ears, tree ferns, and palms of the dense rain forest. A couple of trail-side shelters are provided to rest or escape the short-lived rain squalls that appear suddenly and frequently. On the summit, which is covered by an elfin rain forest, keep to the left of the radio tower for a view unequaled anywhere else on Saba. To the north is Sint Maarten, to the east are Statia and St. Kitts, to the south and west is the open expanse of the Caribbean Sea, and directly below the mountain is the village of Windwardside. A highly recommended, moderately strenuous hike. Because of the high amount of moisture that falls on Mount Scenery, the steps can often be slippery and treacherous. If you do not find a walking stick leaning against the trailhead sign, it might be a wise idea to rent one from the trail shop.

> *A few extra comments about this hike:* For those not used to climbing stairs, this can be a steep and strenuous ascent, so you may need to allow more time than noted. Since the pathway is in the rain forest, the steps are always very slippery. Remember that, as you gain elevation, the temperature will drop. Bring along a jacket or windbreaker.

6. The Maskehorne Hill Track

Walking time: 20 minutes, round trip

This short walk can be reached by either the Crispeen Track (see Walk #7) or the Mountain Road that intersects the Mt. Scenery Steps (see Walk #5). After 300 feet downhill past the shelter, the Maskehorne Hill Track turns off to the right. Passing through the forest, it comes to an overlook of Windwardside.

7. The Crispeen Track

Walking time: 1 hour, one way to "The Rendezvous"

Following the bed of the original road, this track diverges from the new highway a short distance above The Bottom. As you ascend, remember that this route was built with manual labor before any heavy equipment had arrived on Saba.

Coming to the outskirts of St. John's Hill, the route becomes a footpath – one of the old trails that linked the villages before the construction of the road. Continue the ascent in a secondary rain forest and you soon come to an intersection in open pastureland dominated by a small farmhouse. To the left are Bot-

Signs show the way to the Crispeen Track.

tom Mountain (see Walk #9) and Bod's Mountain (see Walk #8) tracks. Keep right, where you'll be accompanied by the national flower of Saba, the black-eyed Susans, whose rich orange flowers grow on creeping vines to overtake and decorate the foliage. Climb over a forested ridge to emerge onto more cultivated fields and the end of the track at "The Rendezvous," where you intersect the Mount Scenery Steps (see Walk #5).

> ✹ **Note:** *This hike can be quite slippery in places.*

8. The Bod's Mountain Track

Walking time: 35 minutes, round trip (not including 30 minutes on the Crispeen Track to reach the trailhead)

Diverging from the Crispeen Track (see Walk #7), the Bod's Mountain Track ascends from open meadows and past a small farmhouse to enter a rain forest of tree ferns, mango, and balsam trees on Mount Scenery's western slopes. Keep eyes and ears open in the hopes of seeing, or at least hearing, a pearly-eyed thrasher, bananaquit, or an Antillean crested hummingbird. The track ends on a small knoll overlooking the southwestern portion of Saba.

9. The Bottom Mountain Track

Walking time: 20 minutes, round trip (not including 30 mins. on the Crispeen Track to reach the start)

The Bottom Mountain Track diverges to the west from the Crispeen Track (see Walk #7). It passes through open, pleasant grazing land and a fern-covered forest floor to end in an overgrown field.

> **Note:** Combine Walks #5, #6, #7, #8 and #9 for a full day of pleasant walking and hiking through varied terrain and vegetation.

10. The Thais Hill Track

Walking time: 25 minutes, round trip

Going toward The Bottom, this easy and enjoyable walk leaves the main highway to the left of the last house in St. Johns. The obvious open country route (no trail) leads to one of the better lookouts on all of the island. With views up to Troy Mountain and down to Fort Bay, Thais Hill is a great place to be for sunset. A moderate walk.

11. The Paris Hill Track

Walking time: 50 minutes, round trip

On the road leading down to Fort Bay is the JPF Radio Station. The Paris Hill Track begins here and works its way to a popular spot in an open pasture. Although the pathway is steep, it is surprisingly easy walking. The excellent scenery is well worth the little extra effort.

> *Inquire locally about the trail's condition. If it has not been maintained recently, you may want to hire a guide.*

12. The Tent Bay Track

This hike leaves the Paris Hill Track (see Walk #11) and heads down toward Tent Bay. However, the route soon becomes tough and should be used only by those employing a guide and ready for a physical challenge.

13. The Ladder

Walking time: 1 hour, round trip

400 steep steps known as The Ladder.

At the end of Ladder Bay Road in The Bottom, the more than 400 steps of The Ladder begin on the left. These steps lead down to the old anchorage. Before the harbor and pier were built at Fort Bay, all cargo (and visitors) had to be brought up these steps. Wildflowers are plentiful here in the winter months, growing amid hundreds of mahogany trees and seedlings.

> ✸ **Note:** *The steps are quite steep and could present a physical challenge to those not used to climbing stairs. Also, they are almost always wet and slippery.*

14. The North Coast Trail

Walking time: 1 hour, 40 minutes, one way to the Sulphur Mines, but allow more time as there is much to see.

The North Coast Trail Hike follows a pathway leading to the now abandoned Mary's Point settlement, from where some present-day Saban cottages were moved in 1934. Even older historical, cultural and agricultural sites exist along the trail. Passing through a stand of mahogany trees on its way to a view of Diamond Rock, the route now sees little foot traffic, so a guide is an absolute necessity. Bird watchers may be interested to know that, in past years, the track was a popular place for observing frigatebirds. The views to the ocean are spectacular, especially those found at Great Point and above Torrens Point. This trail comes to an end as it joins the Sulphur Mine Track (see Walk #2).

A recommended and enjoyable hike if you have a guide to show you the way.

15. "The Road"

The Road should not be overlooked as a unique opportunity to walk and explore. It is only nine miles long and, except in the villages, motor vehicle traffic is light. From the airport on the north end of the island, the road switches back up the mountain to Upper and Lower Hell's Gate for a view onto Flat Point and the airport. From here, you can see why only STOL (short take-off and landing) airplanes can use Saba's 1,300-foot airport runway. Continuing to gain in elevation, the road passes through the gingerbread house community of English Quarter and then leads into the village of Windwardside. A short side street leads to the Harry L. Johnson Museum. This museum, containing exhibits relating to the history of Saba, is worth the few extra steps. The Saba Tourist Bureau and the island's largest grocery store are also in Windwardside.

Having reached its zenith, the road now begins its long descent. On the way to St. John's Hill it passes by open meadows and fields, giving spectacular views of the sea, Statia, and St. Kitts to the east. After St. John's Hill, the road comes to the capital of Saba, The Bottom. Contrary to many stories, The Bottom is so named not because it is in the bottom of a crater. The name is a derivation of the original Dutch name for the village, De Botte, or The Bowl. Once there, you will understand the description.

Saba

A walk along the narrow roads of the capital city will take you to a small garden park, the hospital, an interesting little church, and the Saba Artisan Foundation. Cranston's is the favorite local place to quench the thirst that you will have worked up by now. Continue downhill from The Bottom to Fort Bay, the Pier, the Customs House, and the end of the road (and the island).

The Road is an easy hike. Even though it climbs from sea level to over 2,000 feet and then down again, it is well graded and not strenuous as long as you walk at your own pace.

There is one difficulty in attempting this hike. Sabans are so friendly that almost everyone who drives by will try to give you a ride!

Sint Eustatius (Statia)

Sint Eustatius, commonly called Statia, rises from the sea on volcanic peaks at its northern and southern points. A large, level plain, the Cultuurvlakte, extends between the two. The Quill is an extinct volcano on the southern end of the island and, at 1,965 feet, it dominates the scenery. From anywhere on the island it has the classic look of a volcanic cone. The sides of the mountain rise steeply, ending abruptly on the narrow, jagged rim, with just a hint of the crater inside visible through the low points around the rim.

At one time, the Cultuurvlakte contained 38 sugar plantations. These are now gone and have been replaced by small family plots or open fields. The vegetation increases as the land gains elevation, turning to a rain forest in the mountains and into an elfin woodland on the summit of The Quill.

Statia is only 11.8 square miles and, with such a low elevation, is drier than its neighbors of Saba and St. Kitts. Water shortages have occurred at various times.

Statia has a strong historical foundation, tourism organization, and government. All have taken an active interest in walking and hiking. As a result, there are marked and maintained trails throughout the island. It is now possible to take hikes around the base of The Quill, along the rim and down into its crater, and along the crest of White Wall. These trails are lined with the luxuriant growth of a tropical forest – anthurium, heliconia, philodendron, elephant ear, and orchids.

Trails on the northern end of Statia lead to sandy beaches and pass through areas of sea grapes, manchineel trees, cacti, and century plants. Statia is so far off the beaten tourist path that more than three people on the beach at one time would be considered a crowd. This is an island for those who are truly looking to get away from the masses of tourists found on so many other Caribbean islands.

History

Sighted by Columbus, Statia remained uncolonized until the mid-1600s when the Dutch arrived. They found the beginnings of a small fort deserted by the French; determined to stay, the Dutch enlarged the fortification, naming it Fort Oranje. The island changed hands an incredible 22 times among Holland, France, and England before the Dutch took final possession in 1816.

In the latter part of the 18th century, Statia gained prominence as a world trade center. Goods on their way from the New World to Europe, or in the opposite direction, passed through warehouses that lined the waterfront of Oranje Bay. At its peak trading time, these warehouses stretched for almost two miles along the bay. In addition to the transshipment business, sugarcane production and slave trading were major industries. This small colony was carrying on such a business that the population swelled to over 18,000 and Statia became known as the "Emporium of the Caribbean."

An American brig-of-war arrived in Oranje Bay on November 16, 1776 to pick up munitions and supplies for the army of the rebellious states. The guns of Fort Oranje fired a salute to the ship's flag, becoming the first to recognize America officially as a nation. For the next few years Statia continued to trade freely with the United States, supplying much needed munitions, goods and food. These acts did not sit well with the British and were one of the reasons England declared war on Holland in 1780. In 1781, Admiral Rodney took Great Britain's revenge. After destroying many of the warehouses, Rodney occupied the island and eventually made off with an estimated £48 million of confiscated goods.

The decline of the sugar market a few decades later completed the fall from prosperity. Statia has never again approached its former stature and today the island is a peaceful, sleepy land of only 2,200 people.

Sint Maarten, Saba and Statia in the Leeward Islands and Bonaire and Curaçao in the Windwards make up the Netherlands Antilles. These islands are constitutionally on the same ground as their Dutch homeland. Statians have control over their daily affairs, but are dependent upon Holland for economic help.

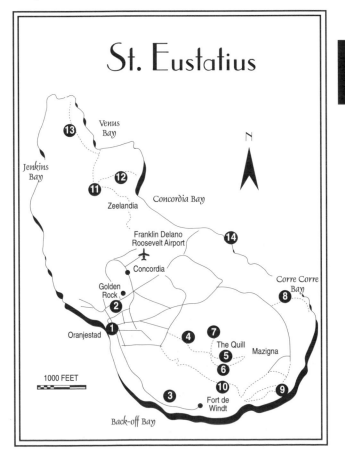

Statia

Data

Transportation to Statia: There are no direct flights from the North American continent or Europe. But short connecting flights are available from Sint Maarten, which has connections to the U.S., Canada, and Europe. The island also has flights to Anguilla, Saba, and St. Kitts.

Statia is off the usual cruise ship tour route; however, it does receive one or two ships a week.

A departure tax is collected.

Entry: No passport is needed for Canadian or American citizens. A birth certificate and proof of an ongoing or return airline ticket are needed. All other visitors need a valid passport and the required transportation ticket.

Currency: The national currency is the Netherlands Antilles florin (guilder). American currency is accepted by most establishments. Foreign money may be exchanged at the banks in Oranjestad. The Barclays Bank is open Monday through Thursday from 8:30 A.M. to 2:00 P.M., with an additional hour from 4:00 P.M. to 5:00 P.M. on Friday. Post Spaarbank has business hours Monday to Friday from 7:30 A.M. to 4:00 P.M. Windward Islands Bank is open Monday to Thursday from 8:30 A.M. to noon and from 1:00 P.M to 3:30 P.M.; Friday it is open from 2:00 P.M. to 4:30 P.M.

Although the major hotels will take them, credit cards are not as readily accepted on Statia as on some of the other islands.

Tourist Information:

   ✍ **In the United States**
    The Caribbean Tourism Organization
    20 E. 46th St.
    New York, NY 10017-2452
    ☎ 212-682-0435

✍ **In Europe**
Minister Plenipotentiary of the
  Netherlands Antilles
Badhuisweg 173-175
2597 JP
'S-Gravenhage, The Netherlands
☎ 070-351-2811

The Tourist Office is located at the entrance to Fort Oranje. There is also a small office open irregular hours at the head of the pier:

✍ Sint Eustatius Tourism Development
    Foundation
  Oranjestad, Sint Eustatius
  Netherlands Antilles
  ☎ 5993-82433

Driving: Rental cars are available. It should be pointed out, however, that Statia is so small that almost all points on the island can be reached within a couple of hours by foot from Oranjestad.

Language: Dutch is the official language; English is the language of everyday life on the island.

Walking and Hiking Guide Companies: There are no formal guide companies, but there are several locals who act as tour guides. Probably the most knowledgeable is Raphael "Charley" Lopes, often referred to as the "Crab-catching King of Statia" for his crustacean hunting ability. He is the official government-paid caretaker of the island's trails and, as such, will be able to lead you to places and point out interesting sites, flora, and fauna that some of the other guides may overlook. Mr. Lopes is most easily contacted through the Tourism Development Foundation. If he is not available, they should be able to recommend another qualified guide.

Except for the hikes on and around The Quill, the walking is easy, the island sufficiently small, and the vegetation open enough that guides are not really needed.

Camping Areas: Camping is prohibited anywhere on the island. Low cost accommodations are available in apartments and guest houses. Contact the Tourism Development Foundation (see above).

Recommended Readings

📖 *Saint Eustatius, A Short History* by Ypie Attema

📖 *Islands to the Windward: St. Martin, St. Barts, Anguilla, Saba, and Statia* by Brian Dyde (out of print)

The Mazinga Gift Shop in Oranjestad has the most complete offering of books and magazines about Statia and other islands of the Caribbean.

Walks

1. The Oranjestad Beach Walk

Walking time: 20 minutes, one way

This is just a stroll along the beach in "Lower Town" Oranjestad. It will take you among the ruins of the formerly busy waterfront area. When Sint Eustatius was known as "The Golden Rock of the Caribbean," the warehouses were crowded with goods destined for Europe or America. The attack by Admiral Rodney and subsequent harsh weather reduced the buildings to the rubble you see now. However, a few have survived and been modernized to house present-day businesses. Several structures, built with ship ballast bricks brought over from Holland, are still used as warehouses and one contains Statia's premier dive center. The Mooshay Bay Publick House is within the confines of a former Cotton Gin Mill.

The beach itself is rough and strewn with boulders. Besides watching the nesting tropic birds, it is also interesting to search for blue beads, five-sided prism glass beads produced in Holland and used by the Dutch as currency for slave purchases in the 18th century. The Bay Road ascending to "Upper Town" on the right marks the end of your walk.

2. A Walking Tour of Oranjestad

Begin the walking tour in Fort Oranje overlooking the bay. The Dutch built this stronghold in 1636, repairing and enlarging a small fortification constructed by the French in 1629, which was subsequently abandoned. Fort Oranje was restored in 1976 in honor of America's Bicentennial and is now one of the most complete historical forts in this area of the Caribbean.

Just outside the fort entrance is the government guest house, built in the 1700s. In 1992, the building and its grounds were restored. They now house governmental administrative offices and the island's court room. Stop in at the small structure next to the guest house to obtain more information on Statia from the Tourism Development Foundation. Walk right for a few steps and come to "Three Widows Corner," which combines a mixture of 18th- and 19th-century architectures. Nearby is the Statian Library, its modern architecture somewhat out of place here. It was built to replace the old library which had been battered by Hurricane Hugo. Going right on Kerkweg Street leads to the ruins of the Dutch Reformed Church. It was built in 1755, but destroyed by hurricane in 1792. In 1981 the ruins were stabilized and you can now ascend the tower to overlook Oranjestad.

Crossing through the grounds of Wilhelmina Park, formerly the slave market place, will bring you to the Manor House on Bredeweg. Behind it is a good example of a hurricane house. The solid walls of these buildings are welcome refuges from the howling winds.

Statia

Go back toward the main part of town on Bredeweg, turn right, walk uphill on Prinseweg for four blocks and reach the Jewish cemetery. The old gravestones dating from 1742 to 1843 are worth studying. Turn left on Bredeweg and pass a decaying Townhouse built in the 1700s. A left on Fort Oranje Straat and another immediate left into Synagoguepath alley leads to the ruins of the Honen Dalim Synagogue. In the middle of the 18th century, Statia had a sizeable Jewish population, but as their numbers declined in the 1800s, the synagogue fell into ruin. Returning to the center of town, at #2 Van Tonningenweg is the Simon Doncker House. Home of a wealthy merchant, Admiral Rodney used it as his headquarters during his occupation of the island in 1781. It now houses the Sint Eustatius Historical Foundation Museum and Library, which is worth a visit. Your walking tour ends here.

A brochure describing these and other sites in greater detail may be obtained at the Tourism Development Foundation or the Historical Foundation's museum. The Historical Foundation is very active on Statia and would be happy to supply a guide for your tour of the city.

3. The Road to White Wall and Fort De Windt Walk

Walking time: 40 minutes, one way

Although this is a paved road, traffic is light, making it a pleasant walk through countryside. From Oranjestad, follow Weg Naar White Wall east out of town. There are few houses along this road and you will have continual views of Gallows Bay and the Caribbean Sea. The road passes the ruins of a 19th-century factory and ends at Fort De Windt, built around 1775 and one of more than a dozen fortifications known to have been constructed on Statia. This spot offers a commanding view of St. Kitts and its towering volcano, Mt. Liamuiga. Directly above you are the southeastern face of The Quill and the cliffs of White Wall, whose limestone sediments were lifted from the ocean's floor by forces within the earth's crust. A recommended walk.

4. The Quill Track

Walking time: 1½ hours, round trip,
to the crater rim and back

The main route up and into The Quill, this trail is reached from Welfare Road in Oranjestad. The starting point should be easy enough to find as there are signs throughout the city directing you there. Beginning as a rutted dirt road, the route soon leaves the scrub brush of the lower elevations behind and provides several good views of Oranjestad, the Cultuurvlakte, and the northern hills of Statia. Within 20 minutes, the route becomes a well-worn footpath climbing a bit more steeply as you enter taller undergrowth and a variety of rain forest-type trees. Once on the rim of the crater, you've reached the end of The Quill Track, but the beginning of three other trails – the Crater (see Walk #5), Mazinga (see Walk #6), and Panorama (see Walk #7) tracks. A moderately strenuous hike.

Views of The Quill from afar.

5. The Crater Track

*Walking time: 45 minutes, round trip (timed from the
rim end of The Quill Track, not including
the 45 minutes needed to reach the beginning
of the Crater Track)*

Reached via The Quill Track (see Walk #4), the Crater Track descends steeply on a rocky and slippery
route into the crater. The main path starts out being quite obvious, but the deeper you go into the crater, the less defined it becomes. There are also
numerous side trails going off in different directions
and leading to sites that should not be overlooked.
As it would be easy to become disoriented in the
thick foliage and/or miss going to these interesting
spots, a guide is recommended.

In previous years, cocoa, coffee, bananas, and cinnamon were cultivated on the floor of the crater.
While the trees and shrubs of these earlier agricultural days may still be seen, the real treat here is
wandering amid the lush growth inside a crater
without having to worry about accidentally falling
into a steaming fumarole or boiling mud pot. Mahogany, corkwood, ironwood, lignumvitae, three
different cedars, and several other trees grow to
great heights, many of them supported on elaborate
and twisting buttresses. At least 18 species of orchids are known to populate Statia, with 15 of them
found inside The Quill. In addition to looking at all
of this, plus heliconia, begonia, and anthurium,
glance downward every once in a while and you
might spot other Quill inhabitants – snakes, lizards, frogs, and soldier and mountain crabs.

➤ Allow much more time than recommended above so than you can properly
explore this wonderland. It is the most
highly recommended outing on Statia.

6. The Mazinga Track

Walking time: 1½ hours, round trip (timed from the rim end of The Quill Track and does not include the 45 minutes needed to reach the beginning of the Mazinga Track)

Reached by hiking The Quill Track to its end (see Walk #4), the Mazinga Track turns right along the crater rim. Within a few hundred yards it comes to an Olympian view out across the green expanse and depths of the inside of The Quill. Following the rim on a steep and slippery route, the pathway gains elevation and the smaller plants give way to the lush growth of the rain forest – philodendron, ferns, and epiphytes (plants that grow on other plants and derive their nourishment solely from rain water and air-borne nutrients). In the rain forest, epiphytes can include a variety of flowering plant species, such as the orchids here on Statia. From the summit of Mazinga Peak there are views of many surrounding islands – Saba, St. Barts, Sint Maarten, St. Kitts, and Nevis. Mazinga Peak, at 1,965 feet and often in the clouds, is the highest point on Statia and is covered by an elfin woodland forest dripping with moisture and hanging mosses.

> **Note:** *This should not be considered an easy or moderate walk. The trail is steep in places and, because of the rain forest, is almost always slippery. Be sure to stay on the trail.*

7. The Panorama Track

Walking time: 1 hour, round trip (timed from the rim end of The Quill Track and does not include the 45 minutes needed to reach the beginning of the Panorama Track)

The Panorama Track is reached via The Quill Track (see Walk #4). It follows the wildly undulating rim of the crater to the left and offers views of the interior of the island, the inside of the crater, and Zeeland Bay. Passing through the rain forest, where orchids, monkey tail, elephant ear, and the hanging grey beards will be seen, keep an eye and an ear out for mountain doves and wild parrots. After about 30 minutes, you should consider turning around, for although a path continues along the rim, it is so steep and slippery that it is not recommended.

8. The Corre Corre Bay Track

Walking time: 1 hour, 20 minutes, round trip

The start of this easy hike may be somewhat hard to locate. The easiest way to find it is to pay close attention to your car's odometer. As you swing around the lower slopes of The Quill, heading eastward out of Oranjestad, you will soon come to the intersection of the English Quarter and the Behind the Mountain roads. You'll now be headed in a southeasterly direction and, in 1.2 miles from the intersection, the Corre Corre Bay Track takes off to the left from the Behind the Mountain Road. More of an open country route than an actual trail, the track goes through private property (please treat the land with respect), whose owners have no objections to your using the trail. On the way to the bay, ruins of an old plantation are passed. Creeping lilac vines grow along the shoreline. An easy hike.

9. The Soldier Gut Track

Walking time: 50 minutes, round trip
(timed from the end of the Behind the Mountain Road)

Another easy walk, the Soldier Gut Track begins at the end of the Behind the Mountain Road. (The last mile of the Behind the Mountain Road is unpaved and rough. It may be necessary to walk, instead of drive, this section. Walking time one way is about 20 minutes.) Along the trail are views of White Wall and Sugarloaf. The gut receives its name from the soldier crabs that use it as a pathway on their trek from the sea to the mountains. Be warned – the slopes are steep and narrow, so do not be tempted to climb down unless you are looking for a real challenge.

The trail makes a circle and on the return trip there are good views of St. Kitts, Nevis and the coastline of Statia.

View of St. Kitts from the Soldier Gut Track.

10. The Track Around The Mountain

Walking time: 1½ hours, one way

This long, but easy hike begins at the end of the Behind the Mountain Road. (See Walk #9.) The trail starts uphill in scrubby vegetation but levels off in just a short while. Once you are on the summit of Whitewall, you can elect to take a side trail for a view of Sugarloaf and the sea. The main trail continues around the side of The Quill, passing by a variety of orchids and other flowers. It ends at Rosemary Lane in Oranjestad.

A moderate, scenic hike. The Track Around The Mountain is one of the least used trails on Statia so it may be wise to check on current conditions if you are not going to hire a guide.

11. The Venus Bay Track

Walking time: 1½ hours, round trip

An easy hike, the Venus Bay Track is actually a dirt road that begins to ascend about 500 feet west of the La Maison Sur La Plage Hotel and Restaurant in Zeelandia. This side of the island is drier than The Quill side; cacti and century plants thrive here. Just as the road begins to descend, the Gilboa Hill Track (see Walk #12) comes in from the right. The route soon drops you into Venus Bay whose rocky beach is ringed by sea grape, manchineel trees (beware of their poisonous fruit and irritating sap), and the parasitic devil's hair. From the beach there is an excellent view of Bergje, Statia's other extinct volcano, formed about 25,000 years ago.

The Boven Bay Track (see Walk #13) starts from Venus Bay, but unless you have someone point it out, it may be hard to find. Return to Zeelandia by way of the Venus Bay Track.

12. The Gilboa Hill Track

Walking time: 1 hour, 20 minutes, round trip
(timed from the road at Zeelandia)

The Gilboa Hill Track, an enjoyable and easy hike, is reached by following the Venus Bay Track (see Walk #11) to its highest point and turning right onto the Gilboa Hill Track. The first good view is of The Quill with St. Kitts in the background. Walking by the numerous Turk's cap cacti, notice that they all lean in the same direction. As this particular species tends to angle toward the equator, it has been given the nickname, the compass plant. When ripe, its pinkish fruit is a succulent treat, not only for birds, but for human beings, too.

Continuing through cacti, other dry land vegetation, and the herds of goats that somehow find enough to eat here, the trail ends with a view of The Quill, St. Kitts, St. Barts, and Sint Maarten. Be on the lookout for the elusive iguanas that inhabit this northern portion of the island.

13. The Boven Bay Track

Walking time: 2 hours, round trip

Follow the Venus Bay Track (see Walk #11) to its end. The Boven Bay Track begins here, but unless someone points it out, you may have a hard time locating it. The route takes you into one of the most remote and seldom visited sections of Statia. For this reason, a guide is highly recommended.

A rewarding, moderate hike into rugged country that few people ever see.

14. Statia's Northern Beaches

On an island not famous for its beaches, Statia's northern coastline makes for rewarding walks. Windswept, with waves crashing in from the Atlantic Ocean, Zeelandia Bay leads to Concordia Bay, which, in turn, leads to Bargine Bay, which runs into Great Bay. Although you probably wouldn't want to go swimming in the rough surf, these miles of nearly unbroken black and beige sands are a great spot to be when a full moon rises from the ocean to cast its silvery light on the green slopes of The Quill.

Statia

Saint Kitts

Sugarcane cultivation has all but disappeared on other Caribbean islands, but the northern part of St. Kitts is ringed by large sugar plantations. There is, in fact, so much cane on St. Kitts that, viewed from a distance, the island is a lighter hue of green than the surrounding islands. The cane rises from the coastline and continues up to the lower slopes of Mt. Liamuiga.

At 3,792 feet, Mt. Liamuiga dominates the cane fields. Evidence of the mountain's younger days as an active volcano is scattered throughout the island. The Black Rocks on the Atlantic coast are the remnants of volcanic rock and lava that came crashing down the sides of Liamuiga years ago. Black sand beaches, such as those at Dieppe Bay, are composed of volcanic ash and dust. The sulphur fumes around Brimstone Hill are a reminder that activity still exists below the surface.

The rain forest, along with the great profusion of ferns, lilies, and orchids, is a result of the moisture-capturing qualities of Liamuiga and the surrounding mountains. In contrast, the southern portion of the island is almost a desert. The southeastern peninsula is much lower in elevation and scrub brush and trees predominate. Deer and vervet monkeys run wild on this part of St. Kitts.

Twenty-three miles long and almost seven miles wide at its widest point, St. Kitts has 68 square miles.

History

In 1493, when Christopher Columbus sighted the island he named it after his own patron saint, St.

Christopher. The Carib Indians were already living there at that time. It wasn't until over a century later, however, that there was real contact between Europeans and the Indians. In 1623, Sir Thomas Warner and a group of 15 others arrived and were welcomed by the Caribs. A short time later, a French colony was established on the island.

St. Kitts, as the British called the island, came to be known as the "Mother Colony of the West Indies." England used it as a base from which to send colonizing parties to Nevis, Barbuda, and Montserrat. The French left from here to settle St. Barth, St. Martin, St. Croix, Martinique, and Guadeloupe.

Alarmed by the growing numbers of settlers, the Indians mounted a doomed offensive. A united effort by the British and French drove the Caribs from the island in 1626. This was the first and only time that the two groups cooperated.

The British began fortification of the "Gibraltar of the West Indies," Brimstone Hill, in 1690. The fortress and the island changed hands a number of times until the French officially ceded the island to Britain by the Treaty of Versailles in 1783. Slave labor and English soldiers continued to add to Brimstone Hill, completing the fortifications around the turn of the 19th century. The island remained under British rule until 1967, when, along with Nevis and Anguilla, it became an associated state of the United Kingdom. In 1983 the Federation of St. Kitts and Nevis was born, giving the sister islands full political independence. Anguilla elected to remain a part of the United Kingdom.

Today, St. Kitts has a population of 35,000, most of whom are descendants of slaves. Sugarcane cultivation is still the principal industry. A narrow gauge railroad, one of the few remaining in the Caribbean, connects the cane fields to each other and to the refinery. Tourism is beginning to play an increasing role in the economy.

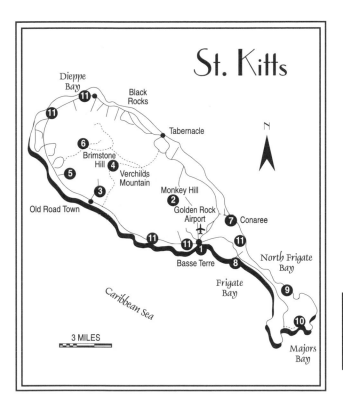

Data

Transportation to St. Kitts: There are no direct flights from North America or Europe, but each continent does have air connections to either Antigua, Sint Maarten, the USVI or Puerto Rico. Each of those islands has daily flights to St. Kitts.

The government-operated ferry, *Caribe Queen*, makes trips daily (except Thursday and Sunday) between Charlestown, Nevis, and Basseterre, St. Kitts.

St. Kitts is becoming increasingly popular with the cruise ship companies.

An embarkation tax is collected from all visitors leaving St. Kitts.

Entry: For American or Canadian citizens, a birth certificate or voter's registration card is all that is required. Other citizens need a valid passport. All visitors must possess a return or ongoing airline ticket. Travelers must be able to provide proof that they have sufficient funds to cover expenses for the full length of their stay. Most countries worldwide use this as an entry requirement and failure to have the required resources could result in a denial of entry.

Currency: The national currency is the Eastern Caribbean dollar. American dollars are usually accepted. The best exchange rate can be obtained at one of the banks in Basseterre. Normal banking hours are Monday-Thursday from 8:00 A.M. to 3:00 P.M. and Friday from 8:00 A.M. to 5:00 P.M. You should be able to find at least one bank open during the morning on Saturday. All banks are closed on Sunday.

Major credit cards are accepted at the hotels and larger tourist shops, but smaller restaurants and stores usually require cash.

Tourist Information:

✍ **In the United States**
St. Kitts-Nevis Tourist Office
414 East 75th Street
New York, NY 10021
☎ 212-535-1234

✍ **In Canada**
St. Kitts-Nevis Tourist Office
11 Yorkville Avenue, Suite 508
Toronto, M4W IL3
☎ 416-921-7717

✍ **In England**
10 Kensington Court
London W8 5DL
☎ 0171-376-0881

On St. Kitts, tourist information may be obtained at the Dept. Of Tourism in the Pelican Shopping Mall on The Bay Road next to the pier. Their mailing address is:

✍ St. Kitts Department of Tourism
PO Box 132
Basseterre, St. Kitts
West Indies
☎ 869-465-2620

Driving: Rental cars are available in Basseterre and other points throughout the island. A local driver's license must be obtained by presenting a national or international driver's license to the Traffic Department in the police station. A fee is charged.

Remember to drive on the left!

Language: English.

Walking and Hiking Guide Companies: Greg Perira, a native Kittitian whose family has been on the island for several generations, is the owner of Greg's Safaris – generally considered to be the premier guide company on the island. Greg is most knowledgeable about the flora, fauna, history and ecological issues facing the island and makes sure that his staff is equally well informed. Besides being able to take you on any of the excursions listed below, the company also specializes in custom-designed tours for those who want to get well off the beaten path.

✍ **Greg's Safaris**
PO Box 65, Basseterre, St. Kitts
West Indies, ☎ 869-465-4121

Kriss Tours operates in much the same way as Greg's Safaris:

✍ **Kriss Tours**
New Street, Basseterre, St. Kitts
West Indies, ☎ 869-465-4042

In case you are unable to make contact with either of the above, the Department of Tourism can put you in touch with other qualified guides.

St. Kitts

Camping Areas: There are no official camp-grounds on St. Kitts. If you make arrangements in advance, Greg's Safaris might be able to set up over-night camping trips.

Recommended Readings

📖 *The Historical Geography of St. Kitts and Nevis, the West Indies* by G.C. Merrill

📖 *A Motoring Guide to St. Kitts* by Amelia Stone & Frank Sharman

Local newspapers are usually the best way to find out about current events. In the case of St. Kitts, two of the newspapers – *The Democrat* and *The Labor Spokesman* – provide more information on their political leanings than they do on the day-to-day social life on the island. Still, it is worth picking up a copy of each to read about the prevailing political climate of the day.

The Observer, established in the mid-1990s, provides a more traditional style of news coverage for the island.

In Basseterre, Walls DeLuxe Record and Bookshop carries a complete line of maps, newspapers, magazines and books about St. Kitts, Nevis and the region:

✍ **Walls DeLuxe Record and Bookshop**
PO Box 87, Fort Street
Basseterre, St. Kitts
West Indies
☎ 869-465-2159

Walks

1. A Walking Tour of Basseterre

As on many Caribbean islands, the best place to begin a walking tour of the capital city is on the pier. The pier bustles with activity whenever the ferry, *Caribe Queen*, arrives from the sister island of Nevis. Saturday is the busiest and most colorful day to visit the pier and the nearby marketplace.

From the pier walk directly into the Pelican Mall, a converted warehouse that is now the home of the St. Kitts Department of Tourism. Literature and advice on sites to see and things to do may be obtained here. After visiting a few of the boutiques and shops in the mall, emerge onto The Bay Road, turn left and you'll come to the St. Kitts Philatelic Bureau next to the Post Office. Although St. Kitts and Nevis are one nation, each issues it own postage stamps, a unique practice that has made the stamps valued by collectors around the world.

Continue on The Bay Road, passing by the Treasury Building, a fine example of the Victorian architecture that is found throughout the West Indies. Turn right onto Fort Street and into the Circus. This circular Georgian-style hub brings a little bit of London to Basseterre. Just up from here is Walls Deluxe Record and Bookshop, the best place on the island to obtain maps, newspapers, magazines, and books about the Caribbean.

Returning to the Circus, check out the Caribelle Batik's retail store (see Walk #3). The banks here will exchange foreign currency for East Caribbean dollars.

One block from Bank Street is Independence Square. This 18th-century slave market area is now a relaxing park and tropical gardens in which to take a rest from the hustle and bustle of the narrow

St. Kitts

streets of downtown. Directly across East Square Street from Independence Square is the Church of the Immaculate Conception.

Go up East Square Street to Cayon Street, turn left for one short block and then right for anpther block onto Burl Street to arrive at Lozac Road and Warner Park, a quiet relaxing park near the downtown area. ln Warner Park on September 19, 1983, the British flag was lowered and the newly designed national flag was raised, marking the beginning of independence for the new Federation of St. Kitts and Nevis.

From Warner Park walk along Lozac Road to Victoria Road. A left onto Victoria and then a right onto Cayon Street brings you to St. Georges Anglican Church. This church is noteworthy for the fact that it has been rebuilt at least four times after being subjected to wars, fires, and earthquakes.

A walk of not quite a mile along Cayon Street will bring you to Springfield Cemetery, where you can read the inscriptions on the headstones. Next to the cemetery is Government House, another fine example of colonial-era architecture.

Walk back into town on Cayon Street, turn right onto Fort Street and into the heart of the shopping district before returning to the pier and the end of your walking tour of St. Kitts' capital city.

2. The Monkey Hill Walk

Walking time: 90 minutes, round trip

This 1,319-foot hill is just west of Basseterre and is certainly worth the easy climb to the top, but you will need to hire a guide to show you where the walk begins and to help you through the maze of private property.

Along the way you will pass the overgrown ruins of "The Glen," a former great house. Monkey Hill obtains its name from the vervet monkeys which inhabit the slopes. They arrived on St. Kitts and

Nevis on board the French ships during the colonial period and from that time they have flourished and spread throughout both islands. If you want a closer look, a primate research station has been established at Estridge Estate near Mansion. It is open to the public on Sundays.

From the summit of Monkey Hill are good views of Basseterre, the Atlantic coast, and the island's mountain range towering above to the north.

An moderate walk that is popular with both tourists and natives. Highly recommended.

3. The Romney Manor - Caribelle Batik Walk

To reach Romney Manor, drive the main highway out of Basseterre to Old Road Town and turn right onto the road marked for Wingfield Estate and Romney Manor. If you wish, you may begin the walk here as the road is a lightly traveled track going through green countryside. It is, however, quite steep in places. Stop along the road near the beginning of the walk to observe the Carib petroglyphs.

In a short while the road arrives at the gates of Romney Manor, once a thriving 17th-century plantation. There are five acres of maintained gardens surrounding the house. You'll discover the plantation's old bell tower, 300-year-old trees, good views, and one of the largest Saman rain trees you'll ever see, right in the front yard. Once you've walked the grounds, visit the Caribelle Batik Workshop housed inside the stately mansion. Master artisans are at work here. Batik is an intricate process involving the application of molten wax to cotton material which is then dipped into dye. The process is repeated a number of times until the desired pattern emerges.

This recommended trip is an easy, enjoyable walk, shopping trip, and history lesson all rolled up into one short excursion.

St. Kitts

4. The Dos D'Ane Pond Trail

Walking time: Expect to spend the better portion of the day hiking from Wingfield Estate to Molineux Estate

A guide is a must for this excursion because it passes through several parcels of private property and into the rain forest where interconnecting pathways may be confusing. The trail may be reached by way of Old Road Town and Wingfield Estate, driving all of the way to the end of the paved road. The pathway leaves the estate along sloping, wooded hillsides leading to the pond. From here, the deciduous forest becomes a seasonal evergreen forest that eventually gives way to the full-fledged tropical rain forest and the slightly steeper side of Verchilds Mountain. The trail itself rises steadily as it works its way to the ridgeline.

This is considered a moderately difficult hike; however, trail conditions change frequently in the rain forest and the current state of the trail should be checked on before embarking on the journey.

5. The Brimstone Hill Fortress Walk

Situated on what is actually a secondary cone of Mt. Liamuiga, Brimstone Hill is reached by way of the main highway from Basseterre. Just beyond the village of Half Way Tree a side road to the right begins the steep and winding ascent to the fortress. To truly appreciate how hard it would have been for an attacking army to fight its way into the fort, begin the walk at the bottom and take the road up to the fort. Not only did the attackers have to scale the steep sides of the mountain, they had to overcome small fortifications along the way and faced gunfire from the fort on the summit.

The fort, started by the British in 1690 as an vantage point to recapture St. Kitts from the French, took more than 100 years of mostly slave labor to construct. Spreading out over 37 acres, all of the structures are built of local volcanic stone. Soon after its completion, however, peace finally came to St. Kitts and the fort was abandoned and fell into disrepair for another hundred years.

Today, much of the fortress has been restored and made into a national park. A museum is housed in several rooms of the Citadel. A booklet describing the complete history of this "Gibraltar of the Caribbean" may be obtained in the museum.

History is not the only reason to take a walk here. Across the blue waters of the Caribbean, five islands can be seen – Sint Maarten, Saba, Statia, Nevis, and Montserrat. Across the grounds on the opposite side of Brimstone Hill is an even more impressive view, inland. Far below the fort, the green sugar cane farmland stretches toward the south. The land gently slopes up to the sides of the island's main mountain range, which rises steeply skyward, disappearing into the ever-present cloud cover near the ridgeline.

The fortress grounds are also a good spot to catch the scampering antics of the vervet monkeys.

6. The Mt. Liamuiga Trail

*Walking time: 4 to 5 hours, round trip,
to the crater rim and back*

The name of the highest spot on St. Kitts may just be one of the most mispronounced words in all of the Caribbean. One book says you should pronounce it "Lie-a-mee-ga," another source says "Lee-a-MOO-ee-ga," a third comes close to that with "Lee-A-mwee-ga," while yet one more reference states it should be "Liar-mweagre." They all do agree, however, that the word, meaning "fertile isle," is what the Amerindian inhabitants called St. Kitts before the arrival of settlers from the Old World. There is also is no doubt that an ascent up Mt. Liamuiga is the most ambitious hike to be undertaken on the island. This is a popular destination, but the fast-

St. Kitts

growing rain forest often overtakes the trail. For this reason a guide is pretty much a necessity.

The hike takes up where the roadway ends in Belmont Estates. The road has gained quite a bit of elevation, but this only means that the trail begins an immediate continual climb through the virgin rain forest. The slopes of Mt. Liamuiga are built of volcanic tuff, which aids in the rapid and thick growth of vegetation such as large gommier, candlewood, and locust trees sprouting growths of orchids, other epiphytes, and mosses. The tuff has also gouged deep ravines that dissect the mountainside.

The crater rim is reached after a climb of over 1,600 feet. Here, at 2,700 feet above sea level, the rain forest becomes an elfin woodland. This area is almost always in a mist and much of the time it is windy, cool, and rainy. (Be prepared with proper clothing.) The harsher climate and the shallower soil of the rim stunt the growth of the trees. However, the constant moisture is conducive to the growth of the mosses, lichens, and ferns. All of this gives the elfin woodland a mystical feeling.

The summit of Liamuiga is still 1,000 feet higher and at one time you could have reached the peak via a pathway. Unfortunately, the route along the crater rim, which was often slippery and overgrown, became so obscured by Hurricane Hugo that it will be quite some time, if ever, before it is cleared enough to be safely used again. Sadly, the hurricane has also stopped any descents into the crater itself. This was never an easy task and often involved clinging to branches, roots, and vines as one dropped steeply down to reach the crater lake. Hugo's winds, measured at more than 200 miles per hour, toppled so many trees that there is now no safe way down.

Only the most experienced of hikers should attempt the trek without a guide.

7. The Conarre Beach Walk

To reach Conarre Beach, drive the main highway out of Basseterre past the airport. About one mile past the airport turn right onto the coconut tree- and sugar cane-lined road, arriving at the beach in another mile. This quiet beach is covered with grayish-black sand. Although the surf is a little rough and there may be an undertow, snorkeling is good here.

8. The Frigate Bay Beach Walk

Frigate Bay is on the southern side of the Southeast Peninsula. The surf here is calmer than on the northern side and the sand is a fine golden powder. Many of St. Kitts' resort hotels are situated in this area, so it is not an isolated, unspoiled beach. However, even though all of the beaches of St. Kitts are open to the general public, you will find days when Frigate Bay Beach is only slightly used, with just a few people taking advantage of the gentle waves and soft breezes.

St. Kitts

9. The Southeast Peninsula Road Hike

Walking time: 3 hours, one way

Seven miles long by a half-mile wide with softly rounded hills, swaying grass fields, and rippling salt ponds, the Southeast Peninsula is bounded by crashing breakers on the north and placid surf beaches on the south. At present, only its northern tip in Frigate Bay and its southern end overlooking Nevis are developed, so you would be hard pressed to find a more visually pleasing strip of land anywhere in the Caribbean. The peninsula is much lower in elevation than the rest of the island and, as a result, receives substantially less rainfall. The vegetation takes on an open, thorny shrub appearance. The reflection of sunlight on golden beaches and deep blue waters and the resulting shadows cast by unmarred hillocks of green, makes this a place a hiking pleasure.

Before 1989, the only way to enter into this unspoiled area was by foot. There is now an excellent two lane highway, not unlike the Blue Ridge Parkway in Virginia and North Carolina, that traverses the full length of the peninsula, climbing hills and crossing vales, with pullout areas for some of the more scenic overlooks. However, traffic is light and walking is still the best way to enjoy the peninsula, especially when you leave the road, climb the lush fields of tall guinea grass and reach rounded hilltops with 360° views.

From the hotel complex in Frigate Bay you'll make the steepest ascent of the road as you climb to Timothy Hill for the first of many spectacular views. Behind you are the manicured golf course and gardens of the hotels in Frigate Bay with a background of rain forest on the island's mountain crest. Ahead lies your route along the peninsula, causing your eyes to wander to Mt. Nevis towering above St. Kitts' sister island in the far distance.

In 1.25 miles the route passes by South Friars Bay and a nice sand beach. Wild monkeys are abundant along this hike; if lucky, you might catch a glimpse of a wild deer or two. Three miles beyond Friars Bay is the Great Salt Pond, an ancient volcanic crater and a good spot to observe the bird life of the area. Be on the lookout for black-necked stilts, plovers, terns, and dowitchers. The dirt road across from the Great Salt Pond leads to another bay, a great area to saunter and ponder life. The beach is another good birdwatching spot; the mature dry woodlands forest behind the sands is home to quite a number of vervet monkeys. As the main road continues south, the vegetation becomes more sparse and desert-like. The southern coast of the island is about 1.25 miles past the Great Salt Pond. Isolated beaches and a good view of Nevis await the walker here.

A most highly recommended hike. Do not miss this excursion! If you don't want to walk it, at least drive

*Green hills are complemented by a blue lake on
the Southeast Peninsula.*

it. You will find rain forests like those on Mt. Liamuiga and Verchilds Mountain on numerous other
islands in the Caribbean, but nowhere will you find
such a piece of undeveloped scenery as you will see
here.

Also, enjoy the isolation of this peninsula while you
can; major development is slated to happen sometime in the very near future.

> An excellent way to spend a full day
> would be to start this hike early (which
> you want to do anyway as shade is non-
> existent and the sun can be brutal), ex-
> plore a couple of the beaches on the
> southern end, have dinner at the Turtle
> Beach Bar and Grill in Mosquito Bay,
> and return to Basseterre along the road,
> letting the glow of a full moon show you
> the way. A word of caution: be sure to
> carry plenty of water with you.

10. Majors Bay - Banana Bay - Cockleshell Bay Hike

Walking time: 2 hours, round trip (does not include the time needed to reach the beaches via the Southeast Peninsula Road)

According to much of the tourist literature, these are the best beaches on St. Kitts. They can be reached only by way of the Southeast Peninsula Road (see Walk #9).

This hike is not on a trail as such. It is just a ramble from one beach to the other through the open scrub land of the coastline. Majors Bay is separated from the other two beaches by a small ridge about 200 feet high. Be careful as you walk over the ridge. The prickly vegetation can do much damage to shoes, clothes, and skin. All three beaches offer good swimming and snorkeling. It is likely that you will be the only person on any of them.

This is a highly recommended excursion. The walking is easy, the views superb, the beaches are the best on the island, the snorkeling is good, and the seclusion is unequaled anywhere else on St. Kitts. Enjoy this area while you can there are plans for major development here.

If you don't want to hike the Southeast Peninsula Road to reach these beaches, drive out to them and you won't regret it.

11. Walks on Hotel and Inn Grounds

Rawlins Plantation is set among the remains of an old sugar factory and has seven acres of tended gardens. **Fort Thomas Hotel** is built on the site of the old fort overlooking Basseterre. The hotel is surrounded by eight acres of tropical gardens.

The **Jack Tar Village Beach Resorts and Casino** contains over 200 acres of gardens, a golf course and tennis courts. **The Fairview Inn** and the **Golden Lemon** also make for enjoyable walks.

If not a registered guest, you should obtain permission before walking through these, or any, hotel grounds.

St. Kitts

Nevis

Nevis, "The Queen of the Caribees," received its title during the colonial period when the great houses and resorts were the playgrounds of wealthy Europeans. The man-made grandeur of those days has now faded and many of the island's natural wonders have returned. There is only one large, resort-type hotel on the beach; a significant percentage of the accommodations are usually hidden away, off the main highways in restored plantation houses. The few tourist shops are small and run by locals. Even the airport is on a modest scale, allowing only small planes to land.

Viewed from afar, Nevis is a perfectly circular, cone-shaped island. From the cloud-enshrouded summit of Mt. Nevis, the island slopes gently down as it approaches the sea, 3,232 feet below. As on the sister island of St. Kitts, tropical rain forests cover the higher elevations, while the summit of Mt. Nevis is elfin woodland. Wild vervet monkeys inhabit the rain forest areas.

Whereas sugarcane is the main crop on St. Kitts, assorted vegetables are the cultivated products on Nevis. On the lower elevations, breadfruit, avocadoes, and papaya are plentiful.

Palm-lined beaches rim the island, with Pinney's Beach on the western coast stretching four miles along the Caribbean Sea. Beaches on the northern shore look out across The Narrows to the sleepy bays of St. Kitts.

Nevis is seven miles long, six miles wide and contains 36 square miles.

History

When Columbus sailed by the island in 1493, its cloud-capped peak reminded him of the snow-covered summits of the Pyrenees in Spain, so he called it "Nuestra Senora de las Nieves" (Our Lady of the Snows). Through time this eventually became, simply, Nevis. Before the arrival of Europeans, the Carib Indians had called their island "Oualie," the Land of Beautiful Water.

In the early part of the 1600s, a group of 80 Englishmen arrived from St. Kitts to establish Jamestown on Nevis, but this first settlement is believed to have been destroyed by a tidal wave in 1680. As with so many of the islands in this area, Nevis was the site of many battles for possession among several European powers. After a one-year French occupation, the 1783 Treaty of Versailles firmly established England as owner of the island.

Alexander Hamilton was born in Charlestown in 1757, emigrated to North America, and went on to become a founding father of the United States.

As a young frigate captain, Horatio Nelson (later Lord Nelson) patrolled these waters and visited Nevis often. Nelson and the Royal Navy used the island as a resting spot for crews and to obtain fresh water. Lookouts were maintained at Forts Charles and Ashby and Saddle Hill. In 1787, Nelson married a Nevisian widow, Frances Nisbet, at Montpelier Estate with Prince William Henry (later King William IV of England) giving the bride away.

When sugarcane was king in the Caribbean, Nevis became "the Queen." This was the time when visiting mineral spring water spas to "take the cure" was the height of fashion and the Bath Hotel of Nevis was among the most popular. The resort catered not only to the plantocracy of the neighboring islands, but also to the aristocracy of Europe. As sugar declined in importance on the world market and the spa fad faded away, Nevis returned to a more peaceful and slower way of life.

Nevis remained under British control until 1967. Along with St. Kitts and Anguilla, it became an associated state of the United Kingdom, gaining full independence in 1983. Anguilla decided to remain with the United Kingdom. Nevis retains the right of secession from the Federation.

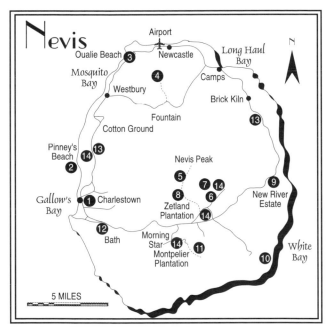

Transportation to Nevis: There are no direct flights from the U.S., Canada, or Europe to Nevis. There are, however, daily short flights from many of the surrounding islands that have direct air connections with North America and Europe. Among them are St. Kitts, Antigua, Puerto Rico, St. Croix, and Sint Maarten.

The government-operated ferry, the *Caribe Queen*, makes trips daily (except Thursday and Sunday) between Charlestown, Nevis, and Basseterre, St. Kitts.

Nevis is visited less often by cruise ships than its sister island of St. Kitts.

A departure tax is collected upon leaving Nevis.

Entry: Although a passport is preferred for American or Canadian citizens, a birth certificate or voter's registration card is all that is required. Other citizens need a valid passport. All visitors must also possess a return or ongoing transportation ticket.

Currency: The East Caribbean dollar is the national currency. American dollars are accepted in many business establishments, but you will probably receive change in East Caribbean dollars. Foreign currency may be exchanged at the banks in Charlestown, whose normal operating hours are Monday to Thursday, 8:00 A.M. to 2:00 P.M. and Friday, 8:00 A.M. to 5:00. The St. Kitts and Nevis National Bank is also open from 8:30 A.M. to 11:00 A.M. on Saturday.

Tourist Information:

✍ **In the United States**
St. Kitts - Nevis Tourist Office
414 East 75th Street
New York, NY 10021
☎ 212-535-1234

✍ **In Canada**
St. Kitts - Nevis Tourist Office
11 Yorkville Ave., Suite 508
Toronto, Ontario M4W IL3
☎ 416-921-7717

✍ **In Europe**
St. Kitts - Nevis Tourist Office
10 Kensington Court
London W8 5DL
England, ☎ 0171-376-0881

The Nevis Tourist Bureau is in Charlestown's main square:

✍ Nevis Tourist Board
Main Street, Charlestown, Nevis
West Indies, ☎ 869-469-1042

Driving: Rental cars are available in Charlestown and at the airport. A local driver's license is required. Presentation of a national or international driver's license and payment of a fee are all that is needed. The permit may be obtained in the Traffic Department of the Police Station on Main Street, Charlestown. Drive on the left!

Language: English.

Walking and Hiking Guide Companies: Before the 1980s it was next to impossible to find someone on Nevis who made a living leading guided walks and hikes. However, the fact that the island has become a major destination for adventure tourists, eco-travelers and walkers and hikers is evidenced by a veritable axplosion of guide companies.

David Rollinson of Eco-Tours Nevis leads informative "eco-rambles." These easy-to-moderate walks in the lower elevations are excellent introductions to the history and environment of the island.

✍ Eco-Tours Nevis
Morning Star
Nevis, West Indies
☎ 869-469-2091

Nevisian Michael Herbert comes highly recommended for hikes up to the higher elevations and into the rain forest.

✍ Heb's Nature Tours
Rawlins Village, Gingerland
Nevis, West Indies
☎ 869-469-2856

Lynell and Earla Liburd operate **Sunrise Tours**, ☎ 869-469-2758, which leads excursions to various parts of the island. One of the favorite hikes goes into the New River Gorge to view three waterfalls.

Top to Bottom Tours (☎ 869-469-9080) runs trips to many of the same places and will also take you on treks most other people overlook. They offer some of the most resonable rates.

The Tourist Board can also put you in touch with these organizations and other qualified guide companies.

Camping Areas: There are no official campgrounds on Nevis.

Recommended Readings

📖　*Swords, Ships, and Sugar: A History of Nevis to 1900* by Vincent K. Hubbard

📖　*Nevis: Queen of the Caribees* by Joyce Gordon (out of print)

Current events are reported by *The Democrat, The Laborers Spokesman*, and *The Observer* – all available throughout Nevis.

Walks

1. A Walking Tour of Charlestown

Begin the walking tour at the pier on the waterfront. Several times a day, one of the ferries arrives from the sister island of St. Kitts. When these boats dock, activity becomes frenzied. Day visitors, local commuters, food, clothing, and other necessities of life all arrive at one time on this vital link between the two islands. Directly in front of the pier is the Ginnery, which processed one of the island's main exports – sea island cotton. A right turn onto the square will lead to the Tourist Bureau and Nevis

Handicraft Cooperative. Another right turn ends at the Nevis Philatelic Bureau. The beauty of the postage stamps of Nevis is world famous and valued by collectors. You can also obtain a detailed map of Nevis here. The Public Market Place, next to the Philatelic Bureau, is especially interesting and entertaining on Saturday morning, its busiest time. Back onto Main Street, turn right and pass Memorial Square and the small monument to the dead of both World Wars.

Continuing on Main Street, pass the Court House and Public Library on your right. Left onto Government Road for one block leads to the Jewish Cemetery, noteworthy for its unique headstones dating from 1690. A left at the cemetery, one block of walking through a residential area, and then another left on Happy Hill Alley and you are at the Nevis Bakery. Normally, a bakery would not be pointed out in a walking tour, but you should not pass up a chance to enjoy the fresh bread and delicious tarts of the Nevis Bakery.

A right onto Main Street will take you past the Treasury Building, an excellent example of colonial Nevis architecture. If you won't get a chance to visit the Caribelle Batik factory on St. Kitts, visit its Nevis outlet in the TDC Store on Main St. Caribelle Batik products are works of art created by the true batik process of melted wax and hand-dipped colors on 100% cotton. Pass by Chapel Street and on the left of Main Street is the Alexander Hamilton Birthplace and Museum of Nevis History. Hamilton, the illegitimate son of a Scotsman and a Creole who rose to become the first Secretary of the Treasury of the United States, was born here in 1757. The small museum, also containing exhibits on numerous aspects of Nevisian life through the centuries, is well worth visiting and will add to your understanding of the island. A small fee is charged for admission.

The walking tour of Charlestown comes to an end here, but if you wish to push on to Pinney's Beach (see Walk #2), you may do so by continuing on Main Street and then making a left onto Island Road.

Nevis

2. The Pinney's Beach Hike

Walking time: 2 hours, one way

One of the least crowded and longest beach walks in the Caribbean. This palm-lined, sandy beach stretches for four miles from Charlestown to the northern coast of Nevis. Along its whole length are white sand, palm trees, and scrub vegetation, with an occasional small bar or restaurant. The only large development is the Four Seasons Resort, which intrudes on less than 10% of the beachfront.

To take a stroll along Pinney's Beach and a swim in the sea is to enjoy the quiet serenity and beauty that is quickly being lost on the more popular and developed beaches of the Caribbean. The relaxing surf, the yielding sand, and the cool breezes passing through the palm trees are what you came to the Caribbean for. A highly recommended hike.

3. The Oualie Beach Walk

Another restful walk, Oualie Beach is on the northwest shore of Nevis and may be reached by the main highway. Here, the vegetation is open, grassy savannah, rather than the palm trees of Pinney's Beach. Not as long as Pinney's, Oualie Beach is enjoyable for its view across The Narrows to Nags Head and the sleepy lagoon of Majors Bay on St. Kitts.

The surf here is rougher than at Pinney's Beach, so use caution when taking a dip.

4. The Round Hill Track

Walking time: 1 hour, round trip

Like many of the hikes on Nevis, the Round Hill Track is not a formal, maintained hiking trail, but rather an excursion on a rarely-used four-wheel-drive dirt road. To reach the beginning of the outing, drive the main highway north out of Charlestown. Four miles out of town, turn right onto Westbury Road and go almost two miles to reach the Methodist Church in Fountain. Just past the church, make a left and follow a two-track concrete road to its end in another 0.2 mile. Park your vehicle (so as not to block traffic) and begin ascending rolling fields on the dirt road to the left.

Rising with an almost constant cool breeze blowing, you'll have extensive views of the western and eastern shores. In 30 minutes trees will block the vistas, but continue on for another five to 10 minutes until you reach Round Hill's summit. At 1,014 feet above sea level, you should walk around the T.V. tower for a cornucopia of changing views –Newcastle Airport, out across The Narrows to the Southeast Peninsula of St. Kitts, around to the dark green slopes of Mt. Nevis, and even back to the huddled buildings of Charlestown. A moderate hike.

5. The Mt. Nevis Trails

Walking time: at least 5 hours, round trip

Nevis

Without a doubt, one of the toughest hikes in all of the Leeward Islands, the Mt. Nevis trails lead to the 3,200-foot crater rim of this extinct volcano. There are actually two trails, one emanating from Zetland Plantation and the other from Hamilton Estate. No matter which one you wish to take, a guide is a necessity here, as even the beginning of either trail might be hard to find.

Both pathways are somewhat similar in the routes they take. Beginning in open fields, the trails enter the forest within 0.5 mile, pass a few lime trees, ascend a small ridge, and then begin their extremely steep ascents through lush, vine-tangled vegetation. On the way, look out for wild vervet monkeys, which were brought to Nevis by early French settlers.

As the trails climb toward the sky they become steadily steeper and extremely slippery. There are places, in fact, that are virtually straight up and down and here it is necessary to cling to roots and vines. Once the crater rim is reached, the effort proves worthwhile. From here, all of Nevis (and the whole of the Caribbean it seems) stretches out below you. The deep green fields of the Gingerland Parish are directly below, sloping gently to the Atlantic. Charlestown, Gallows Bay, and the Caribbean Sea can be seen to the west.

There are trails leading around the rim of the crater and down into the crater itself. These are even harder to find and follow than the ascent trails and should only be undertaken with the direction of an experienced guide.

The wind can be quite cool on the summit and rain storms are rather frequent, so remember to bring a jacket. Be careful on the descent.

This is a highly recommended outing for the decidedly adventurous and truly fit!

> ✣ **Note:** An excellent option that should be discussed with your guide before beginning the hike would be to ascend Mt. Nevis by one trail and descend via the other. Of course, this would involve a vehicle shuttle, so expect the guide's fee to be a bit higher.

6. The Golden Rock Estate Nature Trail

Walking time: 30 minutes, for the complete circuit

The Golden Rock Estate's owner, Pam Barry, whose family has run the estate for five generations, is an active ecology and nature advocate. She has developed a pathway on a portion of the former sugar plantation so that the general public can share in her enthusiasm. Golden Rock Estate is reached by driving eastward out of Charlestown and passing through Chicken Stone and Market Shop. Soon after that small village, be looking for the Golden Rock Estate sign where you'll turn left and follow the road to its end. Stop in at the office to let them know you're going to walk the trail and pick up a trail map. The map is keyed to numbered signs along the route, providing information about plants lining the trail.

From steps next to the car park, the trail ascends by breadfruit, flamboyant, white cedar, soursop, jumbie bead, and wild cilliment before it makes a right turn to descend into a small ravine. (At this point the Water Source Trail – see Walk #7 – continues to the left.) Dropping back down toward the estate office, the lush vegetation here is a perfect place to watch a band of wild vervet monkeys as they swing from limb to limb. Hiking the trail in mid-afternoon will increase your chances of spotting these playful creatures. Continue out of the ravine, into a small open area, and return to the main grounds where you can relax with a cool drink on the patio next to the bar.

7. The Water Source Trail

Walking time: 3 hours, round trip to the steps;
4 hours, round trip to The Source

Nevis

This trail was originally constructed to provide access for workers putting in the pipeline to the main supply of water for the island. It is an excellent choice for those who want to experience the lush rain forest vegetation of Nevis, but lack the time or stamina required to hike Mt. Nevis. The easiest way to reach the trailhead is to follow the Golden Rock Estate Nature Trail (see Walk #6) to where it makes a right-hand bend and descends into a ravine. However, for the Water Source Trail you want to continue forward for a few feet, then make a left onto a dirt road. At the very next intersection, bear right uphill for several yards and make a left onto concrete. Turn around to look behind you for an excellent vista across the Caribbean Sea to Redonda, Montserrat, Antigua, and Guadeloupe. Be paying attention, though; almost immediately you need to turn right onto a dirt road and ascend past several small homes as the roadbed becomes grassy and lined with vegetation. Stay on this main route which, at times, is almost a wide as a two-lane road.

As the journey gains elevation, the vegetation changes from grasses and shrubs to large ground ferns bordering the way. In 50 minutes you'll pass by a water tank and small cave on the left where, to the right, is a deep ravine covered by the green fans of spreading tree ferns. Bromeliads, elephant ears, and other large-leaf plants become more populous as the route swings left to pass through an old gate. Deep ravine cuts reveal a bit of the southern coastline of Nevis, but what may be even more impressive is the nearly vertical slope of Mt. Nevis, rising out of the depths below you only to disappear into clouds hundreds of feet above. The ravine also provides clear views into the vegetation so watch for tremblers, thrashers, thrushes, and hummingbirds.

Inside the confines of a tropical cloud forest, the way soon descends some steps and becomes more of a narrow footpath than a wide roadbed. It is possible to continue from here for another 30 minutes or so to "The Source," but, as the trail only deteriorates and becomes extremely slippery, you are advised to proceed with caution or to end your hike here. A recommended, moderate hike.

8. The Upper Round Road Hike

Walking time: 1 hour, 15 minutes, one way

Following portions of the original late-1600s or early-1700s road that encircled Nevis, the Upper Round Road Hike is an easy trek through predominantly agricultural lands around the base of Mt. Nevis. Local inhabitants have been known to invite visitors to join them in an afternoon fresh fruit snack or a cool Carib beer. As an added incentive, this outing begins and ends at plantation inns that are not only known for their hospitality but, more importantly to a hungry hiker, for delicious West Indian and Nevisian cuisine.

After lunch, or at least a cup of afternoon tea, begin the hike from the Hermitage Plantation by taking the road behind the inn. The route starts out as concrete, but soon turns to dirt as it ascends by old stone walls and plants typical of lower cloud vegetation. At 0.3 mile, avoid the road bearing left uphill and keep to the right on a more or less level plane; the road soon becomes paved again. At 0.6 mile from the Hermitage you'll come to a three-way intersection and an old sugar mill. Bear right, descend, and enjoy the views out across the Caribbean Sea. Be alert! At 0.8 mile, leave the pavement and make an abrupt left onto an unsigned and rutted dirt road.

At the next intersection, keep straight as the road becomes paved, then dirt, and then paved again when you pass by an aqueduct on your left and enter cultivated farm lands. Keep to the left when roads come in from the right at the next two intersections. Breadfruit, mangoes, and tomatoes grow alongside the road. Pay close attention when you walk next to the water catchment tank (1.9 miles from the Hermitage Plantation). Turn right onto a rutted dirt road, only to make an immediate left onto another rough road. A few yards past a small house, turn right and descend the pathway, which is a part of the Golden Rock Estate Nature Trail (see Walk #6).

Within 10 more minutes you'll arrive at the main grounds of the Golden Rock Estate where, hopefully, you have dinner reservations. If you hike on a Saturday during the Caribbean's high tourist season, you'll be able to enjoy the Golden Rock's acclaimed West Indian buffet and the island sounds of a local string band.

Nevis

9. The New River Estate Walk

To better understand the history and ecology of the area, the grounds of the New River Estate should be explored with Eco-Tours Nevis (see Walking and Hiking Guide Companies, above) during one of their eco-rambles. This easy walk amid the prickly pear cactus landscape of the island's eastern side and shore tours the site of a former sugar plantation. You can wander among the remnants of the kitchen, boiling house, windmill tower, lime kiln, and the great house. Be sure to bring a hat, sunscreen, cover-ups, and plenty of drinking water as there is virtually no shade here.

10. The White Bay/Windward Beach Walk

The owners of the Golden Rock Estate have graciously opened this private property to the general public so that all may enjoy the quiet serenity of a windswept coastline. To find the secluded beach, drive eastward from Charlestown on the main road, passing by the turnoff to Saddle Hill (see Walk #11). At the Gingerland Post Office (where the main road makes a hard left), bear right and descend along a paved route through gently sloping grazing lands for a little more than two miles. Just before the road becomes dirt, turn left onto a two-track concrete route and park your car just past the horse racing track. From here it is only a few yards along a dirt road before you arrive at the beach.

There is a very real chance, especially during the off-season, that you will be the only person on the soft sands. Savor this opportunity to discover the natural charms of an unspoiled Caribbean beach. The antics of grazing goats and ghost crabs – which emerge from their dens to make a mad dash to the water's edge and wet their gills – provide humorous entertainment, while the rolling waves make for excellent body surfing.

An important Caribbean plant grows along the upper portion of this shore. Beach morning glory, whose seeds are spread by ocean currents and germinate in the salt water, send intertwining roots into the soil to stabilize the sand, preventing erosion that would result from the constant assault by winds and rains. Incidentally, the beach morning glory also produces a chemical that is used to relieve headache pain by shrinking blood vessels.

11. The Saddle Hill Track

Walking time: 1 hour, round trip

The Saddle Hill Track leads to a viewpoint local lore says was once used by Captain Horatio Nelson. It is accessible by driving eastward from Charlestown on the main highway. Watch for a road sign in Chicken Stone that says "St. George's Parish – the Food Basket of Nevis." Take the second road to the right after the sign and follow it to the first road on the right. Ascend this road. At the top of a small knob, bear left and follow this fairly new concrete road to a dirt road going off to the right.

Park and walk the dirt road as it swings around the base of Saddle Hill for a little more than a mile to bring you an unobstructed view of the Caribbean Sea, St. Kitts, Redonda, and Montserrat. An easy hike.

12. The Bath Hotel, Hot Springs, and Fort Charles Walk

Walking time: 45 minutes, one way

Walk south from Charlestown on Main Street. In less than half a mile, turn uphill on the twisting road to Bath Village (use caution as this main highway sees a lot of traffic).

The Bath Hotel, constructed in 1778, was world famous for its natural hot springs. It was not unusual for Europeans to sail across the Atlantic to bathe in the spring's reportedly healing, sulphurous waters. This was at a time when the voyage took weeks! Even though this grand resort is now in ruins, you can reflect on the hotel's glorious former times and "take the waters," as did European aristocracy. Close to the old hotel is the Nelson Museum, which houses the largest collection of Nelson memorabilia in the New World.

Back on the road, continue toward the shore and you'll soon reach the ruins of Fort Charles. The cannons are a reminder that Nelson once kept a lookout here for French sailing vessels. The fort has a sweeping vista of Charlestown, Gallows Bay, and the Caribbean. A recommended walk.

13. The 'Round the Island Hike

The main highway encircling the island is only 20 miles long. Motor vehicle traffic is not very heavy (except in villages), so consider this hike to explore Nevis and meet her people. You will have company on your journey as foot travel is a way of life for many Nevisians. You may start and stop anywhere along the way, and you will never be far from a restaurant or inn for a rest stop. Remember that you are walking on the island's main highway, so use caution.

Heading north from Charlestown, follow the main highway or walk along Pinney's Beach. There are numerous short paths connecting the beach to the road and you may rejoin the road at any time.

Just north of small Cotton Ground Village are the overgrown ruins of Fort Ashby. Like others on Nevis, this fort was used by the Royal Navy, and a nearby spring supplied fresh water for the fleet. The fort area is also renowned as a good bird watching spot.

Continuing north, the road parallels Oualie and Newcastle Reef beaches. Oualie Beach Pub is a well-liked resting and watering spot.

Heading east, the traffic picks up a little as you pass the Newcastle Airport. In town, stop at the pottery factory for a rest and a lesson in the traditional methods of firing pottery.

Once past Newcastle and the airport, the traffic thins again and the countryside takes on the sleepy feel and look of medieval pastoral paintings. The road passes by livestock grazing in open meadows and the land drops gently to the pounding surf of the Atlantic. You will pass through a number of small villages such as Camps, Brick Kiln, and Butlers.

As the road turns west, take a few extra steps off the main highway to New River Estate (see Walk #9). The sugar mill here, the last on the island to grind sugarcane, closed in 1958.

Back on the main highway you'll pass side roads that lead to old plantations (now converted to inns). Your hike then ascends to a view from Morning Star. This spot is aptly named as the sunrise from this point is truly special.

A short distance from Morning Star is Fig Tree Village. The register in St. Johns, a simple stone church here, records the marriage of Horatio Nelson to Frances Nisbet in 1787 (and makes no mention of Lady Hamilton!).

Before returning to Charlestown, you'll see a road leading to Fort Charles and the Hot Springs Bath Hotel (see Walk #12).

14. Walks on Hotel and Inn Grounds

Situated on the sites of old sugar plantations, a number of the inns on Nevis contain extensive grounds that should not be overlooked in your quest for quality walking spots. **The Golden Rock Estate**, at the base of Mt. Nevis, has its own nature

An old windmill on the Golden Rock Estate.

trail (see Walk #6) and several acres of rain forest and cultivated tropical gardens, which are home to a band of wild vervet monkeys. **Montpelier Plantation** has brick walkways winding through 100 acres of landscaped hillside gardens. **Croney's Old Manor Estate**, a restored 17th-century sugar plantation high on the slopes of Mt. Nevis, contains the ruins of a 19th-century cane-crushing steam engine set amid spacious tropical gardens.

Credited with having had a major positive impact on the economy of Nevis, the sprawling **Four Seasons Resort** connects the sands of Pinney's Beach to the green acreage of a palm-dotted 18-hole golf course via a network of flower-lined paths.

> ⇉ Please remember that if you are not a registered guest it is only common courtesy to ask permission before walking the grounds of any inn or hotel.

Antigua

In recent years, Antigua has pinned much of its hopes upon attracting the large-scale tourist trade. In what were once quiet bays and hidden coves, resorts – complete with golf courses and tennis courts – have begun to spring up, while discos and casinos capture visitors with their nightlife. Make no mistake about it, this is an island that has decided to capitalize on its white, sunny beaches and rolling surf.

This emphasis on the water and modern beach amenities has left the inland mostly ignored. Although Antigua does take an active interest in its history (be sure to visit Shirley Heights and the beautifully restored Nelson's Dockyard), not much has been done to make the hillsides and rolling plateaus accessible to the on-foot explorer. Yet, there are a few signs that the people of the island have begun to realize the value of pedestrian travel, not only for tourists, but also for themselves. The National Parks Authority has published a map of hiking trails near Nelson's Dockyard, the Ministry of Agriculture/Forestry Unit is constructing a network of pathways through the southern highlands, and the Historical and Archaeological Society dispenses information about walking and hiking opportunities.

Antigua has many things going for it. The weather is absolutely perfect and the people are truly warm and friendly. Other islands may boast of having 365 beaches, but Antigua really does offer enough little bays, coves, and inlets that you could visit a different one every day of the year. So, if you dream of spending days strolling on palm-lined beaches, riding the waves on a sailboard, snorkeling in small, hidden coral coves, dancing the night away to pop music, and exploring the well-lit wilderness of a gambling casino, Antigua may just be the place.

History

In 1632, 139 years after Columbus sailed by and named the island after Santa Maria la Antigua of Seville, the first British settlers arrived from St. Kitts. Unlike many early colonists on surrounding islands, Antiguans did not have to endure centuries of conquest and reconquest by various European powers. Only once, in 1666, was the island dominated by France. However, this French rule was ended within three months by the Treaty of Breda.

The island may not have had a turbulent history of its own, but it housed a major British naval base. Admirals Rodney and Hood, and later Admiral Nelson, commanded heavily armed fleets based on Antigua. These patrolled the Caribbean, protecting English merchant ships and Great Britain's interests in the New World.

The abolition of slavery brought decline to the sugar industry and the island became less important to England. Until the 1960s it remained a relatively quiet and unnoticed island. In 1967, Antigua attained associated state status in the British Commonwealth and, in 1981, was granted full independence.

In the last 20 to 30 years, the sleepy island has awakened to the lure of the tourist trade and now draws tens of thousands more visitors than the neighboring islands of Montserrat, St. Kitts, or Nevis. It has also developed into the gateway of the Lesser Antilles. Many international airlines now use Antigua's airport as a transfer point to other islands.

Data

Transportation to Antigua: There are direct flights from the U.S., Canada, and Europe. In addition, Antigua may be reached by air from Puerto Rico, Sint Maarten, Montserrat, St. Kitts, and other nearby islands.

Antigua is a very popular cruise ship port of call. A departure tax is collected.

Entry: Citizens of European countries must bring along a valid passport. Canadians and Americans need some proof of identification, such as a voter's registration card, birth certificate, or passport. Every visitor must possess an ongoing or return airline ticket.

Antigua

Currency: The Eastern Caribbean dollar is the national currency. While it is best to make an exchange at the banks in St. John's, Nelson's Dockyard, or at the airport, American dollars and traveller's checks in U.S. denominations are widely accepted; be prepared to receive change in Eastern Caribbean currency. Normal banking hours are 8:00 A.M. to 1:00 P.M., Monday to Thursday, with Friday hours of 8:00 A.M. to 12 noon and 3:00 P.M. to 5:00 P.M. All banks are closed on Saturday and Sunday.

Credit cards are readily accepted in most hotels, tourist shops, and larger restaurants.

Some establishments quote prices in Eastern Caribbean dollars, while others use American dollars. Be sure to inquire as to which is being used before making your purchase.

Tourist Information:

✍ **In the United States**
Antigua & Barbuda Department of Tourism
610 5th Ave., Suite 311
New York, NY 10020
☎ 212-541-4117

✍ **In Canada**
Antigua & Barbuda Department of Tourism
60 St. Clair Avenue East, Suite 304
Toronto, Ontario M4T 1N5
☎ 416-961-3085

✍ **In Europe**
Antigua & Barbuda Department of Tourism
High Commission
Antigua House, 15 Thayer Street
London W1M 5LD
England, ☎ 0171-486-7073

On Antigua, the Tourist Office is on Lower Nevis Street, about two blocks from the Heritage Pier in St. John's.

✍ Antigua & Barbuda Department of Tourism
Thames Street, PO Box 363
St. John's, Antigua
West Indies
☎ 268-462-0484

Driving: Rental cars are available, but be sure to obtain the required local permit at any police station or at V.C. Bird International Airport. You'll need a valid driver's license and must pay for the permit.

You are in a former British colony, so remember to drive on the left!

Language: English.

Walking and Hiking Guide Companies: Established in the mid-1990s, Bo-Tours specializes in walking.

✍ Bo-Tours
Box 2323, St. John's, Antigua
West Indies
☎ 268-462-6632

On a less commercial level, the Historical and Archaeological Society advises visitors about hikes. Further information may be obtained at the Museum of Antigua and Barbuda on Long Street in St. John's (☎ 268-462-4930).

Camping Areas: There are no campgrounds on Antigua and, in fact, no camping permitted anywhere on the island. Be sure to obey this regulation as it is strictly enforced and violators may be severely fined.

Recommended Readings

📖 *Brief Account of the Island of Antigua* by J. Luffman

📖 *Antigua, Barbuda & Redonda* by Desmond Nicholson

📖 *The Story of English Harbour* by Desmond Nicholson

The Observer is published daily, while *The Worker's Voice*, *The Outlet*, and *The Sun* are weekly newspapers. Each provides its own overview of the daily life and current events on Antigua.

Walks

1. A Walking Tour of St. John's

The best point to start an exploration is at the pier in St. John's. Directly across the pier is the Westerby Memorial, erected in 1888 to honor the work of Moravian Bishop, George Westerby. Walk along High Street to the Post Office, where you can buy the highly prized and colorful postage stamps of Antigua. Turn left on Thames Street and immediately come to the Tourist Office – the best place to learn more about the island.

Follow Long Street to Market Street, where you'll turn left and stop to visit the excellent displays in the Museum of Antigua and Barbuda. This treasury of Antiguan memorabilia is housed in the old Court House. It was constructed in 1750 and is the oldest building in St. John's. One more block will bring you to Newgate Street and the Police Station, built in 1788 and surrounded by a unique style of fence.

Continue right on Newgate Street to the most famous spot of the city, St. John's Cathedral. This impressive structure has a turbulent history. The original building was erected in the late 1600s, but deteriorated to the point that it was replaced in the early 18th century. The stone church then stood for 100 years before it was destroyed by an earthquake in 1843. Having learned from past mistakes, the builders of the present-day cathedral treated interior walls with pitch pine to add stability in the event of further tremors.

Just beyond the cathedral is Government House, now the private residence of the Governor General. Alongside is St. Joseph's Catholic Church, built in 1908 to replace the earlier church that had been erected by 19th-century Portuguese immigrants.

Pass by the World Wars I and II Memorial and use a walkway through tropical flowers, green shrubs, and trees to reach Parliament House and the Administration Building.

Head back toward the harbor on Nevis Street, passing by a number of old colonial homes and a few restaurants. Next to the waterfront is Redcliffe Quay, a former slave-holding area that now serves as a shopping center. The walking tour ends here, just two blocks from the pier.

2. The Long Island and Jumby Bay Resort Grounds Walk

This 300-acre island is just off the northeastern coast of Antigua. Built on the site of a centuries-old sugar plantation, the Jumby Bay Resort is surrounded by beautifully landscaped grounds and is a relaxing spot for lunch or an enjoyable evening in the lounge. White powder sands invite leisurely strolls on the beaches that wrap around the island.

> **Please Note:** All of Long Island is private property, so you should contact the resort before starting to explore.

3. Devil's Bridge and Indian Town National Park

Located on the far reaches of eastern Antigua, Devil's Bridge and Indian Town National Park may be reached by driving from the small village of Willikies toward Long Bay. Look for the sign directing you to make a right onto a side road which is followed to its end at Indian Town Point. You may be the only person exploring this windswept coast of limestone formations and acacia trees.

Throughout the world there are more than 600 varieties of acacia. In the Caribbean they are usually just referred to as cassie trees. Although they may shed their leaves during the dry season and appear to be dead, the trees are very much alive and, if you happen to walk into one or brush against its needle-point spines, you will be harshly reminded of its will to survive.

Prepare to get wet at the blow holes!

Wander around the shore's rocky cliffs to Devil's Bridge, a natural arch of limestone created by the ceaseless pounding of winds, waves, and salt spray on the rocks. When conditions are right, this formation and other blow holes in the park can produce some thunderous effects. Don't stand too close if you wish to stay dry!

4. The Half Moon Bay Beach Walk

On an island famous for its beaches, Half Moon Bay is an outstanding example of a tropical beach and lagoon. Even though part of the area is developed, it is still a pleasant place to stroll on the mile-long, crescent of powdered sugar-white sand. The waves here make for good body-surfing and the palm trees provide a welcome relief from the tropical sun. If you're feeling adventurous, you could explore the rocky northern end of the beach and then round the headland to Exchange Bay. A highly recommended beach walk.

Half Moon Bay Beach.

5. Nelson's Dockyard and The Fort Berkeley Trail

On the southern coast of Antigua, English Harbour is one of the safest foul-weather ports in the world. As early as 1671 these waters were used by the British as a hurricane hole. Adjacent to the harbor, a dockyard was established in 1725 and used in later years by Admirals Rodney, Hood, and Nelson.

Begin this walk in the restored dockyard (admission fee charged), exploring buildings constructed from the early sailing ships' ballast brick, the Officer's Quarters, and the small museum inside the Admiral's House. The museum contains memorabilia from Nelson's days and detailed information on the dockyard and Shirley Heights.

Walk around the wall next to the dinghy pier (beside the hotel and restaurant) to reach the beginning of the Fort Berkeley Trail. This 15-minute path leads

Antigua

through dry scrub brush to the fort itself. The colonial fortification and its batteries were the first line of defense for English Harbour.

Because of the historical perspective you will acquire on this outing, it is a highly recommended walk.

6. The Middle Ground Trails

Adjacent to Nelson's Dockyard are numerous small hills overlooking the Caribbean Sea on which the National Parks Authority has designated pathways called the Middle Ground Trails. As these routes are really not much more than goat paths, it would be wise to check with the National Parks Authority (located inside the museum in the dockyard) for present conditions and to obtain a copy of the trail map.

The easiest way to find the routes is to walk the Fort Berkeley Trail (see Walk #5). Just before you reach the fort, make a hard right to scramble up the rocks of the ridgeline on a somewhat defined route, watching your step to avoid the cacti and other prickly growth. A large percentage of the vegetation you'll encounter on these trails is of the xerophytic type, meaning that it has adapted to the long periods of little or no precipitation common on this side of Antigua. Some of these adaptations include cacti's succulent leaves, or narrow leaves (requiring less moisture to grow) like those found on frangipani, and root systems that spread over a large area to soak up as much moisture from the soil as possible. Once on flat land, aim for the highest point to find the ruins of a small battery and fort. Within 20 minutes from Fort Berkeley, the route drops to an open saddle and comes to a four-way intersection.

The shortest way back to Nelson's Dockyard would be to take the trail on the right. It gradually descends into bushes, trees, and open fields to reach a paved road about 10 minutes from the intersection.

Make a right and in five to seven minutes you'll be back at the dockyard parking lot.

Continuing straight across the four-way intersection, you'll rise to a small knob, descend about 150 feet, and then rise again to reach the site of Fort Cuyler after 20 minutes. Not only did the fort have a commanding view out across the Caribbean Sea but, maybe even more importantly, onto the mouth of Falmouth Harbour. A 10-minute walk from the fort brings you to a paved road. Turn right and 15 more minutes of walking will return you to the dockyard.

A left at the four-way intersection opens up a few more options. Within five minutes, you'll come across a trail descending to the right. This route emerges onto the shoreline of Windward Bay, which can be followed to the paved road. This, in turn, leads back to the dockyard. Continuing to the left and descending for five minutes at the second intersection would deliver you to flat rocks above the impressive 110-foot cliffs of Snapper Point. Of all the Middle Ground Trails, this is the only one that involves retracing your steps. However, on your way back you'll have a chance to study four distinct cacti growing in the area – Turk's cap, pin-cushion, dildo, and sucking cossie.

> ⯈ **Note:** The Middle Ground Trails traverse an area rarely visited by locals or tourists. You could walk every trail here and still spend not much more than three hours.

Antigua

7. The Shirley Heights Lookout Trail

Walking time: 15 minutes, one way, if walked in the direction described; 30 minutes, one way, if done in the opposite direction.

An outing along the 0.5-mile Shirley Heights Trail is not only a scenic walk, but it also provides a chance to study and identify wild xerophytic plants in the largest remaining tract of native dry forest on Anti-

gua. The trail may be reached by driving to English
Harbour and, at the crossroads in town, bearing
onto the road marked for Shirley Heights (a turn in
the opposite direction would lead to Nelson's Dockyard – see Walk #6).

*Shirley Heights offers great views of English
and Falmouth Harbours.*

Climbing toward the summit, you'll pass the remains of barracks, powder magazines, and defensive fortifications. Also on the way is the
commercially-run Interpretation Centre at Dow's
Hill, worth a visit (and the small admission fee) to
view its multimedia presentation about Antigua's
history.

Once on the summit of Shirley Heights, named for
Sir Thomas Shirley who was instrumental in the
fortification of English Harbour, enjoy the view onto
the dockyard for a few moments before walking behind the old kitchen to start your walk. The trail descends at a gradual pace, passing by cinnamon,
jumbie beads, frangipani and Turk's cap cactus.
Follow the slight ups and downs of a ridgeline. Be
on the lookout for a mongoose or two while the pathway winds among turpentine and willow trees, bromeliads, and a variety of orchids. Just before its
final (and somewhat steep) descent, you should be
able to find the remains of several small cottages

dating back to the homesteading days of the mid-18th century. The Shirley Heights Trail comes to an end on a paved road about one-tenth of a mile above the Galleon Beach Club.

8. The Blockhouse to Indian Creek Hike

Walking time: 50 minutes, round trip

From the Blockhouse above Shirley Heights (see Walk #7) you may descend steeply through open scrub brush countryside to the crashing waves of Indian Creek, a meeting place of the Atlantic Ocean and the Caribbean Sea and part of the National Parks Authority land holdings. Archaeological research has shown that the area was the site of an important Arawak Indian village for more than 1,000 years. Today, it is inhabited by goats and an occasional pelican looking for a meal amid the mangrove trees along the shore.

Do not underestimate the steep incline you'll have to hike back up to your car.

Looking out over Indian Creek.

Antigua

9. The Pillars of Hercules Walk

Walking time: less than 40 minutes, round trip

On the road that climbs to Shirley Heights (see Walk #7), a descending road to the right will bring you to the office of the Galleon Beach Club. Ask permission to leave your car, then walk along the beach. At the end of the sand is a path that ascends for a short distance and then drops down to another beach and a rocky coastline which you'll follow around the point. The Pillars of Hercules are such fantastic and noteworthy rock formations towering above the sea that ships' navigators use them to help mark the entrance to English Harbour.

Check sea conditions before beginning this excursion – the cliffs come down to the sea's edge and, if the ocean swells are running high, there would be no place to escape the waves.

10. The Monk's Hill Hike

Walking time: 1 hour, 15 minutes, round trip

To reach this strenuous but rewarding hike, drive from St. John's to the village of Liberta. With the Liberta Pharmacy on your right, make a left onto Ernest Williams Road. At the "T" intersection in 0.2 mile, make a left and follow that road to the small Table Hill Gordon settlement. The road will make a 90° bend, but you'll continue straight to a second 90° turn. Park off the pavement here and begin hiking along a dirt road.

As you rise above open meadows in 10 minutes, the route passes by the ruins of a sugar mill. Just beyond, the beauty of water hyacinths growing in a pond and the shade provided by a few small trees just might tempt you to take a short break before continuing onward and upward (avoiding two roads which come in from the left).

After 1.3 miles you'll arrive on the summit of Monk's Hill, which is crowned by the ruins of Fort George. Completed around 1705, it was to be used as a refuge for women and children in case of an attack. But Great Fort George never once fired its guns and fell into disrepair at the end of the Napoleonic wars. Now, about the only thing standing are the fort's greenstone walls encircling seven acres of acacia bushes, century plants, and cacti growing where mess halls, ammunition magazines, and officers' quarters once stood.

An old entrance gate at Fort George on Monk's Hill.

Head to the far side of the fort for an Olympian 360° vista. To the south are Falmouth and English harbours, Nelson's Dockyard, and Shirley Heights. Turn your gaze eastward to look upon Willoughby Bay and the glistening sea. To the west is Antigua's highest mountain, Boggy Peak, and its numerous connecting ridgelines. Far to the north, across an expanse of green rolling fields, you'll be able to make out Parham Bay, V. C. Bird International Airport, and even the clustered buildings of St. John's.

> ⮞ As an alternative to a round-trip hike, you could take the first road to the right as you descend back toward Table Hill

Antigua

Gordon. This would drop you into the village of Cobbs Cross and arranging a pick-up here would save retracing steps. The length of time for this alternative would be about the same as if you did the round-trip hike.

11. The Rendezvous Bay Walk

Walking time: 50 minutes, round trip

The shortest route to Rendezvous Bay, acknowledged as one of the most beautiful beaches on Antigua, is via a dirt road that is usually too rough for anything but the most sturdy of four-wheel-drive vehicles. This inaccessibility pretty much insures that the beach will never become overrun with hordes of suntan lotion-lathered bodies.

In Falmouth, turn onto Farrel Road (or Avenue – depending on which of the two signs is still standing when you arrive) and follow it as it swings right around Rainbow School and comes onto a dirt road. Make a right at the first intersection, going past a horse riding corral. When the route becomes too rough, park your car well off the road and begin walking uphill to the gap between Sugar Loaf and

Rendezvous Bay.

Cherry Hill. The plant life on the descent to the bay is lush, with bromeliads clinging to many of the trees.

The first portion of the beach you'll come to is composed of coral and shell rubble. Continue along the road (or the shoreline) and you will soon arrive at a beach you've only seen in your dreams – palm trees swaying to the gentle urgings of balmy tropical breezes, soft golden sand arching toward a distant horizon, and turquoise-blue water rolling in on a white-capped surf. Best of all, there are no restaurants, bars, hotels, or development of any kind to disturb the setting.

You should consider making this an all-day outing, including hiking, swimming, picnicking, snorkeling, and sunbathing. Beware of the manchineel trees.

12. The Wallings Walking Trail

Walking time: 4 hours, round trip

Motoring through the "rain forest" along Fig Tree Drive between the settlements of Swetes and Old Road, you'll come across a small roadside stand identified as the "Antigua Cultural Center." Park here and, while enjoying a cold drink at the small bar, ask for directions to the Rendezvous Bay trail.

Traversing the lush green Wallings Woodlands – which has been protected since the early 20th century – the trail winds under large mahogany trees populated by woodpeckers, tremblers, and warblers. Two hours on this route will bring you to the beach on the western end of Rendezvous Bay.

Antigua

➤ An alternative to the round-trip hike once you reach the beach is to follow the sands eastward and use the route of the Rendezvous Bay Walk (see Walk #11). Arrange beforehand to be met in the village of Falmouth, where you'll emerge back into civilization.

> ⚡ **Note:** *Be forewarned that the Wallings Walking Trail is not always well defined, especially when it merges with other pathways. If you are not comfortable with being on such trails, it may be best to forgo this excursion. The Ministry of Agriculture/Forestry Unit does have plans to develop a network of well-defined pathways throughout the hundreds of acres in the Wallings Woodlands area. Contact the Ministry in St. John's for the most up-to-date and complete information.*

13. Boggy Peak

Walking time: 1 hour, round trip

At 1,319 feet above sea level, Boggy Peak is the highest point on Antigua. Although you can drive almost all of the way to its summit, the luxuriant tropical growth and panoramic vistas make it worthwhile to spend some time on the mountain. About half-way between Urlings and Old Road on the island's southern coastline, a dirt road turns inland toward the peak. It is unmarked, so you may have to inquire locally as to which road it is. The route eventually becomes paved. As the vegetation starts to grow very lush, you'll notice a parking area on the right, next to several large buttressed trees. Leave your car here (the general public is prohibited from driving any further) and walk the road for less than a mile to the summit.

Once on top, walk around the perimeter fence enclosing the communications facility to enjoy every perspective. Eastward are the green, undulating ridgelines of Sage, Signal, and Sugar Loaf hills, while beyond are dozens of sailing ships anchored in Falmouth and English harbours. To the south is an interesting phenomenon – the contrasting water colors where the Atlantic Ocean meets the Caribbean Sea near Goat Head and Curtain Bluff. Gazing northward, you'll see many small bays and inlets on Antigua's western coast as your eyes are drawn toward the crowded mass of buildings in St. John's. A moderate hike.

14. The Green Castle Hill Hike

Walking time: less than 2 hours, round trip

Drive the main highway south from St. John's and make a left turn toward Emmanuel. About one mile after the turn, you'll come to the entrance of a brick factory. The hike to summit of Green Castle Hill begins on a dirt road nearby.

This old volcano is the site of the Megaliths of Green Castle Hill, whose origins are subject to debate. Some folks maintain the rock formations are nothing more than a geological happenstance; others claim that the configuration of the megaliths show they were used for worship or study of the heavens by ancient peoples.

Continuing to ponder upon this mystery, you might also have a hard time deciding which direction to gaze from the nearly 600-foot summit. To the north is St. John's and V. C. Bird International Airport. Eastward are long, rolling grasslands, southward are the highest peaks of Antigua, and to the west are the long curving sands of Jolly Harbour and Lignum Vitae Bay.

Antigua

15. Walks on Hotel and Resort Grounds

Grand resorts with extensive grounds and gardens appear to be the rule, rather than the exception, on Antigua. It seems that almost every bay and cove has a resort of some kind and that each is trying to outdo the other in terms of outdoor activities and landscaped surroundings. As each one of these properties leads to a white sand beach, they offer opportunities for easy, relaxing strolls.

> ➤ Remember, if not a registered guest, it is a courtesy to ask permission before walking.

One of the grandest resorts, the **St. James Club**, is situated on 100 acres overlooking Mamora Bay. Blooms of tropical flowers line woodland trails on the hillside, and the land slopes down to, not one, but two beaches.

North of St. John's, in beautiful Dickinson Bay, is the **Halcyon Cove Beach Resort**, with nicely landscaped terraces overlooking the sea. Around the northern coast, in Soldiers Bay, the **Blue Waters** is surrounded by coconut palms and blooming flowers and shrubs. The Mediterranean-style accommodations of the **Hodges Bay Club** are set between tropical gardens and a curving beach overlooking the Atlantic.

The 37 acres of **Hawksbill Beach Resort** include four light chestnut-colored sand beaches, one of which permits sunbathing *au naturel*.

The **Long Bay Hotel** is smaller than any of the above properties and, because of that, it retains the charm of a family-run Caribbean inn. The 20 balconied rooms and six cottages of the hotel are nestled among tended tropical foliage and sandwiched between a reef-protected beach and a quiet lagoon.

Guadeloupe

The Carib Indians called their island Karukéra –
Isle of Beautiful Waters. The title is just as true
today as it was then. The two butterfly-wing islands
that make up Guadeloupe, Grande-Terre and
Basse-Terre, are surrounded by the clear azure
waters of the Caribbean Sea and the Atlantic Ocean.
Jacques Cousteau traveled here on some of his most
rewarding explorations.

Basse-Terre, the western island, is truly the isle of
beautiful waters. The rugged volcanic mountains
thrust their heads 4,000 feet into the sky, drawing
the moisture of the tradewinds to them. There is no
water shortage here; the rains come crashing down
the mountains creating high and mighty waterfalls
and cascades. The three falls of the Carbet River cre-
ate such a white water spectacle that Columbus and
his crew imagined the hillsides to be covered by
snow.

With this abundant rainfall, of course, come the lush
and vibrant colors of tropical foliage. The slopes of
the mountains are covered with thick forests of bamboo, chestnut, mahogany, palm, and gum trees.
These forests produce a cornucopia of flowers, ferns,
and vines. Throughout Basse-Terre you will discover
a new flower around every bend, be it heliconia, orchid, or hibiscus.

Guadeloupe owes its existence to volcanic activity,
as do most islands in the Caribbean. The island is
crowned by volcanoes, with Soufrière, the highest
point on Basse-Terre, the most significant. This
mighty volcano is now dormant, but just barely so.
As recently as 1977, Soufrière spewed volcanic ash
and debris and, to this day, steaming fumaroles and
boiling sulphur pots attest to the mountain's tem-
peramental nature.

From its southern point to its northern tip, Basse-
Terre is dominated by a series of massive mountain

ranges that, for the most part, lie within the National Park. The Park Service and the Mountaineers Club have done an excellent job of making this imposing natural wilderness area accessible to the general public. Nearly 200 miles of well-built and maintained trails penetrate these highlands. Some lead to crashing waterfalls, others cross the open, windswept ridgelines, and still more skirt the edges of hidden ponds and swamps. It is even possible to ascend to the summit of Soufrière and see its volcanic nature first hand.

Cutting across the central mountain range, the Route de la Traversée allows access by car to those who do not have the time or inclination to explore on foot. Even here, however, footpaths lead into the deep, dark rain forest.

In contrast to Basse-Terre, Grande-Terre, the eastern island of Guadeloupe, is low lying, drier, and composed mostly of limestone. While Basse-Terre produces a great variety of agricultural products (bananas, coffee, and vegetables), the rolling plains of Grande-Terre are dominated by fields of sugarcane. Although it may lack the scenic forested slopes of Basse-Terre, it does have miles of white sand beaches that stretch to the horizon.

The city of Basse-Terre is the administrative capital of Guadeloupe, but is smaller and less cosmopolitan than Pointe-à-Pitre, the commercial center of the two islands. Even Pointe-à-Pitre does not present the air of sophistication of Fort-de-France in Martinique. This is the charm of Guadeloupe. It offers all that Martinique does – French fashions, hotels, chic boutiques, delicious foods, modern highways, superb beaches, national park lands and nature reserves – but it does so in a more rural, less harried atmosphere.

History

The Arawak Indians are believed to have been the first inhabitants of Guadeloupe. They were driven off by the cannibalistic Caribs sometime before Columbus arrived in 1493. The Caribs remained the sole inhabitants for another century and a half, fighting off an occasional Spanish attempt at colonization.

Arriving from Martinique, the French established settlements on Guadeloupe in 1635. This set in motion many of the same events that occurred on other Caribbean islands. The French and the English battled for domination over nearly two centuries, with France controlling most of the time. Settlers became dependent on slave labor in their sugar plantations. Infuriated by the Rights of Man Declaration, which abolished slavery, the island declared itself independent of France and soon came under British rule in 1794. The Treaty of Paris (1814) returned Guadeloupe to the French and, except for a short period of British domination in 1815-1816, it has remained there ever since.

In 1946, Guadeloupe (including St. Martin and St. Barth) became a department of France, conferring on the inhabitants all of the rights, privileges, and responsibilities of full French citizenship. In 1974, the islands were made a region of France, administered by a prefect and two sub-prefects appointed by the government in Paris. While this status is agreeable to most, Guadeloupe has experienced small amounts of social unrest in past years, but these outbreaks, which last for only a day or two, have become extremely rare in the last couple of decades.

Sugar and bananas are the chief agricultural products, but fishing also plays a role in the economy. Tourists are discovering this French-Creole island in ever-expanding numbers.

Guadeloupe

Special notes about walking on Guadeloupe

◆ The highlands of Guadeloupe receive far more rainfall and less sunshine than the rest of the island. Be prepared for lower temperatures, more rain, and stronger winds in the higher elevations.

◆ Many of the walks listed in this guide cross crystal clear rivers and streams that may look more than clean enough to drink. These waters, however, have been known to harbor bilharziasis, a snail-borne parasite that may cause damage to the human liver. Be sure to carry enough bottled water (or water obtained from a purified source).

◆ In addition to the walks described below, the outlying islands of La Désirade and Marie-Galante also have trails that should not be overlooked. Also, be sure to contact the National Park Office for the latest hiking information. More and more trails, such as the boardwalk across the marshes of the Grand Cul-de-Sac Marin Nature Reserve, are being built as hiking and ecotourism become increasingly popular.

Exciting News!

For those who truly love walking and hiking, one of the most exciting trail projects ever to be undertaken in the Caribbean was opened to the public in 1994. Patterned after its long-distance counterparts in Europe, the Grande Randonnée G.1 is a marked and continuous hiking route from Vieux-Fort on the southern coast of Basse-Terre to the island's northern tip at Pointe Allègre near Ste.-Rose. In cooperation with the National Park Office, the trail was conceived, built, and is maintained by volunteer members of the Mountaineer's Club, Friends of the National Park, and others who are willing to give their time and labor.

Making use of pre-existing trails connected by newly constructed pathways, the Grande Randonnée (which translates as Great Walk) stays as close as possible to the main crest of several mountain ranges. Yet, it also skirts swamps and ponds, passes next to numerous impressive waterfalls, traverses the flanks of Soufrière, follows above-tree-line ridges with outstanding views, and snakes through some of the lushest tropical rain forest in the Caribbean.

Various bisecting roads make it possible to day hike the trail section by section. However, if you have the time and stamina, it would certainly be more exciting to make use of the six hiker shelters (or refuges as they are known on Guadeloupe) to complete the entire trail. The whole trip is about a week's worth of leisurely hiking, backpacking, and camping. In addition to the refuges, you may camp anywhere along the route as long as you sleep in a hammock and don't build any fires.

Guadeloupe

Contact the National Park Office for further detailed information and to obtain a to-poguide to the entire route. By any means possible, coerce your boss into granting you more vacation time! This is an excursion that, by itself, is more than enough reason to extend your stay in Guadeloupe.

Data

Transportation to Guadeloupe: Flights from the U.S. bring you to hub airports in either Puerto Rico or Antigua, where nonstop connections are made to Guadeloupe. Canadians may fly directly here from Montreal. For European travelers there are, of course, daily direct flights from Paris and other French cities. In addition, Guadeloupe may be reached by air from many of the surrounding islands, such as St. Martin, St. Barth, Martinique, Dominica, and St. Croix.

All of the populated outlying islands – La Désirade, Marie-Galante, and Iles des Saintes – can be reached by daily ferry service from Guadeloupe. Ferry service is also available between Guadeloupe, Dominica, and Martinique. For a number of decades now, Guadeloupe has been a popular cruise ship stop.

Entry: A valid passport is required of American and Canadian citizens for visits of 90 days or more. For a stay of less than three months, a birth certificate or voter's registration card will fulfill the entry requirements. Citizens of the European Economic Community need either a valid passport or an official identity card.

Currency: The national currency is the French franc. American dollars are widely accepted; you will probably receive change in francs. Usually, your money will go farther if it is exchanged at a bank or foreign currency exchange center. A curious exception to this rule is that a few establishments will grant up to a 20% discount when payment is made by traveler's checks or credit card. Yet, other establishments will refuse even to accept foreign traveler's checks.

Tourist Information:

✍ **In the United States**
French West Indies Tourist Board
610 5th Ave., New York, NY 10020
☎ 212-757-1125

✍ **In Canada**
French Government Tourist Office
1981 McGill College Ave.
Montreal, Quebec H3A 2W9
☎ 514-288-4264

✍ **Europe**
French Government Tourist Office
178 Picadilly, London W1V OAL
England, ☎ 0171-493-9232

On the island, the tourist office is in Pointe-à-Pitre in a large white colonial building on the waterfront (next to the place de la Victoire). An English-speaking hostess is usually available.

✍ Office de Tourisme de Guadeloupe
5, Square le Banque
97110 Pointe-à-Pitre, Guadeloupe
French West Indies
☎ 590-82-09-30

Driving: Cars and mopeds are available in Pointe-à-Pitre, at the airport, in the city of Basse-Terre, and through many of the larger hotels.

Guadeloupe is second to none in the quality of its well-built and maintained road system. Most roads, except for those climbing into the mountains, easily measure up to North American standards.

An excellent public transportation system allows you to reach almost any part of Guadeloupe by bus.

Guadeloupe

The tourist office is the place to obtain schedule and fare information.

Language: This is a French island; hotels may have English-speaking employees, but you will be unable to communicate with most of the inhabitants unless you brush up on your French. A small pocket phrase book is a wise idea.

Walking and Hiking Guide Companies: A superb guide service, the Bureau des Guides de Moyenne Montagne, operates within the guidelines of the National Park. This knowledgeable group is able to arrange trips of varying lengths and difficulties to meet your needs. It is usually able to supply an English-speaking guide and is an excellent source of information concerning the geography, geology, flora, fauna, and walks and hikes of Guadeloupe. You may reach them by contacting the tourist office in Pointe-à-Pitre or by writing the National Park.

> ✍ Parc National de la Guadeloupe
> Habitation Beausoleil, Montéran
> 97120 St.-Claude, Guadeloupe
> French West Indies
> ☎ 590-80-24-25

Two local hiking clubs sponsor informal excursions on a regular basis and welcome visitors to join them. Both the Club du Montagne (the catalyst for the development of the Grande Randonnée G.1) and the Association of the Friends of the National Park (whose members are mostly retired senior citizens) may be contacted through the tourist office or National Park. A list of commercial guide companies may also be obtained from the tourist office.

Camping Areas: In a somewhat unusual twist, camping is permitted within the confines of the National Park, but you must use a hammock and cook on a portable backpacking stove; no fires are allowed. You may also stay overnight inside the refuges along the Grande Randonnée G.1. As regulations can change, it would be wise to contact the National Park for current information.

There are three small commercial campgrounds on Guadeloupe, but do not expect typical American standards with designated sites and a few feet of space between them. Guadeloupe's facilities sit on small parcels of land close to the beaches and are almost always extremely crowded during the heavy tourist months. Crowded, in this case, means that tents often touch other tents, with scant space to walk between. However, each site does have a central comfort station area and, when you bring your own gear, provides a low-cost alternative to the hotels and guest houses. On the beach at Deshaies is:

✍ Les Sables d'Or
Plage de Grande Anse
97126 Deshaies, Guadeloupe
French West Indies
☎ 590-28-44-60

Providing low-cost bungalows and bare tent sites is:

✍ Hotel de Plein Air "La Traversée"
Anse de la Grande Plaine
97116 Pointe-Noire, Guadeloupe
French West Indies
☎ 590-98-21-23

On Grande-Terre and far removed from the hiking trails of the National Park, but providing the most pleasant tenting sites is:

✍ Camping de Voyageur
Bais Jolan
97180 Ste.-Anne, Guadeloupe
French West Indies
☎ 590-88-36-74

Recommended Readings

 The French in the West Indies by A. Roberts

 Balles d'Or by Guy Tirolien

📖 *A Woman Named Solitude* by Andre Schwarz-Bart

📖 *Les Plus Belles Balades à Guadeloupe* by Gerard Berry and Bruno Pambour. An impressive guidebook to 40 of the trails – and geography, history, geology, and flora – of Guadeloupe. Published in French. Contains so much information that it is almost worth learning the language just to be able to put the book to its fullest use. A highly recommended resource.

Walks on Basse-Terre

1. The Sofaïa-Baille Argent Trail
Walking time: 4½ hours, one way

This long trail, which wanders through the forest of the northern end of Basse-Terre, is reached by driving Route N.1 west from Pointe-à-Pitre and turning north on Route N.2 toward Lamentin. Continue on N.2 to Ste.-Rose; in the village, turn onto the road for Sofaïa (D.19) and follow it to the sulphur spring.

The trail begins to the left of a forest road. Although not as lush as the rain forest to the south, the woodlands of the north are interesting for the great variety of plantlife there. The Sofaïa-Baille Argent Trail is a relatively straightforward pathway that stays in the woods and offers an occasional view. The trail climbs a low ridge, drops down to a tributary of the Rivière Moustique and ascends again, this time to the main crest of the Barre de l'Ile mountain range. Turning south, it makes use of the Grande Randonnée G.1 (see "Exciting News!" in the chapter introduction above) for a short distance before leaving that route, continuing west, and descending along a spur ridge. Continue on the Sofaïa-Baille Argent

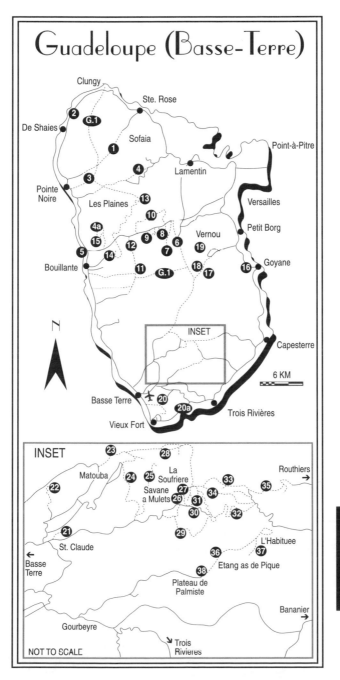

Guadeloupe (Basse-Terre)

Clungy

Ste. Rose

② **G.1**

De Shaies

Sofaia

①

④

Lamentin

Point-à-Pitre

Pointe Noire

③

Les Plaines

⑬

Versailles

4a

⑩

⑮

⑫

⑨ ⑧

⑥

Vernou

Petit Borg

⑤

⑭

⑦

⑲

⑪

G.1

⑱ ⑰

⑯

Goyane

N

INSET

Capesterre

6 KM

Basse Terre

⑳

⑳a

Trois Rivières

Vieux Fort

INSET

㉓

㉘

Routhiers

Matouba

㉔ ㉕

La Soufriere

㉝

㉟

㉒

Savane a Mulets

㉗

㉞

㉖

㉛

㉜

㉚

L'Habituee

㉑

㉙

St. Claude

㊲

←
Basse
Terre

㊱

Etang as de Pique

㊳

Plateau de
Palmiste

Bananier
→

Gourbeyre

↘ Trois
Rivières

NOT TO SCALE

Guadeloupe

Trail and arrive at the road in Beausoleil, which leads to the main highway (N.2) just north of Pointe-Noire. Due to its length, this should be considered a moderate hike.

2. The Grande-Anse Beach Walk

Generally regarded as one of the finest beaches on Basse-Terre, Grande-Anse is just north of the picturesque village of Deshaies (a charming town which deserves a few minutes of exploration). Stretching for a couple of miles, the golden sands of the crescent beach are a sharp contrast to the black sand beaches in the south. Gentle surf and abundant aquatic life are inviting to the swimmer and snorkeler, and large tropical trees bordering the beach offer welcome relief from the ever-present sunshine.

Still fairly uncrowded and undeveloped, Grande-Anse Beach has one of the few commercially-operated campgrounds on Guadeloupe. You may also be interested to know that a few miles north of Grande-Anse it is possible to do your swimming and beachcombing *sans* clothing on the Plage de Cluny.

3. The Piton de Belle Hôtesse Trail

Walking time: 2 hours, round trip to the summit of Piton de Belle Hôtesse and back

Drive Route N.2 north from the city of Basse-Terre along the coast to Pointe-Noire and, just after this village, turn right onto the road to Gommier. From here it is a 60-minute hike along a scenic track through the forest to the beautiful views on the summit of Piton de Belle Hôtesse.

➤ At the summit, it is possible to turn left for 45 minutes along the Grande Randonnée G.1 (see "Exciting News!" in the chapter introduction above) to intersect the Sofaïa-Baille Argent Trail (see Walk #1). A right turn at the top of Piton de Belle Hôtesse would take you to the Grande Randonnée G.1 to connect with the Contrebandiers Trail (see Walk #4) in approximately 90 to 100 minutes.

4. The Contrebandiers Trail

Walking time: 3½ hours, one way

From the city of Basse-Terre, drive Route N.2 north along the coast. About two miles past the intersection with the Route de la Traversée (D.23), turn right onto the road to Les Plaines (D.17). Stop by the Maison du Bois located at this intersection. The museum is an introduction to the many different kinds of woods to be found in Guadeloupe's forests. You may also obtain books and information about the National Park. Paralleling the Rivière-Petite Plaine, follow Route D.17 to its end.

The Contrebandiers Trail, once used as a route to smuggle rum across the island, begins here and climbs through beautiful woodlands. At the ridgeline, it crosses the Grande Randonnée G.1 (see "Exciting News!" in the chapter introduction above) to continue its westward journey.

>> A turn northward at the intersection would bring you to a junction with the Piton de Belle Hôtesse Trail (see Walk #3) in approximately 1½ hours; a southward turn would connect you with the Morne Lèger Trail (see Walk #13) in about two hours.

Gradually descending westward from the Grande Randonnée G.1, the Contrebandiers Trail, which may be overgrown from here on out, follows a spur ridge to emerge from the woods and end at a forest road in Duportail. The road from Duportail can be

Guadeloupe

driven to the main highway (N.2) just north of Lamentin. A moderate hike.

4a. The Saut d'Acomat Walk

Walking time: 30 minutes, round trip

With a small cascade and an inviting basin, the
easily-reached Saut d'Acomat is an ideal swimming
spot often visited by the local people. From the city
of Basse-Terre, drive Route N.2 north along the
coast. Just after crossing the Rivière Grande Plaine
(approximately 1.5 miles beyond the Route
N.2/Route de la Traversée intersection), bear right
onto Route D.16 toward Acomat. In less than two
miles from the intersection – at the second crossroads – you will see an obvious parking area for the
beginning of the walk.

A small trail gradually descends to the river which
you can follow upstream a few hundred yards to
reach the falls. After only 15 minutes of walking,
you arrive at what could not be a more alluring setting. The white water of the falls tumbles down a
narrow cleft in the hillside to form an intensely-
colored aquamarine basin. Encompassed by moss-
covered rocks and lush tropical foliage, this is the
perfect spot to enjoy a picnic, take a swim, and escape the heat of mid-afternoon. A recommended
easy walk.

5. The Littoral Malendure Trail

Walking time: 2 hours, one way

This easy hike (marked with orange and blue
blazes) goes along a portion of the hidden western
coastline of Basse-Terre. The Littoral Malendure
Trail is reached from the city of Basse-Terre by
driving Route N.2 northward. Soon after passing
through the small village of Pigeon, watch for a trail
sign on the left. You will not begin, but will end,
your hike here; make arrangements to be picked up

at this point. Continue northward on Route N.2 to the crossing of the Rivière Colas, where you'll start your walk southward.

Traversing an area that receives little rainfall, you'll be walking by organ pipe cactus and the wonderfully showy spider lily. Be careful when descending into and crossing several river gorges. This may be a dry part of the island, but the rivers have their headwaters in the mountains and can become raging streams if the highlands have had a significant amount of rain. With views of the I'let de Pigeon resting in the Caribbean Sea, the trail swings around the Pointe de Malendure and ends at Route N.2. An easy hike.

The Walks of the Route de la Traversée

Walks #6-#15 are all located along the Route de la Traversée, the scenic highway which crosses the central highlands of Basse-Terre. For 10 miles the route offers access to many of the natural wonders – waterfalls, rain forest, vividly colored flowers, and majestic views – of the 74,000-acre National Park.

The Route de la Traversée is reached by driving Route N.2 out of Pointe-à-Pitre, continuing south on N.1 at the major intersection on Basse-Terre, and then turning right onto Route D.23 at Versailles. The National Park boundary is just beyond the intersection with Route D.1. Even if you don't want to walk any of these trails, it is recommended that you drive along this scenic highway.

For convenience, Walks #6-#15 are arranged as they would be encountered when travelling west on the road.

6. The Ecrevisses Cascade Walk

Walking time: less than 30 minutes, round trip

Shortly after the intersection with Route D.1, the Route de la Traversée continues to the Corossol River Picnic Area (on the right).

To the left of the highway, a short trail parallels the Corossol River and ends at the Falls of the Ecrevisses River. An exceptionally beautiful spot in the tropical forest, this is one of the most photographed scenes on the island. The pool at the base of the falls is a popular local swimming hole. (Sadly, it has also become a place of vandalism and robbery, so guard your valuables.)

A highly recommended walk. The lush rain forest and rushing falls are a major reward for the minor effort expended to reach them.

7. The Rivière Corossol Walk

Walking time: 55 minutes, round trip

Just beyond the bridge over Rivière Corossol is a paved forest road to the left. Leave your car here and begin the walk through the woods.

In a few minutes take the road to the left, which leads to the ford of the Corossol River. Although the road continues on the opposite bank, it is suggested that the walk end here. This is a favorite local swimming and picnic spot. Unfortunately, this place too has been the scene of several recent crimes. Do not carry much money here and watch your belongings closely.

8. The Bras David Tropical Park Walks

Located on the central portion of the Route de la Traversée, Bras David is a showpiece of the National Park. The Maison de la Forêt contains a visi-

Lush vegetation along the Bras David trails.

tor's center, a small museum, and outdoor displays explaining the natural and scenic features of the area. Unfortunately, the signs and exhibits are in French. Picnic shelters are nearby. There is a group of interconnecting trails that give easy access to the luxuriant foliage of the tropical forest. Signs (in French) identify the different trees, plants, and flowers. These three trails (20-, 30-, and 60-minute easy walks) all pass by giant gommier trees, elephant ears, bromeliads, ferns, and mosses.

If you don't have the time to enjoy any other walks on Guadeloupe, be sure to stop at the Bras David Tropical Park; it is the most accessible spot to receive a quick, thorough introduction to the tropical forests of the Caribbean.

9. The Ruisseaux Circuit Trail

Walking time: 2 hours for the complete circuit

Also emanating from the Bras David Tropical Park, the Ruisseaux Circuit Trail permits a longer exploration of the rain forest than do the trails close to the Maison de la Forêt. Following the south side of the

Rivière Bras David, the trail makes for a moderately easy hike.

10. The Rivière Bras David - Rivière Quiock Hike

Walking time: about 2½ hours, one way

The hike begins across the road from the Bras David Tropical Park visitor's area. Follow the trail downstream along the Rivière Bras David for a short distance before ascending a small rise to reach the Rivière Quiock.

The pathway now changes directions and climbs the river in a westward direction. The route offers a number of small challenges since it fords the stream at least 17 times as the path meanders back and forth.

The Rivière Bras David-Rivière Quiock Trail is a lesson in the different types of vegetation growing along the river of a rain forest. The waterway creates a gap in the forest canopy, allowing more sunlight to reach the banks. The plants become fuller and healthier than their relatives deep in the forest.

The trail crosses the river one more time before emerging back onto Route de la Traversée about one mile west of the Bras David Tropical Park parking area.

11. Des Crêtes Trail

Walking time: 5 hours, one way

Offering some of the best continuous views on Guadeloupe, Des Crêtes Trail (a part of the Grande Randonnée G.1 – see see "Exciting News!" in the chapter introduction above) heads south from Route de la Traversée in the pass between the two prominent peaks of Les Mamelles.

Passing by the Mamelle de Petit-Bourg Trail (see Walk #12), the pathway makes a quick ascent to the ridgeline, which it then follows for the rest of the trek. After rising out of the rain forest, the trail follows the up and down contours of minor peaks and enters open highlands. The mountains to the east capture much of the moisture brought by the trade-winds, leaving this crestline with clear skies most of the time. Therefore, when there are rain squalls on other trails, this pathway will usually have good views. Looking to the east you'll see the heavily forested slopes of the National Park and Route de la Traversée. To the west are beaches and to the south, from certain spots along the way, it is even possible to see 4,800-foot Soufrière, its summit hidden by the ever-present cloud cover. Two side trails coming from the west intersect Des Crêtes Trail and could be used as alternatives to walking the complete route. They are not as well maintained or as frequently traveled as the main trail, but should still be easily negotiated.

From the summit of Pitons de Bouillants, the highest point of Des Crêtes Trail, the first side trail drops to the right, tracking a spur ridge to a 1,900-foot peak and making a final descent to the highway (N.2) just south of the village of Pigeon. Also from the summit, the Grande Randonnée G.1 bears left on its way southward. To stay on Des Crêtes Trail, continue straight for a little over one hour past Pitons des Bouillants. A second side trail drops quickly (and challengingly) to the west for 45 minutes and arrives at a paved road leading to the village of Bouillants in a few miles.

Soon after the second side trail, Des Crêtes Trail begins its rapid, but fairly easy descent of the ridge and ends at a paved road leading to the small settlement of Village. Coastal highway N.2 is reached shortly thereafter.

This is a strenuous hike due to its distance and the number of ups and downs that are encountered on the rugged, open ridgeline. However, it is also one of the more rewarding hikes on the island. Just be sure

Guadeloupe

to allow enough time, since the trail from Route de la Traversée to the paved road of Village is almost six miles long.

12. The Mamelle de Petit-Bourg Trail

Walking time: 1 hour, 40 minutes, round trip

The first few hundred yards of this trail run concurrent with Des Crêtes Trail (see Walk #11) before turning off to the left to make a slippery ascent to the 2,400-foot summit of Mamelle de Petit-Bourg. Views include the forested slopes of northern and central Basse-Terre and its northern coastline.

13. The Morne Lèger Trail

Walking time: 3 hours, round trip to
the summit and back

Just past Des Crêtes Trail (see Walk #11), the Morne Lèger Trail (a part of the Grande Randonnée G.1 – see "Exciting News!" in the chapter introduction above) leaves Route de la Traversée to the right. Making use of an old road along the forested ridge, the path continues with a relatively easy ascent to the summit of Morne Lèger. A little over 2,000 feet in elevation, the limited view from the top is of the windward coast of Basse-Terre, with even a hint of the skyline of Pointe-à-Pitre. (From here, the Grande Randonnée G.1 continues north for many miles to Pointe Allègre on Basse-Terre's northern coast.)

14. The Mamelle de Pigeon Trail

Walking time: 1 hour, 20 minutes, round trip

Almost directly across the road from the Morne Lèger Trail (see Walk #13) the Mamelle de Pigeon Trail begins its ascent of the mountain. The pathway winds around Mamelle de Pigeon through a forest of olive and palmetto trees. From the summit (2,526 feet), the views are of Pointe-Noire and the western coastline and, eastward, across Route de la Traversée and Basse-Terre, all the way to the other island of Guadeloupe, Grande-Terre. A moderate, but slippery hike to an excellent overlook.

15. The Morne Louis Road Hike

Walking time: 1 hour, 20 minutes, round trip

Mentioned as a hike because of the easy grade and superior views, this excursion follows a road from the highest point of Route de la Traversée, heads around the mountain and leads on to the summit of Morne Louis. At the 2,438-foot peak is a television tower and a view into the wilderness of the mountains of northern Basse-Terre, inaccessible by car. The panorama also includes the eastern half of Guadeloupe, Grande-Terre.

A relatively easy hike along a smooth road.

16. The Chutes de la Rivière Moreau Trail

Walking time: 4 hours, 15 minutes, round trip

Every bit as spectacular as the Chutes du Carbet (see Walks #33 and #35), the waterfalls on the Rivière Moreau are further away from any road, take longer to reach by foot and, therefore, are less visited. To reach the trailhead, drive Route N.2 out of Pointe-à-Pitre and head south on Route N.1 from the major intersection on Basse-Terre. Stay on N.1, passing by the Route de la Traversée and going through the town of Petit-Bourg. In less than four miles from the town, turn right onto the forestry road to Douville. (You might have to inquire locally for the location of this small road.) Driving this route for six miles will bring you to the trailhead.

In a dense tropical forest of châtagnier and gommier trees, which attain heights of more than 100 feet, the trail crosses a low ridge and ascends along the Rivière Moreau. Be careful when crossing the river, which you will do not once, not twice, but eight times during your progression up the Ravine Racoon. Approximately 2.5 miles of hiking will bring you to the falls where, dropping from more than 300 feet above you, the water cascades via three distinct shelves to come rumbling into the basin pool. Surrounded by the large leaves of trumpet trees, don't pass up this chance for an energizing swim before heading back.

An easy hike, but beware of the stream crossings if it has been raining heavily.

17. The Victor Hugues Trail

Walking time: 8 hours, one way

This is one of the longest and most isolated hikes that can be undertaken on Guadeloupe and possibly in all of the Leeward Islands. The trail attains the heights of the central mountain range and passes by peaks and valleys that are still, to some degree, unexplored and impenetrable.

To reach the beginning of this ambitious excursion, drive through Versailles on Route N.1. (See the second paragraph of the "Trails of the Route de la Traversée" for directions to this point.) Beyond the village of Petit Bourg, turn right on the road to Carrère and Montebello. When the road forks, bear left and follow this to the banana plantation. A short path (which is unmarked, so you'll probably have to inquire locally to find it) leads through the banana trees to the beginning of the hike.

Cross the Palmiste River and begin the long, steady climb. Working its way through the forest between two ridgelines, the trail reaches the open crests of 3,000 feet. The Merwart Trail comes in from the right after about four hours (see Walk #18).

Continue to the left on the Victor Hugues Trail (which is now part of the Grande Randonnée G.1 –

see "Exciting News!" in the chapter introduction above) and arrive at the hiker's shelter near the peak of Matéliane. For the next three hours the pathway meanders along the highest walkable ridgeline on Guadeloupe and the views are magnificent. To the west are the bright green, wooded slopes that descend to the western coast of Basse-Terre and to the east are the waves of the Caribbean Sea lapping at the beaches of Goyave and Ste.-Marie. To the south, usually in the clouds, is Soufrière and the rugged Mts. Caraïbes on the southern tip of Guadeloupe.

Remain on the ridgeline through the Savane de l'Herminier and skirt the slopes of Grand Sans Toucher. With Soufrière growing ever larger, it is now possible to look across the steep gorge of the Class River. Just beyond these cliffs is the rolling mountain plain of the Savane aux Ananas (Pineapple Mountain).

Continue to the intersection with the Carmichael Trail (see Walk #28), which comes in from the left. This pathway, also part of the Grande Randonnée G.1, leads to Soufrière (see Walk #27). Keep to the right, leaving the white and red blazes of the Grande Randonnée G.1, and begin the descent of the Victor Hugues Trail along the Rouge River. In one hour from this intersection, you'll reach the end of the expedition at the Maison Forestière near Matouba.

> *Note: Although this hike does not require mountaineering skills (such as on some of the narrow ridges and dangerous trips that can be taken on Guadeloupe's sister island, Martinique), its length and difficulty should not be underestimated. The trail has a number of ups and downs and the pathway can become faint and indistinct due to the quickly growing vegetation. Mountain mangle covers much of this ridgeline and picking your way through it may slow your progress. It is recommended that you*

> *check with the National Park Office for*
> *current trail conditions. If you are un-*
> *sure of yourself on long hikes in ex-*
> *tremely isolated places, it would be wise*
> *to hire a guide.*

Remember to bring plenty of water as there is none available along the route. Be prepared for long periods of hot sunshine and/or cold, misty weather.

> ⚡ ***One further warning:*** *Since the route*
> *remains above the trees on open, ex-*
> *posed ridges for much of the time, do*
> *not attempt this hike if the weather is*
> *threatening to take a turn for the worse.*
> *Should a storm occur, you would be to-*
> *tally exposed with virtually nowhere to*
> *turn.*

Do not let these warnings deter you. This is one of the best hikes in the Caribbean, and the views, isolation, and duration of the hike make all of the efforts worthwhile. Highly recommended.

18. The Merwart Trail

Walking time: 4 hours, one way, to the intersection
with the Victor Hugues Trail

The Merwart Trail is an alternative route to reach the high crestline of the Grande Randonnée G.1 Trail (see "Exciting News!" in the chapter introduction above). Drive Route N.1 through Versailles (see the second paragraph of the "Walks of the Route de la Traversée" for directions to this point). Just beyond the small village, turn right onto Route D.1 and proceed to Vernou. Beyond Vernou, follow the road marked for La Glacière to its end.

Following a route somewhat similar to the beginning of the Victor Hugues Trail (see Walk #17), the Merwart Trail gradually makes its way through the forest, rising steadily between the ridges, and arrives at the Grande Randonnée G.1 in about three hours. To the left, that route leads to the summit of Morne Merwart in 30 minutes. Bear right along the crestline and, in another hour, just before the hiker's shelter at Matéliane, the Merwart Trail comes to an end as it meets up with the Victor Hugues Trail.

Due to its length and almost continual climb, this should be considered a moderately strenuous hike.

19. The Saut de la Lézarde Trail
Walking time: less than 1 hour, round trip

Drive Route N.1 through Versailles (see the second paragraph of the "Walks of the Route de la Traversée" for directions to this point). Just beyond the small village, turn right onto Route D.1 and proceed to Vernou. A short distance beyond Vernou, stay on D.1 as it makes a left turn where the road to Glacière bears right. In less than 0.1 mile, you will come to the parking area for the Saut de la Lézarde Trail.

Making a slippery descent into planted fields of breadfruit, bananas, and other tropical fruit, the trail switchbacks for 20 minutes to arrive at the 40-foot waterfall and its basin pool. Do not be tempted to take a swim, as the current is swift and people have been injured here.

A recommended hike because of the ease of reaching such a beautiful setting.

The Mt. Caraïbes Hikes

20. The Champ Fleury to Marina de Rivière Sens Trail
Walking time: 4 hours, one way

An ambitious excursion along the ridgelines of the rugged southern mountains of Basse-Terre, this

Guadeloupe

hike is reached by driving Route N.1 eastward from the city of Basse-Terre through Gourbeyre. Turn onto the road for Champ Fleury and continue to its end.

Now a part of the Grande Randonnée G.1 (see "Exciting News!" in the chapter introduction above), the route begins as a wide graveled, and sometimes paved, track as it ascends through open countryside with views of the southeastern coast. In a little over a mile, the trail becomes narrower and steeper and enters the hardwood and bamboo forest. It reaches a trail junction one mile later. To the left is the Mt. Caraïbes Trail (see Walk #20a) and the continuation of the Grande Randonnée G.1.

Bear right, ascending along the crestline to another junction. The right fork leads to the summit of Morne Cadet (2,200 feet), one-third of a mile away. Continue to the left and reach the summit of Vent Souffle. The highest point (2,253 feet) of the Mts. Caraïbes, this summit is the payoff for your efforts. The open peak has a grandstand view in all directions. To the south are the green, rugged mountaintops of Bout Morne and La Voute, with the Iles des Saintes shimmering on the horizon across the Caribbean Sea. The city of Basse-Terre is to the west, and Trois-Rivières and the island of Marie-Galante are to the east. Towering above everything to the north is cloud-capped Soufrière.

From the summit, continue south and then west along a series of ridges to pass by a number of lesser peaks. These add quite a number of ups and downs, so expect your forward progress to slow in this area. Eventually, the trail begins a long, steady, and, at times, steep drop from the heights. Recent work at a rock quarry near the end of this hike has obliterated the actual route of the trail, but it is obvious as you descend which route will lead you to a secondary road. Follow this secondary road to the coastal highway (D.6) and the Marina de Rivière Sens.

Do not underestimate the number of ascents and descents that must be negotiated on this hike.

20a. The Mt. Caraïbes Trail

Walking time: 2 hours, to the intersection with the Champ Fleury to Marina de Rivière Sens Trail

Another trail that follows the ridgelines of the southern mountains and is a part of the Grande Randonnée G.1, the Mt. Caraïbes Trail starts in a cultivated field just north of the village of Vieux-Fort. The National Park Office suggests that you inquire locally to find the trailhead, which starts by ascending along planted fields and soon enters the forest. Continue the ascents, steep in places, cross a number of ridgelines, pass by two unmaintained trails and, in one hour, you'll be at the head of a major river valley – Ravine Grand-Fond. The steep ravine has a heavy concentration of royal palms and is a prime run-off area for the frequent rain squalls.

Climb slightly to where the trail splits for a few hundred feet. The right fork passes by an old hut that could be used as an emergency shelter before returning to the main route. Continue beyond another deep ravine to a steep, rough, rocky, and somewhat dangerous ascent to a viewpoint of the southern coast and Iles des Saintes. Fifteen more minutes of walking among the bamboo and heliconia will lead to the intersection with Walk #20. To the right it is one hour to Champ Fleury; to the left, two hours, 50 minutes to Marina de Rivière Sens.

Highly recommended, but only if you are in good shape.

Trails of the Soufrière Area

Walks #21-#34 are all accessible by driving Route N.3 out of Basse-Terre toward St.-Claude and then taking Route D.11 on the quickly rising flanks of Soufrière. Individual directions are given for Walks #35-#38.

21. The Cascade Vauchelet Trail

Walking time: less than 1 hour, round trip

Look for the prefect's residence in the village of St.-Claude and turn left on the road directly across Route N.3. Follow this to the police station and begin the walk here. (Even with these directions you will probably have to ask locally for the location of the trail as it is rarely used and is not marked.)

This easy walk follows along the top of a deep, narrow gorge of the Noire River. The pathway is through a rich hardwood forest thick with ferns. In 20 minutes, near the meeting of the Noire and Roche rivers, it drops down to cross the river on a bridge and arrives at the magnificent Cascade Vauchelet. The water comes crashing down for 100 vertical feet in this narrow gorge. This beautiful place makes an ideal swimming spot.

A highly recommended walk; this is the most easily accessible large waterfall on the island.

22. The Saut d'Eau du Matouba Hike

Walking time: less than 1 hour, round trip

Another easy, short trail to a waterfall, the Saut d'Eau du Matouba Trail is reached by driving Route N.3 from St.-Claude toward Matouba. Bear right at the Louis Delgres Monument, staying on N.3. The road will soon bend left and then make an almost immediate right. Here, you need to turn left onto a minor road which you'll follow for just a short distance. Like the Cascade Vauchelet Trail, the path to the Saut d'Eau du Matouba is unmarked, so you'll have to inquire locally as to where it leaves the road.

After a good view across the high mountain fields, the trail enters woods and, in a few minutes, drops to the banks of the Saint Louis River, where you'll soon come to the Saut d'Eau du Matouba. Although the falls are only 30 feet high, they flow between volcanic rock walls and can be very impressive. An easy hike.

> ⚡ **Special Note:** *The pool at the base of the falls may look inviting, but resist the urge to go swimming. A whirlpool is created by the falls and a number of accidents have occurred here.*

23. The Hauteurs de Papaye Trail

Walking time: 3 hours, one way
(this includes the side trip to the Hot Springs)

This is an easy hike through forest and open meadows on the western side of Soufrière. It may be reached by driving Route N.3 through St.-Claude to Matouba. Proceed through Matouba toward Fond Bonard and park at the Maison Forestière.

The Hauteurs de Papaye Trail begins by making use of the Victor Hugues Trail (see Walk #17) as it leaves the Maison Forestière. In a very short time the pathway leaves open fields and enters forest. The Victor Hugues Trail continues left, while the Hauteurs de Papaye Trail turns to the right (this is about 30 minutes from Maison Forestière) and descends to the Rouge River. Cross the river, ascend, and 0.3 mile later you will arrive at a side trail to the Hot Springs of Matouba.

Take this trail to the left. As you gain elevation the vegetation diminishes to gnarled branches of mountain mangle. In less than 30 more minutes, you'll arrive at the Hot Springs, whose 104° waters are used for therapeutic treatments at the Clinique des Faux-Vives near Matouba. Return to the main Hauteurs de Papaye Trail and turn left. In an additional mile the path descends to cross the Chaude River

Guadeloupe

and passes through the forest, emerging onto the bucolic open meadows of the Papaye Plateau. This is a major livestock and agricultural producing area of Guadeloupe. The trail ends at the parking area for the Clinique des Faux-Vives.

A recommended hike due to its ease and variety of forest, fields, and streams.

24. The Delgres Trail

Walking time: 1½ hours, one way

A worthwhile hike through rain forest, the Delgres Trail is reached by driving on Route D.11 through St.-Claude toward Savane-à-Mulets and Soufrière. Park at the Beausoleil Picnic Area. The trail leaves the picnic pavilions and, in a few hundred yards, comes to the intersection with the Nez Cassé Trail (see Walk #25). Turn left on the Delgres Trail, following the Rivière Noire through heavy rain forest. This pathway is an excellent introduction to the forests of the central heights of Guadeloupe. Philodendron and anthurium grow well among the giant trees and are supported by their large root systems. Thick vines wind their way up from the ground, attached to the trees higher branches. Cross a number of small streams and in 30 minutes, ford the Noire River and ascend steeply for 15 more minutes. Continue through the forest, again crossing a number of smaller streams, and arrive at a cultivated plateau. A short walk in the cattle pasture leads to some vegetable gardens and to the hike's end on the road near Clinique des Faux-Vives.

Except for the steep climb out of the Noire River valley, this is an easy to moderate hike.

25. The Nez Cassé Trail

Walking time: 4 to 5 hours, round trip

A rugged trail to the summit of the mountain crest, the Nez Cassé Trail begins at the picnic area of Beausoleil and follows the same pathway as the Delgres Trail (see Walk #24).

Cross the stream, arrive at the intersection with the Delgres Trail, and continue on the Nez Cassé Trail by taking the right fork. The trail more or less parallels the canal of the Noire River through a rain forest of chestnut, epiphytes, and areas of bamboo. In 30 minutes, cross the river on a dam amid thick vines and heavily buttressed trees. If you are not in the best of shape, it is suggested that you end the hike here.

For the next 0.5 mile you will gain quite a bit of elevation, after which the trail becomes only slightly less steep. Eventually, it comes out into the open along a narrow ridge overlooking the Noire River Gorge and the Mts. Caraïbes to the south. Continuing the ascent through the mountain mangle, the trail reaches the knife-edge crest and summit of Nez Cassé. This is the reward for your efforts – a 360° view of Soufrière, the open heights of La Carmichael and the southern and western coasts of Basse-Terre.

> **Note:** *This is a rough hike, evidenced by the length of time required to walk just a few miles of trail. The ascent of Nez Cassé should not be underestimated. If you are intimidated by narrow ridges and precipitous heights, you should probably hire a guide.*

26. The Piton Tarade Walk

Walking time: 20 minutes, round trip

After driving Route D.11 through the forest and taking in the views as it heads up the slopes of Soufrière

Guadeloupe

to the Savane-à-Mulets parking lot, this pleasant little walk is almost an anti-climax. However, for those who don't wish to invest the time or energy needed to walk around the volcanic summit of Soufrière, the Piton Tarade Walk is an easy introduction to the geology and plant life of the area.

The trail begins at the upper end of the parking lot, winds around the small plateau, and ascends to the summit of Piton Tarade (3,931 feet). The grasses, thyme, and mountain mangle are evidence that nature is working hard to recover from the devastating effects of Soufrière's last eruption in 1977. The views from the peak are of Soufrière, L'Echelle, La Citerne, the Caraïbes Mountains, and the southern coast.

Such an easy walk as this should not be passed up.

27. The Soufrière Hike

Walking time: 3 hours for the complete circuit hike (subtract a little over an hour if not exploring the mountaintop)

Soufrière is one of the crowning glories of hiking in the Caribbean – a chance to walk about in a very-much-alive volcano. The power of that life, the destruction and devastation, are still very evident. To this day there are over 150 earth tremors registered every year around Soufrière. The fumaroles emit sulphurous hot gases, mud pots still bubble and belch, and even the ground around the base of the summit is warm to the touch.

The exploration of Soufrière begins just beyond the Savane-à-Mulets parking lot and, after a short ascent on a series of switchbacks, the trail makes a gentle climb on the contour of the land around the summit of the volcano. The path first passes by an area that was destroyed by the latest eruption and the foliage is now re-establishing itself. Crossing the cleft of l'Eboulement Faujas, the vegetation thickens as the trail proceeds into and out of the deep ravine of the Grande Faille and arrives at a side trail to the summit. Turn right and make a short, steep ascent to the eerie, fascinating world of a volcanic summit. (The climb is made easier by the use of switchbacks.) The top of Soufrière is often encased by a cloud mist which adds to the other-wordly feeling, but sometimes makes it difficult to see where the trail is going. However, the footpath is easily identified as there are markers showing the way. Just wait for the wind to part the clouds and reveal the nearest marker.

The pathway on the top of the mountain passes by peaks of volcanic rocks, giant steaming fumaroles, and craters of boiling water and mud. At the first intersection, continue to the right past the concrete hiker's shelter and ascend to the highest point of the mountain (and Guadeloupe), 4,800 feet above sea level. Beyond the summit, go by a side trail to the right, staying on the main trail to another intersection. Turn left and pass between two large steaming craters. From here, a right turn leads to a circular path around the largest steaming crater and eventually back to the main trail. Another right will take you back to the side trail, which has a series of switchbacks leading down to the trail around the base of the summit.

Once back on this trail turn right, descend a bit more and go by a side trail to the left that crosses the fields of mountain pineapple and mangle of the Grand-Savane (see Walk #28). The views of the highlands to the north are spectacular here. Continue on the path to the right and you'll soon enter the moonscape of the Pass of l'Echelle. This was the site of major eruptions in 1976-77, and the ground is peppered with rocks and boulders literally hurled from the depths of the earth.

Circle below the summit of Soufrière, passing side trails to the Carbet Falls (see Walk #33) and L'Echelle (see Walk #31). The trail makes a rather steep descent to the road; a right turn will return you to the parking lot of Savane-à-Mulets.

Guadeloupe

> ⚡⟩ **Please take note** that this is *the* most
> highly recommended excursion of this
> entire guidebook. As stated before, it is
> one of the crowning glories of hiking in
> the Caribbean and you should not pass
> up the opportunity to explore a moun-
> tain such as Soufrière. Except for the
> few short ascents and rocky and slip-
> pery footing, the Soufrière Hike is sur-
> prisingly easy.

28. The Carmichael Trail

Walking time: 1 hour, 15 minutes, one way, to the
second Victor Hugues Trail intersection (add about 30
minutes to reach the trail via the Soufrière Hike and
the time needed either to retrace your steps or
continue along the Victor Hugues Trail to Matouba)

This spectacular hike (which is a portion of the
Grande Randonnée G.1 – see "Exciting News!" in
the chapter introduction above) begins on the north
slope of Soufrière, about a half an hour's walk from
the Savane-à-Mulets parking lot. See Walk #27 to
arrive at this point. The trail leads north in the
high, open country amid tangled branches of mountain mangle. Last century this gentle, rolling plateau was a mountain lake and the ground remains
moist and slippery.

The vistas are continuous along this route, with
grand views of Soufrière, Nez Cassé, the high,
twisting ridgelines to the north, and even the coast
of Grande-Terre. In 40 minutes from the beginning
of the Carmichael Trail, ascend to the summit of
Carmichael (4,600 feet) for an even more commanding view. Descend slightly and then rise easily to
Morne du Col. (Beyond this summit is a faint path
to the left which leads to the Victor Hugues Trail –
see Walk #17.)

You will now make a quick descent into the forest,
coming to another spur trail of the Victor Hugues
Trail to the left. This is officially the end of the Car-

michael Trail, so you may either retrace your steps, continue northward along the Grande Randonnée G.1, or descend to Matouba via the Victor Hugues Trail – about one hour's worth of additional walking.

A moderate hike recommended for its continuous views.

29. The Chutes du Galion - La Citerne Hike

Walking time: 1½ hours, one way

Beginning almost directly across the road from the Savane-à-Mulets parking lot, this hike follows a path, known as the Pas du Roy, which descends through the heavy vegetation of the southern flank of Soufrière. An intersection is reached shortly – the right fork, via the Trace de l'Armistice, climbs back to the road at the Maison du Volcan. Take the left fork and descend in the mountain mangle and other low growing foliage. Views to the south and south-east begin to appear and, shortly thereafter, the trail switches back down to the Citerne River. It will take 35 minutes to reach this point.

You are now just below the Galion Falls. The base of the falls may be reached by following the river upstream. This is, however, a slippery and somewhat dangerous climb along the river bed. The best route is to cross the river and ascend steeply for 10 minutes on the wet pathway to an overlook of the 130-foot falls.

Leaving the rain forest of the river valley, the trail climbs into the low lying vegetation of the higher elevations, and the crater of La Citerne is reached in 40 minutes from the river. Follow the crater rim right, toward the television tower. This is the classic volcanic cone with a lake in the bottom of the crater. The views of Soufrière, L'Echelle, and the windward coast are especially impressive from here.

The hike ends at the road leading back to the Savane-à-Mulets (see Walk #30). A moderately difficult hike.

30. The Road Walk

Walking time: 25 minutes, one way

The road from the Savane-à-Mulets parking lot to the TV tower on La Citerne may be driven. However, for those who wish to experience the volcanic activity of the area without any strenuous hiking, it makes a pleasant and easy walk.

Along the almost-level road there are continuous views of the Caraïbes Mountains, the southwestern coast, and of Soufrière and L'Echelle looming directly above. The route passes a number of steaming fumaroles and hot springs that have discolored the landscape in varying shades of green, red, and orange. Even the ground in some spots is warm to the touch. Twenty minutes into the walk, L'Echelle Trail (see Walk #31) climbs to the left and, a few hundred yards beyond that, the Route en Lacets Hike (see Walk #32) goes down to the left. Your walk continues along the road to end at the TV tower parking lot.

A walk around the crater of La Citerne would add an additional 10 to 15 minutes and provide some grand views of Basse-Terre's eastern coastline, of Grand-Terre, and of Marie-Galante further off on the eastern horizon.

31. L'Echelle Trail

Walking time: 1 hour, 15 minutes, one way, to the Pass of l'Echelle and the intersection with the Soufrière Hike

On The Road Walk (see Walk #30), just before reaching La Citerne, take the pathway to the left, which goes uphill. The work done here is a true monument to the efforts and labors of trail builders. Even though the slope of L'Echelle is extremely steep, switchbacks make the ascent fairly gradual.

After 30 minutes of climbing among the mountain pineapple, mountain mangle, and orchids, the summit of L'Echelle is reached. Be extremely cautious here since the ridgeline is very narrow, the foliage almost non-existent, and the pathway muddy, slippery, and, at points, threatens to slide you down the nearly-vertical wall of the mountain.

Having made it past this precarious section, skirt the moss-covered Morne Mitan and drop quickly into the volcanic rock-strewn Pass of l'Echelle with its smoking fumaroles. L'Echelle Trail ends here.

To return to Savane-à-Mulets, turn left onto the Soufrière Hike (see Walk #27) and descend to the road near the parking lot – an additional walk of about 30 minutes.

> *The difficulty of the passage on the summit should not be undertaken lightly, especially by those who have a fear of open heights.*

32. Route en Lacets Hike

Walking time: 1½ hours, one way

Originally envisioned as a road connection between the Chutes du Carbet and the Savane-à-Mulets, this route makes use of the groundwork that was done before the project was abandoned. On The Road Walk (see Walk #30), turn left downhill before reaching La Citerne.

Follow the remnants of the paved tract as it makes the long descent on the side of L'Echelle, enjoying the good views of Capesterre and the eastern coastline of Basse-Terre. In 30 minutes the groundwork begins to fade as the road deteriorates into a path of switchbacks down toward the heavy growth of the rain forest.

As the foliage becomes thicker, a side trail comes in from the left. Although it is possible to continue on the Route en Lacets, it is suggested you take this trail to the left, join the Karukéra Trail, turn right and arrive at the Chutes du Carbet Picnic Area in 40

Guadeloupe

more minutes. If, however, you are adventurous, continue to the picnic area by way of the Route en Lacets. Be forewarned that the path is lined with a plant whose leaves have been likened to the sharp edges of a razor blade. They can inflict considerable damage to clothing and skin. Proceed with caution.

33. The Chutes du Carbet Trail

Walking time: 3½ hours, one way (from the intersection with Walk #27 in the Pass of l'Echelle, including the side trips to the two falls). Add 30 minutes to reach the beginning of the hike via the Soufrière Hike

The Chutes du Carbet Trail, which provides access to the most impressive falls on Guadeloupe, begins in the Pass of l'Echelle. To reach this point, leave Savane-à-Mulets and follow the road toward La Citerne. Turn left after .25 mile and proceed uphill, via the latter portion of the Soufrière Hike (see Walk #27) to the pass. Continue beyond the fumaroles and L'Echelle Trail (see Walk #31) and turn right onto the Chutes du Carbet Trail. Walking time to this point is 30 minutes. Descending from the pass, the Chutes du Carbet Trail (also a portion of the Grande Randonnée G.1 – see "Exciting News!" in the chapter introduction above) winds in between the rocks and scruffy vegetation and soon arrives at a trail junction with the Karukéra Trail (see Walk #34). Continue to the left, ford the stream, and begin a steep descent that may require you to hold onto roots and vines to keep from falling.

Thirty minutes beyond the Karukéra Trail you'll reach another junction and turn right. Follow this pathway to the first falls. In this impressive setting the water drops down a sheer rock face for over 370 feet. Return to the main trail (the side trip to the falls will take about 30 minutes) and turn right. Continue down a gentler slope through the thick and verdant foliage of a full-fledged rain forest of gum and chestnut trees. In another mile the Third Carbet Falls Trail comes in from the left (see Walk

#35). Descend on the graded trail to the right and reach another junction.

Turn right onto this side trail, which will lead to another faint junction. Follow the right fork, ford the river twice, and arrive at the second falls of the Carbet River. Not quite as high as the first, this 360-foot waterfall is more dramatic. The Carbet River is bigger and wider here, and the water comes rushing down at a feverish pace. Close to these falls is another, smaller 30-foot waterfall. Its hot pool is often used as a local swimming hole.

Return to the main trail, turn right, and cross the Carbet River on a footbridge. Pass the Karukéra Trail (see Walk #34) and the Route en Lacets (see Walk #32) and arrive at the Chutes du Carbet Picnic Area. The road from the picnic area cuts across cultivated fields to connect with the coastal highway (N.1) south of Capesterre.

This whole excursion is a moderate hike if done in the direction described – strenuous if done in the opposite direction.

34. The Karukéra Trail

Walking time: 1 hour, 20 minutes, one way, from the beginning of the trail at its intersection with the Chutes du Carbet Trail

Paralleling the Chutes du Carbet Trail (see Walk #33), the Karukéra Trail descends from the open heights of Soufrière and L'Echelle into the rain forest and eventually to the Chutes du Carbet Picnic Area. (See the first two paragraphs of Walk #33 for the beginning of the Karukéra Trail.)

From its junction with the upper portion of the Chutes du Carbet Trail this pathway, which is easy to follow yet has steep and difficult footing along some portions, provides a good study of the plant life of Guadeloupe. Mountain mangle and pineapple thrive on the higher elevations and the chestnut and gum trees bristle with epiphytes in the lowlands.

Guadeloupe

The final few yards of the Karukéra Trail are also a part of the Grande Randonnée G.1 (see "Exciting News!" in the chapter introduction above). A good choice would be to combine the Karukéra Trail with Grande Randonée G.1 for a strenuous circuit hike.

35. The Third Falls of the Carbet Trail

Walking time: 2 hours, 15 minutes, one way, to the Chutes du Carbet Picnic Area

These are the smallest falls in height, but the largest in terms of water volume. The Third Carbet Falls Trail may be reached by leaving Route N.1 just south of Capesterre and driving Route D.3 to Routhiers. Continue on the unpaved track through a banana plantation to its end. Begin the hike here.

The well-defined pathway is in a dense hardwood forest. After one mile it crosses a stream and soon reaches the junction to the falls. Take the left fork and descend steeply to the river. The force of the falls, which you have reached within one hour of walking, creates a mist and a roar that hang heavy in this emerald-green river valley.

Return to the main trail, turn left and parallel the Carbet River. Continue in the rain forest on a gentle rise, cross two streams, and ascend more steeply to the junction with the Chutes du Carbet Trail (see Walk #33). To the left, the Chutes du Carbet Picnic Area is reached in 1.5 additional miles.

36. The Etang l'As de Pique Trail

Walking time: 1½ hours, one way, to the junction with the Grand-Etang Hike

From the city of Basse-Terre, drive Route N.1 to Gourbeyre. In the village, turn onto Route D.10 and take it through Moscou to its end in the Plateau de Palmiste.

The trail (which is also a part of the Grande Randonn-ée G.1 – see "Exciting News!" in the chapter intro-duction above) starts amid the plants of a banana farm and, 15 minutes later, crosses the first of sev-eral streams. You are now in the deep rain forest of Guadeloupe. The trees stand tall, the vines are thick and long, and the ferns and epiphytes compete for space. The path continues into a swampy area – your shoes are almost guaranteed to get wet and muddy – and descends to Etang l'As de Pique. Cross the river to reach this small body of water, which derives its name from the shape of the pond –l'As de Pique translates as the Ace of Spades.

Cross back over the river and walk along the right side of the pond to reach a view of Grand-Etang to the east. The trail now makes use of switchbacks for 30 more minutes to reach the junction with the Grand-Etang Hike (see Walk #37). A moderate hike.

37. The Grand-Etang Hike

Walking time: 4½ hours, round trip

To reach this highly recommended and moderate hike, drive Route N.1 north from Trois-Rivières to Route D.4. On D.4, go beyond L'Habituée to the parking area for the Grand-Etang. From the far end of the parking lot, the path (part of the Grande Ran-donnée G.1 –see "Exciting News!" in the chapter in-troduction above) goes down into a forest of mahogany and bamboo. In 10 minutes, at the junc-tion, turn left along the shore of the pond. Grand-Etang is a natural swampy area and has the poten-tial for good bird watching early in the morning and turtle viewing later in the day.

Continue around the pond, crossing the outlet stream (which is actually only heard since it is hid-den below the rocks) and ascend to a mangrove thicket. The roots of the trees are characteristic of mangrove swamps in that they spread out from the trunk, far above ground level, to firmly anchor the trees in the shallow, mushy soil.

Guadeloupe

Descend slightly, cross a couple of small streams, and arrive at another intersection. To the right it is 20 to 25 minutes back to the parking area. Turn left and reach another junction 0.3 mile further. To the right is Etang l'As de Pique Trail (see Walk #36). Take the left fork down to a stream in about another mile. From this water run there is a hard climb to a ridgeline and then an equally steep descent to the mangrove area that surrounds Etang Madère. The path skirts the north side of the swamp to end at a second swamp, Etang Roche. These are truly unique ponds. Much of the time they are dry, and it is possible to explore the grasses and rushes of the swamp without getting wet. The area is also home to a great variety of birds.

A highly recommended hike. On this relatively short, moderate hike you will discover a wide selection of botanical areas and plants – mangrove, pond, bamboo, swamp, rain forest, and river bed.

38. The Bassin Bleu Walk

Walking time: 40 minutes, round trip

This short, easy walk begins at the same place as the Etang l'As de Pique Trail (see Walk #36 for driving directions).

Dropping into a small ravine, the pathway ascends along the Galion River to arrive at the popular swimming spot within 20 minutes. A cascade of about 20 feet drops into the basin, which becomes its most colorful when receiving the direct rays of a midday sun. An easy walk.

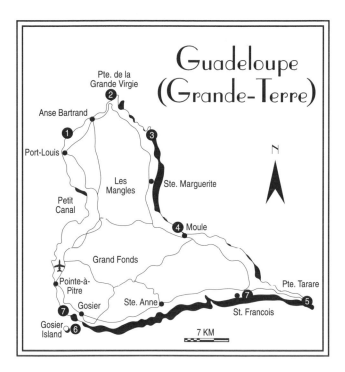

Walks On Grande-Terre

1. La Plage du Souffleur Walk and Anse-Bertrand Hike

Walking time: 3 hours, one way

Located at the small fishing village of Port Louis, La Plage du Souffleur is nearly deserted during the weekdays. Watching the fisherman go about their daily chores is an added attraction to this pleasant beach walk.

If you are feeling adventurous, it is possible to continue northward for several miles. This coastal route passes by a most interesting cemetery whose graves are outlined by pink-tinged conch shells. The coastline here is nearly completely deserted and alternates between soft sandy beaches, mangrove marshes, and rugged, rocky shores. Within three hours of fairly isolated hiking you'll arrive at Anse-Bertrand. Your shuttle car can pick you up here (having driven Route N.6 northward from Port-Louis). A moderate hike.

The white sands of La Plage du Souffleur.

2. The Pointe de la Grande Vigie Walk

Drive Route D.122 north from Anse-Bertrand to its end at the parking area for the Pointe de la Grande Vigie. A short trail loops through the scrub brush to a most imposing view. The Atlantic Ocean crashes onto the rocks almost 300 feet directly below and the indented cliffs of the coast outline the low grounds of Grande-Terre as it swings southeast to a view of La Désirade. On good days, Antigua can be seen on the horizon 35 miles to the north, with just a hint of Montserrat sticking up out of the sea to the west.

Looking out from Pointe de la Grande Vigie.

3. The Falaise Hike

Walking time: 5 hours, one way,
from Lagon de la Porte d'Enfer to Mahaudière

The word "falaise" translates to cliff, and this is exactly the focal point of this long hike along the northeastern coast of Grande-Terre. Signed and marked by paint blazes, the beginning of the route is most easily reached by driving Route D.122 north out of Anse-Bertrand. However, instead of heading north to Pointe de la Vigie, bear right at the first major intersection and follow the road to a picnic area at Lagon de la Porte d'Enfer, "The Gate of Hell." Begin the hike here.

Pass by the Trou Madame Coco, where folklore tells of Ms. Coco, who, while carrying an umbrella to protect her from the sun, purposely walked out into the ocean swells, never to be seen again. Winding its way amongst acacia and tamarind shrubs, the path sometimes stays on the cliffs high above the waves, other times dropping to the shore, so you can explore the tidal environment. Because of the low growing vegetation, the views remain good all of the way to Pointe Petit Nègre, which is about four hours into

Guadeloupe

the hike. Here, the trail officialy leaves the coast to follow a small track inland for 60 minutes to Route D.122 at Mahaudière.

If you wish to stay along the shore, the open country permits an additional walk of at least two more hours to Anse de la Savane Brûlée near Gros Cap.

An easy hike whose only difficulties are its length and constant exposure to the sun. Be sure to bring a hat, cover-ups, and plenty of water.

4. The Moule Beach Walk

Another walk on the sands near a small village. This spot seems peaceful enough, but at one time it was the site of fierce battles between Carib Indians and early settlers. If you're an amateur archaeologist, you may be interested in searching for skeletal remains, as some have been found on the beach in this area.

5. The Pointe des Châteaux Hike

Walking time: less than 1 hour to cover the entire circuit trail

Follow Route N.4 east from Pointe-à-Pitre to its end on the easternmost point of Guadeloupe, Pointe des Châteaux. Waves come roaring onto the contorted rock formations which make up the coastline of this windy and desolate spot. A signed circuit trail wraps around the small knob of the point, permitting further access to this rocky and stark landscape.

In addition to the circuit trail there are miles and miles of white sand that traverse the narrow strip of land leading to Pointe des Châteaux. You could spend hours walking and not cover all of the beaches here. On the north shore is an *au naturel* swimming and bathing spot, Pointe Terrare.

6. The Gosier Island Walk

*Walking time: a half-hour to circumnavigate
the island*

This small island is less than a mile offshore at Gosier. It is so small that a stroll around it can't be considered much of a walk, but its superb little beach
and accessibility make it an enjoyable trip. A lighthouse is near the center of the island. Even though it
is close to a major population center, the odds are
good that you will be the only one here. Another recognized nudist bathing area, Gosier Island is a recommended trip that may only be reached by boat (or
by swimmers with stamina).

7. Walks on Hotel and Resort Grounds

Guadeloupe also has its share of grand hotels and resorts with extensive grounds and maintained gardens. Each offers a good opportunity for pleasurable
strolling.

In St.-Francois, **Meridian Guadeloupe** has 150
acres in which to wander. **Hamak** has five acres of
terrace, gardens, and lands adjoining the Meridian
Guadeloupe's property. Near Deshaies on Basse-
Terre, **Touring Club Hotel de Fort Royal** has a
small golf course and two fine, white sand beaches.

➣ If not a registered guest, you should ask
permission before beginning any of these
walks.

Not to be overlooked are the beach/hotel strips at
Bas du Fort and **Gosier**. Here, it is possible to walk
from one beach to another, stopping at the hotel bars
to quench the thirst worked up from all of that sun,
hot sand, and topless bathing. These areas include
over four miles of sandy beaches and hotels.

Guadeloupe

Walks On Iles des Saintes

Ten miles south of Basse-Terre is the small group of islands named Iles des Saintes. The little archipelago has such delightful weather and fine scenery that many Guadeloupians have vacation homes here. Terre-de-Bas and Terre-de-Haut are the two largest populated islands. All of the walks described here are on the main island of Terre-de-Haut.

Regularly scheduled ferry service connects Iles des Saintes with either Trois-Rivières on Basse-Terre or Pointe-à-Pitre on Grande-Terre. There are also air connections between Pointe-à-Pitre, the city of Basse-Terre and Terre-de-Haut. All of this service means that you can arrive on Terre-de-Haut early in the day, take a couple of the walks listed, have a delicious lunch and a leisurely swim, complete all of the other walks listed, and arrive back on the mainland in time for your evening meal.

1. The Island Road Hike

Walking time: 1½ hours, one way

Begin this walking tour of Terre-de-Haut at the pier in Bourg de Saintes. The small square is the center of activity on the island and it is not uncommon to find a group of musicians performing for passersby. Don't miss the chance to sample a coconut tart from one of the street vendors.

Turn left by the gendarme office onto the main street lined with small restaurants and tourist shops. This little village is a classic small Caribbean French settlement. Soak it all in – this is the French Caribbean at its best.

In only a few minutes you'll reach the edge of town and climb the gently graded road to Fort Napoleon. Situated on a small knoll of 360 feet, Fort Napoleon is a well-preserved 17th-century structure offering a commanding view over the island and surrounding seas. A small admission fee is charged to tour the inside of the fort.

Return to town via the same road and continue beyond the square at the pier. Once again you will pass a number of small shops and restaurants. Pick any of these for lunch – you can't go wrong since the food on the French islands always seems to be excellent. (And the restaurants on Iles des Saintes are also less expensive than those on other islands!) Continue through town, always on the main road. Pass the small open-air market, a couple of grocery stores, and enter the countryside by bearing left onto Route D.124. At the edge of an open field with grazing goats, follow the road uphill for a short distance and it will level off. Soon, on the left, is the route to the summit of Le Chameau (see Walk #5).

Spices are but one of many goods for sale at the open-air market.

Beyond the Le Chameau route is a turn-off to the right that you should follow to one of the most popular beaches on the island, Le Pain de Sucre. The small bay here is usually crowded with dozens of visiting yachts. Return to the main road, turn right, and ascend to the Bois Joli Hotel. From here there

Guadeloupe

are views back to Le Pain de Sucre and Bourg de Saintes.

The road now makes a quick and steep descent to the beach at Anse Crawen where the road and the hike ends. Stop, relax, and take a swim *au naturel*.

A most highly recommended excursion. Again, it cannot be emphasized enough, be sure to experience the beauty and charm of this little island.

2. The Baie de St.-Pierre Walk

Walking time: 45 minutes, one way

Leave the village of Bourg de Saintes by walking the road to the north and arrive shortly at the junction to Baie de St.-Pierre. Continue on fairly level ground, passing the Baie de Marigot and a couple of noteworthy restaurants.

Ascend a small ridge going by open fields and grazing cattle. If you didn't know any better, you could be convinced you were walking through the bucolic scenery of southern Virginia. Near the high point of the ridge is a small camping area. (Check in town about regulations.) Descend the ridge and arrive at Baie de St.-Pierre. There is a small fee charged to use the beach, whose white sands form the classic crescent shape of a tropical beachscape (and also provide access to the Circuit de Crêtes Trail – see Walk #3).

3. The Circuit de Crêtes Trail

Walking time: 2 hours, 15 minutes, to complete the full circuit

From the far eastern end of the Baie de St.-Pierre (see Walk #2 for directions), the signed and marked Circuit de Crêtes Trail climbs through cacti and other scruffy vegetation to the ridgeline separating Baie de St. Pierre from Grande Anse. The pathway soon swings around the sloping cliffs of Grand Souffleur. Be careful since some spots are slippery and the drop-off is steep. Continuing with ever-present views of sandy beaches and the Caribbean Sea, the route reaches the summit of Morne Rouge. Here, you have an almost 360° vista of the island, its neighbors, and the surrounding blue waters. Soon after the summit it is possible, if you don't mind a bit of unsure footing, to take a scrambling side trip down to the beach along Grande Anse (see Walk #4).

The main route of the circuit trail stays on the ridgeline for several hundred more yards before descending to the right and meeting with pavement. Turn right and return to the Baie de St.-Pierre (see Walk #2 for a description of this route) or, if you prefer, bear left and walk into Bourg de Saintes in just a few minutes.

4. The Grande Anse Walk

Walking time: 1 hour, one way

From the pier in Bourg de Saintes turn right and walk for a couple of blocks until you pass the Mairie. Turn left, rise slightly, and descend gradually to the cemetery. It is worth spending a few minutes here to

Conch shells are laid in memory of loved ones.

observe the tile-covered grave markers and conch shell-lined paths.

A beautiful and uncrowded beach lies at the end of the road. While the scenery is pleasing to the eye, the wind and the rough surf usually discourage any swimming. At the far northern end you could hike steeply uphill to join the Circuit des Crêtes Trail (see Walk #3) not far from the summit of Morne Rouge. A recommended, moderate walk.

5. Le Chameau Hike

Walking time: 2 hours, 15 minutes, round trip

The beginning of this hike to the highest point of the island is reached on Route D.124 at a point about half-way between Bourg de Saintes and Le Pain de Sucre. Turn off the main road and ascend, gradually, using the switchbacks of this track.

While on the hillside be on the lookout for iguanas; they inhabit Iles des Saintes in great numbers. You have to be quick since they scamper away at the first sound of humans.

Le Chameau Peak offers a great view of Bourg des Saintes.

The trek continues to climb through vegetation, which becomes progressively smaller as you get closer to the summit of 1,013 feet. This hilltop offers pleasing views of all of the islands of Iles des Saintes, Marie-Galante, and even cloud-capped Soufrière on Guadeloupe.

While it may gain elevation gradually, be aware that this walk rises from almost sea level to over a thousand feet at the summit.

A Very Special Walk

Walking time: less than 2 hours, complete hike around the island

Six miles off the southeastern coast of Grande-Terre is Petite-Terre – two delightful deserted small islands great for exploring. Petite-Terre may be reached only by boat; arrange transportation from charter companies in Ste.-Anne or St.-Francois. The smaller island, Terre-de-Haute, is very overgrown and this tangled growth and cacti prohibit exploration much beyond its small beach. Terre-de-Basse, on the other hand, can be explored at great length.

Begin your discovery of Terre-de-Basse at the lighthouse. Unfortunately, it is usually locked so you won't be able to enjoy the view from the top. Walk west on the long white sand beach that covers the north coast of the island. You have complete freedom here as there will be no one else around. Swim, bathe, or do whatever comes naturally! As you round the corner of the northwest tip, the beach gets wider for a short distance and then narrower as the vegetation edges closer to the sea. Coming to the southern coast, pass by a popular picnic spot used by private yachts. Enter the scrub vegetation onto a part of the island that is rougher, more rocky, and has no sand beaches – just small cliffs overlooking the sea. It may become necessary to pick your way a short distance inland through tangled branches to avoid a couple of precipitous drops to the sea. Don't be alarmed by the sudden movements of iguanas; do be careful of the cacti, whose needles have been known to penetrate the soles of shoes. Also be on the lookout for hundreds of small crabs emigrating from the sea. On this section you'll also discover the old rock walls that stretch south to north. They are reminders that this land was once farmed, with cattle and goats grazing in the fenced fields. Near the end of the walk, the ground becomes a solid rock base, reminiscent of the rugged coastlines of Maine. The tour of Terre-de-Basse ends at the lighthouse.

A very highly recommended excursion. Do not miss this one!

Dominica

One of the most visually pleasing of the islands, Dominica is the nature walker's paradise. The terrain is so mountainous that the island has been called the Switzerland of the Caribbean. About 49% of Dominica is covered by dense rain forest, while 80% remains in its natural state.

Much of the island can be reached only on foot and it is believed that many of its 290 square miles have yet to be explored. Most of the inhabitants live on the narrow coastal plain, leaving the highlands undeveloped. Thanks, in part, to the increase in walkers and hikers, Dominica has taken an active interest in its footpaths by developing new ones and rehabilitating, maintaining, and marking an excellent system of trails throughout the island. Some of these routes make use of original Carib Indian traces, while others were once employed by the local people to get from one village to another. As the update of this book went to press, reception facilities were being constructed at Trafalgar falls, Emerald Pool, and the Cabrits National Park. Each facility will house a reception/information center, restrooms, and a snack bar. The Waitikubuli Trail, which would stretch the length of the island from south to north, is just now in the proposal stage. If it ever does become a reality, it will surely be one of the most spectacular and premier hiking opportunities in all of the Caribbean.

The Caribbean islands are the result of volcanic action and there is much evidence on Dominica that this evolution continues. Trails pass by giant gommier and chestnut trees dripping with cable-thick vines and bristling with bromeliad epiphytes. These routes lead to bubbling sulphur springs, around crater lakes, past steaming fumaroles, and up to a mist-obscured boiling lake. Cascading waterfalls crash through deep gorges created by the once-molten lava.

The plant life on Dominica is truly phenomenal. Bromeliads, orchids, anthuriums, and heliconias bloom throughout the year. In some places there are over 60 species of trees in just a 10-acre area! Bananas, oranges, grapefruit, limes, coconuts, coffee, and cocoa are harvested from the cultivated lower lands. The wildlife is also abundant and varied. There are over 135 species of native birds, the most notable being the endangered Jacquot and Sisserou parrots. Giant frogs, known locally as mountain chickens, inhabit the mountainous forests. Cave

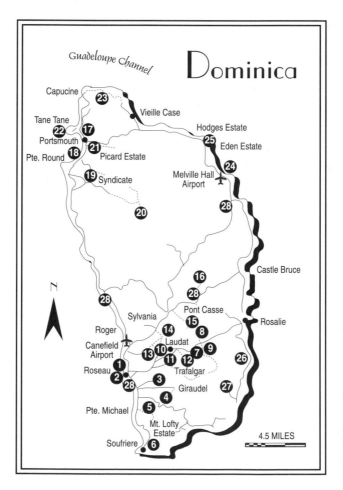

bats, agouti (a rodent), and the manicou (an opossum) live in the lower elevations. Dominica is even home to iguanas, boa constrictors, and 20 species of land crab.

Morne Diablotin, in the north central part of the island, rises to 4,747 feet. Watt Mountain and Morne Trois Pitons also attain heights of over 4,000 feet. This high elevation insures an abundant rainfall, enough so that Dominica exports fresh water to many of the drier islands.

A walk on Dominica allows you to experience the Caribbean as it was for centuries before the first settlers from Europe arrived.

History

On his second voyage to the New World in 1493, Columbus first spotted Dominica on a Sunday, thus naming the island for that day of the week. The Carib Indians on the island were left alone until the early 1700s, when France and England began colonizing the Caribbean. These early settlers met with such fierce resistance from the Caribs that they signed a treaty in 1748, leaving the island in the possession of the Indians.

Enticed by the fertile soil, neither country stayed away for long, and the pattern of battles for dominance was repeated here as it was on so many of the other islands. Construction of Fort Shirley began in 1770 to protect British vessels anchored in Prince Rupert Bay. The matter of possession was settled in 1805. The French burned the capital city, Roseau, to the ground, but finally gave up all rights to the island upon payment of 12,000 British pounds.

While battling among themselves, the settlers still had to contend with Indian attacks. As late as 1930 the Indians staged an uprising against British rule. About 3,000 Caribs now live peacefully on a 3,700-

acre reservation on the northeast coast, the final remnants of a race that once inhabited all of the Caribbean and for whom the entire island chain was named.

Dominica remained under British control until it became an associated state of the United Kingdom in 1967. In 1978 it gained full independence as a democratic republic within the British Commonwealth.

The island is one of the poorest of the Caribbean, but is working to improve the lives of its people. The government accepts foreign aid and the U.S. and Canada have helped to build a modern road system.

Not all Dominicans are happy with the situation and coups were attempted in 1980 and 1981. This political unrest has now subsided, but there is still a feeling of resentment by a few Dominicans toward outsiders. While this should not deter visitors, it is wise to employ local guides when going off the typical tourist paths. To some degree, this helps alleviate the impression that the visitor is enjoying the charms of the island without giving anything in return.

Data

Transportation to Dominica: There are no direct flights from the U.S., Canada, or Europe. Each of these, however, has direct flights to Puerto Rico, Sint Maarten, Antigua, Guadeloupe, Martinique, and other nearby Caribbean islands. Connecting flights to Dominica from all of those islands are available.

Two ferry companies provide sea connections between Guadeloupe, Martinique, and Dominica.

With the construction of the cruise ship berth in Prince Rupert Bay, next to Fort Shirley and Cabrits

National Park, Dominica is quickly becoming a regular port of call for cruise ships.

There is a departure tax imposed upon leaving.

Entry: Proof of citizenship – a voter's registration card, birth certificate, or valid passport – and a return or ongoing airline ticket are required of U.S. or Canadian citizens. Valid passports and a return or ongoing ticket are required of all other visitors.

Currency: The East Caribbean dollar is the national currency, but American dollars are widely accepted. Banks in Roseau will exchange money. Usual business hours are Monday to Thursday 8:00 A.M. to 3:00 P.M. and Friday 8:00 A.M. to 5:00 P.M. Before the 1990s credit cards were not readily accepted here but, as evidence that Dominica is fast becoming a major tourist destination, they are now widely used at tourist establishments.

Tourist Information:

✍ **In North America**
Dominica Tourist Office
10 East 21st Street, Suite 600
New York, NY 10010
☎ 212-475-7542

✍ **In Europe**
Caribbean Tourism Organisation
Suite 315, Vigiliant
120 Wilton Road, Victoria
London SW1V 1JZ
England, 0171-233-8382

On Dominica, the National Development Corporation (next to the Botanical Gardens) provides tourist information:

✍ National Development Corporation
PO Box 293
Roseau, Commonwealth of Dominica
West Indies
☎ 767-448-2045

Dominica Tours, located in the Anchorage Hotel just south of Roseau, is most helpful and will also supply you with much information.

Driving: Rental cars are available in Roseau and Portsmouth. Visitor driver's permits may be obtained at the Police Traffic Department in Roseau or from the Customs and Immigration Office at either airport. Presentation of a valid national or international driver's license and payment of a fee are required. Drive on the left!

Language: The official language is English. French is extensively spoken and the natives have a patois language all of their own. Many of the inhabitants can use all three languages.

Walking and Hiking Guide Companies: Janice Armour of Dominica Tours has a vast knowledge of the flora, fauna, history, and geography of Dominica. All of the walks for Dominica in this guidebook can be arranged through her. Ms. Armour's tours are some of the most comprehensive on the island and she goes as far as employing different guides for different hikes or tours based upon the guide's area of expertise. Also, as proprietor of the hotel, she offers many package deals that provide for room, board, transportation, guided walks, hikes and tours, and even scuba and whale watching trips. These are often cheaper than making arrangements on your own.

    ✍ Dominica Tours
       c/o Anchorage Hotel, PO Box 34
       Roseau, Commonwealth of Dominica
       West Indies
       ☎ 767-448-2638

Another excellent choice, which also has a contingent of well-trained guides, is:

    ✍ Ken's Hinterland Tours & Taxi Service
       PO Box 447
       Roseau, Commonwealth of Dominica
       West Indies
       ☎ 767-448-4850

If you are unable to make arrangements with either of the above, the National Development Corporation can put you in touch with other qualified guide companies.

Be aware that, in order to finance improvements and maintenance of pathways and related facilities and activities, the government has recently instituted user fees for different sites and/or trails. These apply both to when you are with a guide company or hiking solo.

Camping Areas: Motivated by environmental preservation concerns, camping is not permitted on the island.

Recommended Readings

Dominica: Isle of Adventure by Lennox Honeychurch

The Dominica Chronicle is the island newspaper. It provides a good overview of what is happening politically, economically, and socially on the island.

Walks

1. A Walking Tour of Roseau

Begin your walking tour in the open air New Market Square on the banks of the Roseau River. As on many of the other Caribbean islands, Saturday morning is the most colorful time to visit the marketplace. In addition to the usual fruits, vegetables, and native handicrafts, you may find some "mountain chickens" for sale. The chickens are actually large land frogs, used in a number of local recipes.

One block from the market, stop in at the post office for some of the most colorful postage stamps in all of the Caribbean. Continue along Bay Front, which was renovated in the early 1990s. It features reconstructions of original storefront architecture and a tree-lined walkway. Passing by the Court House you will eventually arrive at the Old Market –in former days a slave trading site and now a crafts center and tourist information office. Turn left here onto King George V Street, the main commercial area.

After shopping your way through several blocks, turn right onto Queen Mary Street and, in one block, you'll come to the Roman Catholic Cathedral. Stop in and take a look at the superbly handcarved wooden pews. Another block along Queen Mary Street brings you to Tropicrafts. Fiber rugs, world-renowned for their durability, are handwoven in this shop. Roseau was named after the reeds that grow along the city's rivers and are now used to weave these rugs and other handicrafts.

Take Turkey Lane and return to the waterfront and the Fort Young Hotel, impressively built within and upon the ruins of the original structure of the 1700s. A left turn here takes you past the public library and eventually to Bath Street. Bearing uphill on Bath Street leads to the Botanical Gardens.

2. The Botanical Gardens

Established in 1890, the 40 acres of Dominica's Botanical Gardens were once recognized as some of the finest in the Caribbean. At one time, landscaped with a fountain, ponds, and elaborate ironwork, the gardens boasted more than 500 types of trees and shrubs, including nearly 100 species of palm.

Although time, financial constraints and, most notably, the ravages of hurricanes have reduced the overall grandeur of the gardens, a Forestry and Wildlife Division brochure still lists more than 50 plants found here. This area of shaded greenery makes for a quiet, restful walk. The Agricultural

Experiment Station is also within the gardens and you are allowed to wander through their experimental gardens to see what new vegetables are being grown and tested.

(Detailed information on the Trois Pitons National Park may be obtained at the Park Headquarters next to the Agricultural Station.)

In the upper end of the Botanical Gardens is a shaded route leading to the summit of Morne Bruce. A large cross and a few benches overlook the city, giving an excellent view of the town, the Roseau River, and the Caribbean chain stretching out to the west.

The gardens and Morne Bruce are both recommended respites from the hustle and bustle of downtown Roseau.

3. The Castle Comfort - Ridgefield Estate Hike

Walking time: about 2 hours for the complete circuit

Except during morning and evening rush hours, this is an easy hike along a series of lightly traveled roads. Just south of Roseau is the Anchorage Hotel and just past that is a road bearing left uphill. Walk this road, passing by newly constructed houses (a sure sign that Dominica is becoming slightly more prosperous), through the village of Bellin, and then out into the open country of tiny family-owned farms. Just past the village of Giraudel is the Ridgefield Estate. A previous landlord had turned this place into a show garden with over 50 plants, including a variety of lillies, orchids, hibiscus, and even carib wood, the national flower of Dominica. Sadly, the general public is no longer permitted access.

Continue on the main highway past the Ridgefield Estate and return to Roseau. Along the way are good views of Roseau, the ocean, and Scotts Head (Point Cachacrou) to the south.

4. The Morne Anglais Trail

Walking time: 2 hours, one way

This steep mountain trail begins in the village of Giraudel. Leading through cultivated fields, it eventually enters the Trois Pitons National Park. With good views (when not covered in a cloud mist) of the surrounding countryside, the route ends amid the stunted epiphytes, ferns, and mosses of an elfin forest on the summit of 3,683-foot Morne Anglais.

> **Note:** *It is advisable to obtain a local guide for this hike. The trail is steep, slippery, and hard to follow in places.*

5. The Mount Lofty Estate Hike

Walking time: 1 hour, one way

In the village of Pointe Michel, south of Roseau, walk the road leading uphill. For 45 to 60 minutes, the road will gradually rise, taking you through open farming and estate lands. At Mount Lofty Estate the road ends and you have views of the sea, lush green valleys on both sides, and Morne Anglais looming above to the north. An easy hike.

6. The South End of the Island Hike

Walking time: about 3 hours, one way

From the village of Soufrière drive uphill on the road to the sulphur springs. These springs are evidence of the true nature of the islands – volcanic. The minor earth tremors felt here in 1994 were an emphatic reminder!

From the sulphur springs walk back downhill and make a left turn onto the road marked for the Petit Coulibri Guest Cottages. Follow this rural route for approximately two miles to the cottages, which stand on the site of a former aloe plantation estate.

The grounds provide a view across aquamarine waters to the cloud-covered summit of Montange Pelée rising high above the lower verdant slopes on Martinique.

From the cottages there is a route (you may have to inquire locally to find it) which drops almost 1,000 feet and delivers you back to the main coastal highway and Scotts Head. This knoll that juts out into the sea offers a spectacular view. Martinique lies in the mist of the horizon across the waters of the channel, the deep green forests of Dominica slant above the lime and banana plantations of the valleys, and the waves of the Atlantic tumble onto the rocky southern coast of the island.

After visiting Scotts Head, take the time for a swim or maybe even some snorkeling in Soufrière Bay on the northern side of the peninsula.

7. The Freshwater Lake Hike

Walking time: 1 hour for the complete circuit

To reach Freshwater Lake, drive out of Roseau on the highway that crosses Roseau River at the Botanical Gardens. At the first intersection keep left toward Trafalgar. At the next intersection bear left again, this time toward Laudat. Passing through the settlement of Laudat, continue on the road to the left. In two more miles the road ends at the parking area for Freshwater Lake. There is a rough trail going completely around Dominica's largest lake.

Freshwater Lake, which is the source of the Roseau River, has been dammed to provide water for hydroelectric plants. The lake, in the crater of a volcano, is in Trois Pitons National Park and is an excellent place to explore the montane and cloud forest. Due to the shallow soil and continuous winds, the trees are short, trunks are thin, and foliage sparse. This permits shrubs, ferns, and flowers, such as the blue wax flower and multicolored heliconia plants, to grow abundantly from the forest floor.

Mang blan and mang wouj trees are predominant here. Their roots extend high up onto the trunks, helping to anchor the trees in the soggy soil. Be on the lookout for hummingbirds, mountain whistlers, and an occasional agouti. Anolis lizards are often spotted moving about near the purple blossom clumps of water hyacinths, as are the brown and yellow Siwik (or river) crabs which make their home among the boulders of the shoreline. An easy and recommended hike.

8. The Boeri Lake Trail

Walking time: 1½ hours, round trip

This trail takes off north from the parking area at Freshwater Lake (see Walk #7 for driving directions). Ascending through former agricultural lands, the pathway goes by both cold and hot springs and into the montane forest and elfin woodland on the sides of Morne Macaque. This mountain is actually the cone of a relatively young volcano that separates Freshwater Lake from Boeri Lake, both of which are inside the craters of more ancient volcanoes.

During the hike, which passes by cabbage palms, heliconias, anthuriums, and tree ferns, it is possible to peer down onto the eastern coast and the Atlantic Ocean. To the south are Freshwater Lake, Morne Nicholls, and Morne Watt. A moderate hike.

9. The Freshwater Lake - Rosalie Trail

Walking time: 2 hours, one way

This is another trail leading from the Freshwater Lake parking area (see Walk #7 for access directions). From the mountains this moderate and very pretty hike has a series of switchbacks that lead quickly down through the forest and into the farmlands below. The trail joins a road near Grand Fond, about two miles outside of Rosalie.

Note: Although once a popular local route, the path is now rarely used. A guide is recommended.

10. The Papillote Wilderness Retreat Rain Forest Gardens

Since 1969, Papillote Wilderness Retreat proprietors, Anne and Cuthbert Jean-Baptiste, have been developing their rain forest gardens along the sloping sides of Morne Macaque. In an area that receives 250 inches of rainfall a year, footpaths now wander over a terraced garden of bromeliads, aroids, heliconias, ferns, begonias, fruit trees, herbs, orchids, and much, much more. Yellow-crowned night herons are often spotted during early morning walks and one track, which will usher you by Damsel Falls and hot springs, contains the nests of broad-winged hawks. Agoutis, the rabbit-like rodents found only in the Caribbean, may be seen stealing "dinner" here.

The gardens are only open to registered guests of the hotel (which makes an excellent base from which to explore Dominica's highlands) or to those who make reservations for the guided nature walks led by Ms. Jean-Batiste. Papillote Wilderness Retreat is reached by driving out of Roseau on the highway that crosses Roseau River at the Botanical Gardens. At the first intersection keep left, toward Trafalgar. At the next intersection bear right, still headed toward Trafalgar. Once past this small settlement you will see the grounds of the retreat on the left. Papillote's mailing address is:

✍ PO Box 2287
Roseau
Commonwealth of Dominica
Windward Islands

11. The Trafalgar Falls Walk

Walking time: 20 minutes, round trip

Begin this pleasurable walk just a few yards up the
road from the Papillote Wilderness Retreat (see
Walk #10 for driving directions). The mostly downhill path leads through the thick rain forest of central Dominica. It has been estimated there are over
60 different types of trees in just a 10-acre area on
this part of the island. Large-buttressed chataignier are the dominant trees here.

*The Trafalgar Falls Trail cuts through
dense vegetation.*

In about 10 minutes you will reach a platform from
which to view the spectacular double Trafalgar
Falls. Tumbling hundreds of feet down the mountainside, the two falls come together forming a
large, cool pool at the base (which is the beginning
of the Roseau River). Tree ferns, orchids, and heliconia cling to the steep mountainsides, adding a diversity of color to this majestic spot.

Although it is not necessary to have a guide lead
you to the waterfall, you could hire one to show you
the way beyond that point. A scramble up the boulders of the stream will bring you to a 104° hot spring

hidden behind the roaring thunder of one of the waterfalls.

12. The Valley of Desolation and Boiling Lake Trail

Walking distance: round trip is more than 10 miles;
allow at least 7 hours for this ambitious hike

A true adventure for the truly adventurous. This hike is so strenuous that Dominicans have dubbed it "the once-in-a-lifetime walk." It should only be undertaken with the help of a local guide; once it reaches the Valley of Desolation, the trail is unmarked and hard to follow. Do not let these warnings deter you, for this is an excursion through the most unusual area of Dominica and possibly in the entire Caribbean.

The trail begins in Titou Gorge, close to Laudat. Before starting your hike, take a dip in the pool at the beginning of the trail and experience the thrill of sitting in a cold mountain stream while leaning your back into the hot springs water dripping down the gorge walls. This trough was formed when the molten lava from a volcano cooled and split apart. Hopefully, your guide will take you for a swim up the gorge, less than four feet wide in some places, to sit under the rushing waterfall just a short distance upstream.

As the trail leaves the gorge you'll be find yourself listening to the melodious song of the mountain whistlers. The trail quickly tops a ridge and drops down to Trois Pitons River. This waterway continues westward, eventually becoming a part of the magnificent double Trafalgar Falls.

After fording the river, the trail begins a long, steep climb to the summit of Morne Nicholls. From here, you have a grand view of Watt Mountain to the south. The stunted growth of the elfin woodland also allows you to see the steam rising from your final destination, Boiling Lake.

Dropping down a constructed footpath, the trail enters the Valley of Desolation, its route parallelled by a hot water stream. Even though the air around you may be cool, you can warm your hands by dipping them into this rivulet.

Walking into the Valley of Desolation will take you back in time to when the earth was young. Fissures release gasses with such force that they almost sound like steam engines, and hot springs send plumes of sulphur fumes streaming into the cold mountain air. These fumes and springs have transformed the valley into an eerie and barren area dotted with green, blue, orange, and white mineral deposits. Be sure to stay on the trail here to avoid breaking through the thin crust to the hot lava below!

Rising out of the valley, the path finally reaches Boiling Lake, the second largest such lake in the world. Usually enshrouded in its own cloud of vapors, the lake contains bubbling, grey water of 190° Fahrenheit that can cook an egg in less than three minutes. Runoff from the surrounding mountains seeps through the porous lake bottom and then rises back to the surface, heated by the hot lava below.

When you return from this excursion, you not only will bring back the mud and sweat of your efforts (so wear old clothes), but also the memories of this unmatched hike through the interior of Dominica.

> ⤷ A very highly recommended trip. In other words – for those who are up to it – don't miss this one!

13. The Lower Middleham Trail

Walking time: 3 hours, one way

This trail was built and is maintained by the Dominica National Park Service. It begins in Providence, just west of Laudat. From Providence, begin walking through the rain forest and reach a trail intersection. To the right is the Upper Middleham Trail (see Walk #14). Continue on the Lower Middleham Trail to another intersection. Bear left past once-cultivated banana and breadfruit trees to an overlook of one of Dominica's highest waterfalls, the imposing 275-foot Middleham Falls. Return to the main path and continue through the rain forest to a trail-side shelter.

Another trail, coming in from the right, also leads to the Upper Middleham Trail. Just past this side trail is Tou Santi, "The Stinking Hole." This hot air lava fissure is home to numerous bats. Proceed on the path, emerging from the forest and into the cultivated lands of Cochrane.

14. The Upper Middleham Trail
Walking time: 2½ hours, one way

The Upper Middleham Trail makes use of the first portion of the Lower Middleham Trail near Providence (see Walk #13). The access point near Sylvania (at the other end of the path) is rarely used and hard to find. This description will take you from Providence to Sylvania.

Following the combined Upper and Lower Middleham Trails from Providence, the Upper Middleham Trail bears off to the right at the first intersection in about 30 minutes.

Due to the dense forest canopy, the ground is relatively open and tempts one to do some off-trail walking. Stay on the trail, though, as it is easy to become lost. As you walk in the forest, be on the lookout for quail doves, red-necked pigeons and, in the early evening, listen for the peeping of tree frogs. At the next trail intersection a left turn would lead to Tou Santi and the Lower Middleham Trail. The Upper Middleham Trail continues to the right. A number of switchbacks lead to a former coffee plantation before the trail ends at the road near Sylvania.

Note: Using both Middleham Trails would make a pleasant all-day hike.

15. The Morne Trois Pitons Trail

At 4,550 feet, cloud-covered Morne Trois Pitons is Dominica's second highest peak. The trail leaves the main highway near Pont Cassé. It begins in a rain forest and climbs to montane and finally elfin woodland. A guide should be used for this trail.

 Note: The trail is steep, slippery, extremely difficult to follow, and not used on a regular basis.

16. The Emerald Pool Trail

Walking time: 25 minutes for the complete circuit

The Emerald Pool Trail is the showpiece of the Dominica National Park system. Easily accessible about 3.5 miles northeast of Pont Cassé on the road to Castle Bruce, this pathway is even paved for a short distance. Dropping down from the picnic tables and outhouses next to the road, the trail soon comes to an overlook of the falls. On the way, it follows an old stone road that Dominicans used in earlier times to travel from Roseau to Castle Bruce.

Within 10 minutes, the pathway arrives at Emerald Pool at the base of the falls. This is probably the most visited tourist spot on the island. The beauty of the area, with the clear water dropping past lush tropical foliage and sparkling as it splashes into the pool, ensures that it will remain a favorite for many years to come.

Continue on the loop trail, where stones laid by the Carib Indians are still in use, and pass by two viewpoints – one looking out across the mountains of central Dominica and the other onto the island's Atlantic coast. Accompanied by scampering lizards, you'll ascend back to the parking area.

This is a highly recommended moderate walk.

17. A Walking Tour of Portsmouth

A short walk through this town is worthwhile. Portsmouth is the only natural harbor on Dominica and, as a result, there are always a few visiting yachts anchored here. At any given time there will be several people on the two miles of white sand beaches shaded by overhanging coconut palms. Most of the homes in town have a small garden plot next to them and you may even catch a cricket match in the field on the edge of town. Stop at the bakery for some very delicious fresh bread.

A resting lizard.

18. The Portsmouth to Pte. Ronde Hike

This pleasant hike goes along the shore through the village of Glanvillia to the secluded beaches of Pte. Ronde. Stop and take a swim at one of these white sand beaches.

19. The Syndicate Nature Trail

Walking time: 30 minutes for the complete circuit

At Dublanc, just south of Pte. Ronde, is a road leading uphill into the forest. Drive this lightly travelled route to the parking area for the Syndicate Nature

Trail. This superb path runs through property which was purchased for Dominicans with funds provided by several international organizations and, most importantly, with moneys raised by Dominicans through radio appeals and school fund-raisers.

The circuit trail loops by orchids, anthuriums, and bromeliads as it threads through a climax forest of mang blanc, gommier, and chataignier trees – some of which are supported by enormously buttressed trunks. Two viewpoints overlooking the Picard River gorge provide the best opportunity of catching a glimpse of Dominica's native parrots.

Nesting in tree cavities of old-growth forests such as the one this trail traverses, both species of parrots are internationally listed as endangered. The Sisserou, or Imperial parrot has kelly-green wings and a dark purple breast. It grows to more than 18 inches long. Smaller in size, the Jacquot, or red-necked parrot, has red highlights on the bottom part of its neck and wings. You'll have a much better chance of seeing them if you start your walk by 5 or 6 in the morning.

The ease of this walk through Dominica's most accessible dense rain forest and the possibility of sighting a parrot makes it a highly recommended excursion.

20. The Morne Diablotin Trail

There are two trails leading to the summit of Morne Diablotin which, at 4,747 feet, is the highest peak on Dominica. The shorter trail begins near the Syndicate Nature Trail (see Walk #19 for driving directions) and starts almost immediately on a steep climb to the top. The longer trail begins near Picard Estate, just south of Portsmouth. Both routes are long, slippery trails that start in a rain forest. As they climb into the montane forest, the canopy thins and you'll notice more ferns, ginger, and other growth on the ground. As the two trails meet in elfin woodland for the final steep ascent, you may have to get on hands and knees to wriggle over, under, and around the gnarled and moss-coated branches of kaklin trees.

Since the summit is almost always enshrouded in clouds, don't be disappointed if you have no views. If you do happen to arrive on a rare clear day, you're in for a real treat. To the northwest lies Portsmouth, outlined by sunlight playing on the waves of Prince Rupert Bay and the curves and swells of the Cabrits peninsula. Northward, across the Guadeloupe Channel, lie the small islands of Marie-Galante and Isles des Saintes, the pale green mountains of Basse-Terre and the lowlands of Grande-Terre on Guadeloupe. Gazing eastward, you'll see the white foam of ocean waves rolling onto the jagged coast-line. Most impressive, though, might be the view south across much of Dominica's rugged topography. Morne Trois Pitons, Morne Macaque, Watt Mountain, Morne Anglais, and many others thrust their peaks into the clouds, rising high above the surrounding, thickly-forested slopes.

> **Note:** A strenuous, but rewarding hike for those who like a challenge. Both routes are arduous and should not be undertaken lightly. Begin your hike early in the day to ensure enough time. Also, check on trail conditions before you depart; most visitors employ a guide to show the way.

21. The Indian River Boat Ride, Walk, and Swim

Walking time: 30 minutes on the boat and 30 minutes on foot to the swimming hole

The mouth of the Indian River, just south of Portsmouth, is bordered by swamps, while further upstream mangrove trees grow numerous and large. A trail along the river's southern bank would permit an easy stroll, but to fully appreciate the area's tranquil beauty its best to hire one of the guides based at the mouth of the river to row you upstream.

Passing silently on top of the almost-fluorescent green water, the boat will glide you into a world reminiscent of the Amazon. Bwa mang, or swamp bloodwood trees, spread out their amazingly large, swirling, and twisted buttressed roots across the river bank and drape their canopy into the water. What little sunlight does filter through creates dancing shadows upon the foliage and stream. A variety of crabs crawl along the muddy banks, green herons troll the waters in search of a meal, and other birdlife, such as the Antillean crested hummingbird and the pearly-eyed thrasher, flitter about. Orchids, ferns, and anthuriums vie for growing space; the strangler fig makes it own space by wrapping itself around and down the bwa mang trees.

Sunlight filters through dense vegetation onto Indian River.

After about 30 minutes of rowing you'll come to a small landing dock and a bush bar built of native materials. Most guided trips end here with a drink of rum or local juices at the bar. However, behind the bar is a pathway, and this is where your walk will begin. It starts in an old banana plantation, but soon enters the forest. Paralleling the stream through additional mangrove copses, the trail will bring you, within 30 minutes, to one of the most isolated swimming holes on Dominica.

> **Note:** *This is a recommended excursion. However, choose your guide carefully. Some of these young men are very knowledgeable about the flora and fauna of the area; others will just take you on a boat ride. Also, make sure it is understood that you not only want a guided tour upstream, but that you also want to continue to the swimming hole.*

22. The Cabrits National Park

This national park is a short drive north of Portsmouth. British garrisons were located on two peaks of extinct volcanoes here in 1770. The French had possession of the fort for five years from 1778 to 1783. Many of the original structures of Fort Shirley and its adjacent batteries, accessible by marked pathways, remain and make for an interesting afternoon's exploration. There is also a short trail leading through a swamp area (inhabited by doves and herons) and out to Douglas Bay. After exploring the rock

A view from Fort Shirley across to Portsmouth.

and coral formations along the beach, take a swim in the cool, clear waters of the bay.

A detailed brochure about Cabrits National Park may be obtained in the fort's visitor's center or from the National Park Headquarters at the Botanical Gardens in Roseau. All of the walking in the Fort Shirley area is easy to moderate.

23. The North End of the Island Hike

Walking time: 5 hours, one way

Drive the road north out of Portsmouth through Tenetane, Cottage, and Clifton. From Clifton, begin hiking along the track which will connect with the old road once used by French soldiers as a link between Fort Shirley and Rosalie. This track winds around the north tip of the island and along the way are majestic views across the Guadeloupe Channel. Continue on the road, bypassing the village of Dimitre to reach a gravel road at the Delaford Estate. You may end your excursion here or continue with a pleasant walk on the roadbed to a larger highway near Vieille Case. This hike is strenuous only because of its length.

24. Woodford Hill Estate Walk

A walk from Eden Estates to Woodford Hill. The road passes by a lake and through banana and grapefruit plantations. Take a swim at Woodford Hill Beach.

25. The Hodges Estate and Islands Exploration Walk and Swim

This begins as another trip along a network of roads going through coconut and banana plantations. After walking on the roads for a while, be sure to side-track down to the white sands of Hodges Beach. For the adventurous swimmer, there are three small islands 150 yards offshore just waiting to be explored.

> ⋙ **Note:** Both of the above estate walks are on roads that wind through plantation and wooded areas. Your walks can be as long or as short and as easy or as difficult as you wish, depending upon whether you decide to walk the level roads or the ascending routes. If you stay on the main roads you will always be able to find your way back. Both walks are enjoyable.

26. The Sari Sari Falls Hike

Walking time: 3 hours, round trip

Departing from La Plaine on the southeastern coast, this rough trail passes initially by banana plantations before dropping steeply to the Sari Sari River. Continuing onward involves scrambling over slippery rocks and boulders as the route enters the heavier growth of a true rain forest. After fording the river several times, as well as making use of the stream itself, the trail will deliver you to Sari Sari Falls. With all the toil it took to get here, don't forgo the opportunity to bathe in the pool as the water comes crashing down from 125 feet above you.

A guide is necessary to show you the way. Second and third visits, which you will surely want to make, can be done independently.

27. The Victoria Falls Hike

Walking time: 2½ hours, round trip

Minerals rising to the surface in the Valley of Desolation find their way into the water system, turning streams and rivers into faint hues usually not associated with free-flowing streams. Thus, the White

River, which originates in the valley, receives its name from its distinctive milky color. Picking up more and more water as it flows down the mountains, the river makes such a roaring and dramatic plunge over a rock facing near the village of Delices that many Dominicans find it more spectacular than Trafalgar Falls.

Victoria Falls is reached via a rugged hike that involves entering a narrow gorge in the rain forest, negotiating slippery rocks, clambering over boulders and crossing the river numerous times at difficult fording spots. The trail is hard to identify as it comes to an end near the falls.

(If you feel like more hiking after a swim in the pool at the base of the falls, you might be able to talk your guide into bringing you to nearby Jack Falls.)

◆ *A guide is a must.*

28. Walks on Hotel and Resort Grounds

The hotels and resorts on Dominica tend to be small, family-run operations and not the sprawling multi-story concerns of international corporations. As a result, they do not have the vast groomed grounds found around the resorts on other islands. Yet, many are nicely landscaped and do make for genial meanders.

The Anchorage Hotel has cultivated more than 30 different flowers and ornamentals within the small confines of their property. **Floral Gardens** at Concord Village has a small tropical botanical garden to explore. It is perched just above the tumbling waters of the Pagua River. **Emerald Bush Hotel**, close to the Emerald Pool, offers several hours' worth of tropical hiking trails. **Castaways** is about the only hotel on the island situated on a black sand beach more than two feet wide.

➤➤ If not a registered guest, it is a courtesy to ask permission before beginning your walk upon any hotel or resort grounds.

Dominica

Martinique

The Amerindians originally called Martinique "Madinina," island of the flowers. Indeed it is. Except for the dry lands of the Ste.-Anne Peninsula, flowers are just about everywhere on the 425-square-mile island. You can hardly walk or look anywhere without seeing bromeliads, orchids, anthuriums, heliconias, bougainvillea, poinsettias, roses, hibiscus, and the impressive porcelain rose. The Parc Floral of Fort-de-France brings some of this color to the city, as do the flowered window boxes lining the streets. Near harvest time even the sugarcane fields in the Lamentin plains become oceans of breeze-rippled white plumes.

The rain forest covering the northern portion of the island adds its own variety of color. The green of gommier, chestnut, redwood, and magnolia leaves forms the roof of the forest. The mosses, vines, lichens, and epiphytes growing on the trunks and branches contribute their own contrasting hues.

As on Dominica, almost anything will grow on Martinique. Agricultural products add another dimension of color. Bananas, pineapples, mangoes, limes, and avocados are grown in abundance. In addition to the fruit, many fields are planted with tomatoes, pumpkins, and two other common Caribbean vegetables, christophine and the yam-like igname.

The variety on Martinique extends to its topography. You can visit this one island and experience almost every type of geographical and environmental feature in the Caribbean. All around its rugged coastline are tranquil, sandy beaches. A few are composed of black sand just to remind you of the volcanic origin of the islands. Montagne Pelée, highest point on Martinique, rises to almost 5,000 feet above sea level and is only dormant, not extinct. Hot springs and sulphur fumes are evidence that Pelée still lives.

Close to Fort-de-France are the near-vertical walls of the Pitons du Carbet. This mountain range, so rugged that it has been called the "Alps of the Caribbean," attains heights of over 3,700 feet and contains ridges so narrow that many are traversed on hands and knees. Dense jungle-like growth and hardwood forests cover the slopes.

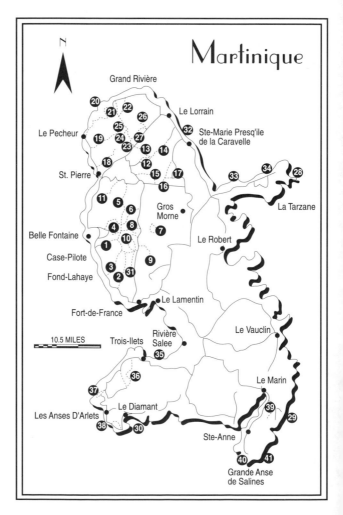

South of Fort-de-France are the central plains. What industry there is on Martinique is here. The dominant feature, however, is the miles of sugarcane plantations stretching across the gently rolling land.

The dry, open Savane des Pétrifications is on the southeastern tip of the island. A unique area, it contains a large salt pond, a variety of cacti, and scattered boulders of petrified wood and volcanic rock.

The Office of the National Forest does an excellent job of building and maintaining walking trails throughout Martinique. Ranging from leisurely strolls to challenging mountaineering climbs, the trails and walks go through the forests, up to volcanic craters, down into narrow gorges, along open savannahs, past hot springs, near mangrove thickets, and out to cliffs overlooking the crashing surf.

Martinique is, without a doubt, the most popular tourist destination in its part of the Caribbean. Most visitors come from France and the European continent, but increasing numbers of North Americans are discovering the island. It is a place where you can enjoy the comforts of a modern hotel, feast on Creole cooking and French pastries, purchase the latest Parisian fashions, and then escape, within minutes, to a deep, lush rain forest, a bubbling hot spring, or an isolated beach.

Walking on Martinique

◆ The Office of the National Forest has marked, blazed, and numbered 31 trails throughout the island. The first 31 walks described below correspond to those numbers. The numerical designations for the walks beyond Walk #31 are relevant to this guidebook only and will not correspond with any outside resources or information.

◆ Some of those walks pass through private property. Be sure to stay on the pathways and respect the rights of the landowners so that others may continue to use the trails.

◆ There are quite a few short, easy walks that are less than an hour's duration and are not listed separately in this guide. These include the Floral Park at Trois-Ilets, the Zoological Gardens near Carbet, Habitation Clement, the Botanical and Floral Trail near Ajoupa-Bouillon, a short pathway through the forest of the Montravail Picnic Area, the wonderful waterfall known as Cascade de Saut Gendarme near Fonds Saint-Denis, and the Balata Botanical Gardens. Also, many backroads in the countryside can be made into pleasant walks around cultivated fields and through small, peaceful villages.

Precautions:

◆ The peaks of Martinique are often in the clouds and are on open, exposed ridges. The temperature, wind, and weather are usually harsher than at lower elevations. Always be prepared for a wetter, cooler environment when going into the mountains.

◆ Although not aggressive, there is a poisonous snake that lives on Martinique. Bites from the fer-de-lance are rare, but you should keep in mind that the mountains and sparsely populated lands are its home. When walking into deep vegetation, or if walking alone, it is a good idea to tap the ground in front of you as you go. This will alert the snake that you are near; most bites are a result of the snake being taken by surprise.

History

Columbus first sighted Martinique in 1493, but he didn't go ashore until his fourth voyage to the New World in 1502. Some reports state the Carib Indians gave him a less than friendly welcome and he retreated to his ship amid a barrage of arrows.

Colonization began in 1635 with the arrival of the French. Most of the neighboring islands changed hands a number of times during the 17th and 18th centuries, but not Martinique. Only once, in 1762, did England gain possession. However, in exchange for the Canadian lands of North America, the British relinquished all claim to Martinique in 1763.

The 1763 treaty did not stop the British from occupying a small, steep rock island off the southern coast. For a year and a half, in 1804 and 1805, English guns kept the channel closed to maritime traffic. The rock was, in fact, even commissioned as an official vessel of the British navy, the *HMS Diamond Rock*.

The French imported large numbers of black slaves to labor in the sugarcane fields. France was, however, one of the first in the New World to grant freedom to the slaves, in 1848. Victor Schoelcher, immortalized with statues, librar-

Cascade de Saut Gendarme.

ies, roads, and towns on Martinique named after him, is credited with bringing about the emancipation.

St.-Pierre, on the northwestern Caribbean coast, was at one time the most important city on Martinique. Also the cultural center of the Caribbean, it was known as the "Little Paris of the West Indies."

On May 8, 1902, Montagne Pelée, which rises above the city, erupted. So much volcanic ash and lava came rushing down the side of the mountain that the 30,000 inhabitants of St.-Pierre perished in less than two minutes. The only person to survive was a prisoner locked in an underground cell. St.-Pierre never quite recovered; today it is a pleasant village, but only a shadow of its former self.

Martinique became an overseas department of France in 1946 and a region in 1974. As such, the population enjoys the same status as citizens on the French mainland. The population is now 360,000, mostly descendents of the slaves. Sugar is still an important agricultural product, as are rum, pineapples, and bananas. With every passing year tourism plays an increasing role in the economy.

Data

Transportation to Martinique: There are direct flights from Canada and Europe. The United States is linked to the island via the airport on Puerto Rico. There are also daily flights connecting Martinique with Guadeloupe, Dominica, and other surrounding islands.

Two ferry companies provide transportation between Martinique, Dominica, and Guadeloupe.

Fort-de-France is a popular stopover for cruise ships, most of which cater to Europeans.

Entry: While a valid passport and visa are required for stays longer than three weeks, a birth certificate or voter's registration card will suffice for shorter visits from U.S., Canadian, and EEC citizens.

Currency: The national currency is the French franc. American dollars are widely accepted, but you will receive change in francs; you get a better exchange rate at banks. You may, however, find an even more favorable rate at the international exchange offices located throughout the island.

As strange as it may seem, some places will give a substantial discount when payment is made with a credit card or travelers checks.

Tourist Information:

  ✍ **In the United States**
    French West Indies Tourist Board
    610 Fifth Ave.
    New York, NY 10020
    ☎ 212-757-1125

  ✍ **In Canada**
    French Government Tourist Office
    1981 McGill College Ave., Suite 490
    Montreal, Quebec H3A 2W9
    ☎ 514-288-4264

  ✍ **In Europe**
    French Government Tourist Office
    178 Piccadilly
    London W1V 0AL
    England , ☎ 0171-493-9232

On Martinique the office is located on the waterfront in Fort-de-France:

  ✍ Office de Tourism
    rue Ernest Deproge
    97200 Fort-de-France
    Martinique, French West Indies
    ☎ 596-63-79-60

Driving: Rental cars are available in a number of cities throughout the island. Camping vans, which can accommodate up to five people, are popular here and may be rented in Trois-Ilets. Mopeds can also be rented at many places. The roads are highly devel-

Martinique

oped and are some of the best in the Caribbean. There is a sufficient public transportation system, and virtually every village and town may be reached by bus. Contact the tourist office for specific routes and schedules.

Language: Definitely French. While major hotels usually have someone who speaks English, it is not extensively spoken or understood. Brush up on your French and your visit will be more pleasurable.

To confuse you even more, many locals also speak a lilting Creole that is unique to Martinique.

Walking and Hiking Guide Companies: The Parc Naturel office has organized hikes on a regular basis and is able to arrange specialized hikes with guides for groups or individuals:

✍ Parc Naturel Regional de la Martinique
Maison du Tourisme Vert
9 boulevard Général de Gaulle
97200 Fort-de-France
Martinique
French West Indies
☎ 596-73-19-30

There is also an active group of professional guides who are at least as knowledgeable about the trails, flora, fauna, and geography of the island as the staff of the Parc Naturel. This group can usually arrange for an English-speaking guide:

✍ BASALT
Fonds Capot
97222 Bellefontaine
Martinique
French West Indies
☎ 596-55-05-46

The tourism office can supply you with the names and addresses of other commercial guide companies.

Camping Areas: Camping is permitted in the backcountry of Martinique, but regulations change from place to place and season to season. The best advice is to contact the Parc Naturel (see address above) or the Office of the National Forest (route de Moutte, BP 578, 97207 Fort-de-France, Martinique, French West Indies) for current information.

Commercial campgrounds include Vivre et Camper in Ste.-Anne (☎ 596-76-95-52) and Nid Tropical at L'Anse a l'Ane (☎ 596-68-31-30). Privately-operated campgrounds come and go on Martinique, so it's best to contact the tourism office for up-to-date information.

Most of the designated non-commercial campsites are on beaches, become crowded on the weekends, and have few, if any, facilities. They are more geared toward camping vans, but tent camping is permitted. The advantage of these areas is that most are informal sites and no fees are charged.

The most popular spots are Anse Corps de Carde, Anse du Diamant, Grande Anse-d'Arlets, Anse Macabou, Cap Chevalier, Grande Anse des Salines, Grand'Rivière, and the Baie du Gallion near Tartane.

Recommended Readings

📖 *The French in the West Indies* by W. A. Roberts

📖 *His Majesty's Sloop of War Diamond Rock* by Vivian Stuart and G. Eggleston

📖 *31 Sentiers Balisés en Martinique*. An excellent guide to the trails and communities of Martinique published (in French) by the Office of the National Forest. Contains detailed descriptions and maps of the trails and topography.

Special Walk - A Tour of Fort-de-France

Being one of the larger islands, Martinique may be the most cosmopolitan in the Caribbean. This air of sophistication is most evident in the capital city, Fort-de-France, a growing city of over 100,000 people. Sidewalk cafés line the street along the inner city park, La Savane. The women walk about in chic outfits and the iron grillwork on the balconies is reminiscent of New Orleans. The narrow, crowded streets are now winding their way up the hillsides surrounding the Bay of Fort-de-France. This walking tour concentrates on the downtown area.

Begin the tour at the pier on the waterfront. (The ferry to Pointe du Bout leaves from here.) The Tourist Office Visitor's Center is also on the waterfront and is a good place to obtain detailed information about the island. Directly across Boulevard Alfassa is La Savane. Take the main walkway through the greenery of the park and you'll reach the impressive statue of Empress Josephine. Born on Martinique in 1763, she later became the wife of Napoleon.

Turn to your left and gaze upon the hard-to-miss Bibliothèque Schoelcher. This elaborate library, honoring the famous abolitionist Victor Schoelcher, was originally a pavilion in the 1889 International Exhibition in Paris. The building was disassembled, shipped to Martinique, and reassembled here. Continue on Rue de la Liberté for five short blocks to arrive at the Musée de la Martinique. The museum has excellent exhibits with artifacts and records of the Arawak and Carib Indians. Also included are displays from colonial life and depictions from the days of slavery.

After a visit to the museum, turn left onto rue Blénac for one block to the 17th-century iron St. Louis Cathedral. The cathedral has been destroyed several times, was last restored in 1895, and recently had the gilded bell tower added. Turn right onto rue Schoelcher for two blocks, make a left at the statue of Victor Schoelcher, pass the Palais de Justice and, in one block, bear left onto rue Isambert. In two blocks you'll arrive at the vegetable market-place. The yams, pumpkins, christophines, mangoes, tomatoes, avocados, and bananas make a colorful display. A myriad spices, often sold for homemade remedies, flavor the air. Continue for a couple of blocks to the banks of the Rivière Madame, turn right and walk to the fish market. Among other exotic choices, you could dine on shark or turtle to-night.

Across the street from the market is the Parc Floral. Wander through the tropical flowers, study the fishlife in the aquarium, get some refreshment from one of the vendors, rest, and enjoy the beauty of the park. The walking tour ends here.

Walks

1. The Verrier-Absalon Trail
Walking time: 3 to 4 hours, one way

This difficult trail, marked with blue and yellow blazes, may be reached by way of the Route de la Trace (N.3). About five miles north of Fort-de-France, turn left and follow the road all the way to the Station Thermale d'Absalon.

At the parking area, the trail begins with a steep climb through mahogany and gommier trees. In 25 to 30 minutes there is an intersection; the left fork descends to the Rivière Duclos. Continue straight on the Verrier-Absalon Trail, passing through the mahogany plantations of the Plateau Concorde and the Savane St.-Cyr. Twice the trail will come to junctions with the La Demarche-Plateau Concorde Trail (see Walks #2 and #3). Continue straight at both of these intersections. Up to this point the terrain has been relatively easy and on a gentle slope. After the Savane St.-Cyr, the ascent of Morne Châpeau Nègre begins. The pathway becomes much steeper and rougher in places as it leaves the forested hillsides and comes to the elfin woodland of the mountain top. Due to the harsher climate on the ridgeline, the trees are stunted and mosses and ferns flourish.

The summit of Morne Châpeau Nègre (3,000 feet) is often in clouds. However, when these do clear away, the view is magnificent. To the northwest is the Caribbean coast of Martinique, to the south are the Baie de Fort-de-France and the lush green, forested hills of Morne Rose and Morne Bois d'Inde. To the southeast are the vast cultivated plains in central Martinique, Lamentin. You may also be able to see the Atlantic coast and the Caravelle Peninsula lying far to the northeast.

> From this viewpoint you have the option to follow a trail across the ridgeline and over the crest of the Pitons du Carbet to the Route de la Trace and the village of Colson. This is an arduous journey that will take at least three hours from the summit. See Walks #6 and #8.

The Verrier-Absalon Trail descends Morne Châpeau Nègre to the west along the forested ridgeline. It becomes less steep and finally ends at the road near Verrier, one hour from the summit. The road in Verrier connects with the coastal highway (N.2) in Bellefontaine.

The ascent of Morne Châpeau Nègre is steep and long. While the footpath is not dangerous, the terrain does require quite a bit of physical exertion. This trail is recommended only for those in good shape.

2 & 3. The La Demarche - Plateau Concorde and Morne Rose - Savane Saint-Cyr Trails

Walking time: 3 hours, one way

These trails are both marked with yellow and white blazes. As a relatively easy excursion with far-reaching views, the beginning of this hike is reached by following the coastal highway (N.2) north of Fort-de-France to Fond-Lahaye, a traditional French-Caribbean fishing village. Just past Fond-Lahaye, take the road to the right all the way to la Demarche. The road ends and the trail begins.

As the trail rises gradually through fields of vegetables and spices, there are good views of Fort-de-France, Case-Pilote, and the Caribbean Sea. You might see (and will definitely hear) a diversity of birdlife as the trail moves beyond the cultivated savannah to enter the forest and begin the ascent of Morne Bois d'Inde. About an hour from the beginning of the hike you'll reach the Plateau de la Concorde and a mahogany tree plantation. Shortly afterward is a trail junction. The path to the right leads to d'Absalon and the Route de la Trace in a little over one hour (see Walk #1).

The route you want runs to the left and follows the Verrier-Absalon Trail for a short distance before coming to another junction in the Savane St.-Cyr. Continuing straight would lead to Morne Châpeau Nègre (see Walk #1). Turn left and begin a descent through an area of young pine and mahogany trees. The television station and road in Morne Rose will be reached in an hour. This road leads to Case-Pilote and the coastal highway (N.2).

➤ **Note:** The beginning of the trail is on private property, so be sure to stay on the path.

4. The Montjoly-Caplet Trail

Walking time: 5 to 6 hours, one way

An extremely difficult hike marked with yellow and white blazes, the Montjoly-Caplet Trail involves quite a number of climbs over rock faces, vertical mountainsides (while clinging to roots and vines), and descents through muddy, narrow ravines. The trail is reached by following the coastal highway (N.2) to Bellefontaine. In the village, turn right onto D.20, which parallels the Rivière Fond Capot up to the village of Morne-Vert. Just before reaching the village take the road to the right, marked Canton Suisse, and follow it for almost two miles to the small settlement known as Montjoly, described by some tourist brochures as "a very French-looking mountain village."

The trail ascends through vegetable gardens and open pastures. It soon enters a forest of white gommier and begins the climb to Morne Tranchette, which will be reached in 45 minutes. The climbing has just begun. The trail gains more than 1,400 feet of elevation through the forest to the summit of Piton Lacroix. The route is steep and you should allow almost two hours of climbing, clinging, and scrambling to reach the summit.

Your effort will prove worthwhile. The open summit has a 360° view and it is possible to see much of the 425 square miles of Martinique. To the southeast are the Lamentin plains, Montagne Du Vauclin, and the Savane de Pétrifications. Directly south is Fort-de-France, Trois-Ilets, Morne Larcher and even the neighboring island of St. Lucia. To the north and east lie the Atlantic Ocean, the Presqu'Ile de la Caravelle, and the jagged ridgeline of Morne Jacob. About the only place on Martinique that can't be seen from here is the extreme northern coastline. That view is blocked by towering, mist-covered Montagne Pelée.

Your route now makes use of Walks #6 and #8 as it heads northward on the open ridgeline with continuous views of cultivated and settled lands to the west and the rugged slopes of the Carbet Range to the east. In a half-hour, the two other routes you joined will split to the right. Continue to the left for another half-hour and arrive at the summit of Morne Piquet, just 100 feet lower than Piton Lacroix.

The trail now starts a precipitous descent along the ridgeline to Caplet. At some points the ridgeline is less than a foot wide! At other times the trail makes use of near-vertical, muddy ravines, which are always slippery and treacherous even in dry weather. After an hour of this kind of descending, the trail comes to an intersection. A right turn leads to Fond-St.-Denis (see Walk #5). Continue straight along the pathway on a much gentler slope. An hour of walking through open fields leads to the Caplet settlement near the village of Morne-Vert. A paved road leads from Caplet to Morne-Vert and Route D.20, which, in turn, descends to the main coastal highway, N.2.

With the ascent of Morne Châpeau Nègre and the descent of Morne Piquet, this is possibly the most difficult hike on Martinique. Start early in the day and do not underestimate the difficulty of this trail. A guide might be a wise idea.

5. Caplet - Fond Saint-Denis Trail

Walking time: 3 hours, one way

This moderate and enjoyable hike through woodlands and fields is marked with white and red blazes. It may be reached by following the coastal highway (N.2) to Bellefontaine. A short distance past Bellefontaine turn right on D.19 to Morne-Vert. Turn right at the church, cross the river, and then make a left. The trail begins behind the last house in the valley.

Leaving the inhabited area, the trail rises gradually through cultivated fields, with views of the valley dropping farther and farther below. In less than an hour the mahogany forest is reached, and shortly thereafter the pathway leads to a waterfall surrounded by verdant tropical vegetation.

The trail now makes a short, steep climb through the forest to arrive at an open ridgeline giving good views of the area. Along this ridge the trail enters a Caribbean pine forest and then descends to cross a small river.

Climb for just a few minutes from the river and reach another ridgeline. Follow the trail alternately through open savannahs and woodlands. In one hour from the river crossing, descend, somewhat steeply, to the farmlands along the Rivière du Carbet. Cross the river on a bridge and ascend to the highway (D.1) in Fond St.-Denis.

This is a moderate hike requiring only light physical exertion, and is recommended for its views and stroll through the forests.

6 & 8. The Plateau Boucher - Morne Piquet and Des Pitons Trails

Walking time: 6 to 7 hours, one way

One of the most difficult hikes on Martinique, this trek also offers some of the most magnificent vistas on the island. It is marked with blue and white blazes and then yellow and white circle markings. Following the crestline of the Pitons du Carbet Range, the trail has a number of steep, slippery ascents and descents. At one point, it traverses a knife-edge ridge less than a foot wide! However, those adventurous enough to hike this crest trail will be amply rewarded. Also, birdwatchers often hike the Plateau Boucher-Morne Piquet route in search of the blue-headed hummingbird.

The hike starts at Plateau Boucher on the Route de la Trace (N.3), about an hour's drive north of Fort-de-France. It begins an immediate steep ascent through thick tropical rain forest; in less than an hour it climbs almost 1,400 feet. As it gains elevation the rain forest begins to fade away and is replaced by the shorter growth of elfin woodland. Growing among the twisted and stunted trees are a variety of mosses, ferns, orchids, and even mountain pineapple.

As you near the summit of Piton Boucher (3,300 feet), take in the views to the north. At the top, it is possible to look down onto the Route de la Trace, over to Morne Jacob and up to the cloud-covered volcanic cone of Montagne Pelée. The summit of Piton Lacroix is to the south, over 400 feet higher than Piton Boucher.

The magnificient Pitons du Carbet.

The trail now levels out somewhat with a slight descent and then a gradual ascent along the ridge that connects Piton Boucher to the main crestline of the Pitons du Carbet. It takes about an hour to reach the crestline of Morne Piquet. (A right turn here heads to the summit of Morne Piquet and beyond; see Walk #4.) New views of Le Morne-Vert and the Caribbean coastline emerge once the crestline is reached.

Turn left and begin the long, gradual ascent to the summit of Piton Lacroix, gaining less than 300 feet in an hour. At 3,725 feet, Piton Lacroix is the highest point of the Carbet Range. Much of Martinique now lies below you. The forests of Savane St.-Cyr reach almost all of the way down to the city of Fort-de-France. Beyond the Baie de Fort-de-France is the southern coast of Martinique and Diamond Rock. Off in the haze of the horizon – across the sparkling waters of the Canal de St. Lucia – lies the island of St. Lucia, over 30 miles from where you now stand. To the east are the sugarcane fields of Lamentin and the white surf of the ocean crashing onto the rugged Atlantic coastline.

Turn left from the summit and continue on your way. (Straight ahead leads to Morne Châpeau Nègre; see Walk #1. Following the trail to the right leads to Montjolly; see Walk #4.) Follow the open ridgeline with unlimited views. Along this portion of the trail is the extremely narrow knife-edge ridge. Exercise caution here, especially in wet weather. In an hour you'll reach a major trail intersection where you now encounter routes marked by the yellow and white circles.

At this point a decision must be made. To the right lies a short, steep ascent to Piton Dumauzé, which is just 40 feet lower than Piton Lacroix. From this summit the trail leaves the open heights and makes a long, steep descent back to the woodlands, across the Rivière Dumauzé and finally out onto the savannah at the Colson Hospital.

If you decide to take the left turn at the intersection you'll encounter a sharp ascent that just misses the summit of Piton de L'Alma and then requires the use of ropes as it drops dangerously down the face of a 50-foot cliff. After the cliff, this trail follows a long ridge down into the forest and back to the Route de la Trace in the village of Colson. Either trail will require about two hours of hiking from the major trail intersection.

> ⚡ *Do not underestimate the difficulty of this hike. If you are in good physical condition, start early in the day and enjoy the wonders of hiking along the open ridgelines for four or five hours. A guide might be a good idea.*

7. The Rabuchon Circuit Trail

Walking time: 3 hours for the complete circuit

This trail, marked with yellow and white circles, provides several nice vistas. It is an easy hike through central Martinique's rain forest. The trailhead is reached by driving north from Fort-de-France on the Route de la Trace (N.3) for about one hour to make a turn onto the Forêt de Rivière Blanche road. (If you come to Plateau de Boucher and the trailhead sign for Walk #6 while still on the Route de la Trace, you've gone just a bit too far and need to turn back.) Follow the forest road for three miles to the Coeur Bouliki picnic area and the trailhead.

The hike begins by crossing the Rivière Blanche to enter a forest of mahogany trees. Soon, you'll cross over the smaller Rivière Mahots before ascending for about 45 minutes to reach a ridgeline. It offers a pleasant view of the river winding its way through the valley.

The route then passes by a trail coming in from the right, which goes to the Route de la Trace near the village of Colson. Keep left in a more southerly direction for another hour of rain forest walking to reach a viewpoint overlooking Fort-de-France and the lower slopes of Morne Cesaire.

The Rabuchon Circuit Trail then returns to Coeur Bouliki, one of the first designated picnic areas to be developed on Martinique. The small pools in the river are good swimming spots.

You will remain close to rivers throughout most of this excursion. Think twice before embarking upon this hike if there has been heavy rainfall within the last few days.

9. The Morne Cesaire Trail
Walking time: 2 hours, round trip

This moderate hike, marked with yellow and white blazes, is reached by taking the Route de la Trace (N.3) north of Fort-de-France. A short distance past the National Forest office's picnic area and arboretum, you need to make a hard right onto the Forêt de Fond L'Etang road. After a couple of sharp switchbacks you'll arrive at the beginning of the trail.

Within 30 minutes of climbing you'll reach a cultivated field planted in fruits, vegetables, and anthuriums. The excellent view to the north is of the Pitons du Carbet. The trail now enters an old mahogany plantation and in another half-hour ends at the summit of Morne Cesaire. From here is an impressive view of Fort-de-France, the jagged coastline of the bay, and Trois-Ilets lying to the south across the bay.

10. Circuit D'Absalon Trail
Walking time: 2½ hours for the complete circuit

This easy, enjoyable hike, marked with blue and white circles, is a circuit trail beginning at the same point as the Verrier-Absalon Trail. (See the first paragraph in Walk #1 for access information.)

After an initial short, steep ascent, the hike bears to the right (the Verrier-Absalon Trail takes off to the left). For 50 minutes it follows a gently wooded ridgeline that parallels a branch of the Rivière Duclos. There are occasional limited views along the way. The trail descends the ridge, fords two small water runs, and comes to another junction. The path to the left leads to the Colson Hospital in about an hour. The circuit trail you are following continues down to the right and arrives back at the paved road within 50 feet of the parking area.

After the initial ascent, this is an easy hike through dense forest.

11. The Canal de Beauregard Trail

Walking time: 1 hour, one way

The Canal de Beauregard, marked with yellow and white blazes, was built in the late 18th century to bring water to distilleries in the Rivière du Carbet Valley. It is still used today as an irrigation channel and may be reached by taking the Route de la Trace (N.3) for a little over an hour north from Fort-De-France. Turn left on D.1 and continue to Fond-St.-Denis. Just after entering the Fond Mascret village take the road to the left and descend to the canal.

This is a moderate hike that uses the narrow pathway along the hillside above the canal. Although the walking is easy, it may intimidate some people since it does, at times, become very narrow, with the waters of the canal directly below.

The route passes through fields of vegetables, flowers, and fruit trees. Along the way are views of the Rivière du Carbet valley and the towering Pitons du Carbet. Entering a forest of kapok and gommier trees, the trail ends at an irrigation station where a small road will eventually lead down to the main coastal highway (N.2) near Le Carbet.

12. The Circuit de Ste.-Cécile Trail

Walking time: 4 hours to complete the circuit

This difficult ascent of Morne Jacob begins in the community of Ste.-Cécile and is marked with blue and white circles. Follow the Route de la Trace (N.3) from Fort-de-France and, a short distance before

Morne Rouge, turn right onto the signed road leading to a pineapple factory and Ste.-Cécile. This will
be a little over an hour from Fort-de-France. The beginning of the trail is marked.

Along a heavily forested ridgeline, the trail reaches
the base of Morne Jacob in an hour. A most strenuous and dangerous ascent of another hour leads to
the summit. At one point, a sheer rock cliff must be
negotiated. The view from the summit is of Petit Jacob, Le Lorrain, the Atlantic, Presqu'Ile de la
Caravelle, Morne Rouge, and the Pitons du Carbet.
The path to the right is the Carabin-Morne Jacob
Trail, which leads to the Carabin settlement (see
Walk #14). Continue straight across the summit on
the Circuit Trail. Follow the ridge in open savannah
land and, in 45 minutes, you'll reach a junction.
Turn left, downhill. (The trail to the right is an extremely steep, narrow, dangerous, and seldom used
route ascending to Morne la Piguonne – see Walk
#13.) Follow the Circuit Trail as it winds its way
down through the forest. In an additional 45 minutes it arrives in Ste.-Cécile, just a short distance
from where you began your ascent.

This is a strenuous hike that involves much climbing and good mountaineering skills. A guide is
highly recommended.

13. The Crête du Cournan Trail

Walking time: 3 hours, one way

This hike, marked with blue and yellow blazes, provides a few views of the surrounding agricultural
countryside. It is a strenuous hike as it follows
ridgelines under a heavy forest canopy. Driving the
Route de la Trace (N.3) north from Fort-de-France,
pass through the town of Morne-Rouge and watch
for the right turn onto D.12., 0.2 mile after crossing
the Rivière Capot. The trailhead sign is on the left.

Although it begins by passing through agricultural
lands, such as banana plantations, the pathway is

obviously headed toward the tropical forest. Fording a few streams, you'll begin the ascent and eventually reach the heights of the Crête d'Or, only to rise further in elevation to the Crête du Cournan and the summit of Morne la Piquonne. Beyond the peak, this pathway comes to an end as it meets up with the Circuit de Ste.-Cécile Trail (see Walk #12). A moderately strenuous hike.

14. The Carabin-Morne Jacob Trail

Walking time: 5½ hours, round trip

This trail is marked with yellow and white blazes. It goes to the summit of one of the oldest volcanoes on the island and is reached by following the Route de la Trace (N.3) through Morne-Rouge and continuing north to N.1. Turn east (right) onto N.1. Just past the town of Le Lorrain, turn right onto D.22 and follow it to the small settlement of Carabin. The beginning of the Morne Jacob Trail is marked.

The trail starts with an immediate long and steady climb. Follow the ridgeline through a forest laden with bromeliads and orchids, pass by the summit of Morne Quatre-Vingts and then begin the steeper ascent to the summit of Petit Jacob. One hour into the hike, you'll have a superior view of the Atlantic coast stretching all the way from the Lorrain Valley to the easternmost tip of the Caravelle Peninsula. The soaring peak of Morne Jacob looms directly ahead.

Drop slightly from the summit and begin the ascent of another peak. The trail will repeat this pattern three more times before reaching Morne Jacob's summit. The pathway gives occasional views through the moss- and lichen-covered stunted growth of the windswept ridgeline. The final climb to Morne Jacob is the steepest. In addition to the waves rushing onto the Atlantic coast, it is now possible to view Morne-Rouge, Montagne Pelée and, to the south, the Pitons du Carbet. (If you wish, continue beyond Morne Jacob's summit for a short distance to

Martinique

intersect the Circuit de Ste.-Cécile Trail – see Walk #12).

The easiest of the ascents to Morne Jacob, this hike should not be considered an easy one. Its length and the number of ascents and descents make it a moderately strenuous outing.

15. Des Jésuites Trail

Walking time: 2 hours, 45 minutes, one way

Des Jésuites Trail is exceedingly popular with both locals and tourists. It begins on the Route de la Trace (N.3) a half-mile north of the Deux-Choux Tunnel. There is ample parking space and the trail is marked.

Before the descent into the river valley there are good views of Montagne Pelée, Morne-Rouge, and the forest lands lining the Route de la Trace. In an hour, the pathway fords the Rivière du Lorrain. It is not a difficult crossing, but you will get your feet wet. The river valley is a popular outing and picnic destination. A gradual ascent of another hour brings the trail to an end at D.1, about two miles east of the Route de la Trace.

This is a popular hike for a very good reason. There is possibly no other place on Martinique where you can so easily pass through the colorful and lush rain forest. The birdlife and wildlife is abundant, as is the great variety of vegetation. The whole length of the trail is lined with magnolias, gommiers, chestnuts, orchids, bromeliads, bougainvillea, bamboo, and palms.

For those in search of an easy stroll through a tropical rain forest, this hike is strongly recommended.

16. The Morne Bellevue-Reculée Trail

Walking time: 3½ hours, one way

About one hour north of Fort-de-France, turn right from the Route de la Trace (N.3) onto D.1 and head toward Gros-Morne. Approximately four miles from this intersection, look for a steep, unmarked road going off to the left. The trail, marked with yellow and white blazes, begins on the right side of this road a few yards from highway D.1.

Leaving the road, the trail climbs almost to the peak of Morne Bellevue and then makes a quick descent to the summit of Morne de l'Etang, 45 minutes after starting the hike. The blue and white blazed Pérou-Morne de l'Etang Trail heads off to the right (see Walk #17), but the Morne Bellevue-Reculée Trail bears left to make a number of short ascents and descents as it follows along the uneven ridgeline.

In 2.5 hours, the forest opens up and there are good views of the villages of Ste.-Marie and Trinité. Further to the east is Presqu'Ile de la Caravelle pushing its way out into the Atlantic Ocean. For 45 additional minutes the trail drops gradually along the ridge and ends at a forest road. This leads to the main highway, D.15, near Reculée.

This is a moderate hike, although the numerous short ascents and descents may become tiresome.

17. Pérou-Morne de l'Etang Trail

*Walking time: 30 minutes, one way
(to the intersection with the Morne
Bellevue-Reculée Trail)*

The beginning of this short, moderate walk is most easily reached by following D.24 out of Sainte-Marie. When you come to D.15, cross it by bearing slightly to the right and continuing uphill on the secondary road. There will be a couple of intersections, but each has a sign pointing you to the marked trailhead, which appears suddenly in a cultivated field on the left. The trail is marked with blue and white blazes.

Ascending gradually into a mahogany forest, there is a view back onto Sainte-Marie and farther out to Presqu'Ile de la Caravelle. Arriving at Morne de l'Etang, the route comes to an end as it intersects the Morne Bellevue-Reculée Trail (see Walk #16). A moderate walk through pleasant woods.

18. The Sources Chaudes Trail

Walking time: 5½ hours, round trip

Translated, Sources Chaudes means hot springs, and this trail leads to the famous sulphur springs of Martinique. The trail, marked with yellow and white blazes, begins on the coastal highway (D.10) about 1.5 miles north of St.-Pierre. A sign marks the trail at a gate and gravel road leading off to the right of the main highway.

➤ **Important Notice!** The armed forces of Martinique use this gated, gravel road for military maneuvers and firing practice. The road and the trail are closed to the public on Tuesdays, Wednesdays, and Fridays!

Follow the gravel road as it gently rises through open, dry savannah lands up to the western slopes of Montagne Pelée. The eastern slopes of the volcano capture most of the moisture of the trade winds as they sweep across Martinique, leaving very little water for the vegetation on this side of the mountain.

Gaining elevation, the road fades into a pathway as savannah vegetation gives way to ferns and some greenery. After 1.5 hours, the Rivière Chaude is reached. Walk upstream and in 15 more minutes you'll enter a narrow gorge. The walls of the canyon begin to close in, making it necessary to actually walk in the river. The sulphur content and heat of the water have transformed the gorge into a primeval area of multi-hued rocks and emerald algae. Use caution as you reach the source of the river. The rock debris in the canyon is unstable and could make for a steep and dangerous slide if you are not careful.

A moderate hike, the trail becomes slightly difficult near the end as it reaches the narrow confines of the gorge. It is, however, a recommended excursion due to the unique nature of the gorge.

19. The Montagne Pelée Par Grande Savane Trail

Walking time: 2 hours, one way, to the intersection with Walks #24 and #25

Marked with yellow and white blazes, this is the easiest ascent to the summit of Montagne Pelée. The trail begins at the end of the Grande Savane, just south of Le Precheur. (See Walk #20 for directions to this point.) Walk the jeep road along the gentle slope of the Grande Savane, passing through vegetable fields and fruit trees. In 45 minutes the road fades away and views of the northern coast appear. Fifteen more minutes and you'll have views down into the deep gorges.

As you continue a fairly gradual ascent, the lower altitude vegetation disappears, and there are now good views of the Caribbean coastline and the village of St.-Pierre. The elfin woodland of the higher elevation begins, as does the final ascent to the volcanic rim of Montagne Pelée. After 30 minutes of fairly steep climbing, the crater rim is reached. The trail you have been following technically comes to an end here, but it is possible to walk around the crater rim and up to Montagne Pelée's highest point by following the descriptions for Walks #24 and #25.

This is the easiest ascent of Montagne Pelée.

20. The Precheur - Grand'Rivière Hike

Walking time: 6 hours, one way (not including the optional two-hour side trip to the Rivière Trois Bras waterfalls)

Following what is actually an old road along the northwestern coast, this long hike is reached by taking the coastal highway (N.2) north from Fort-de-France to St.-Pierre. Pass through the village and continue along the coast on D.10 all the way to Le Precheur. Continue north and begin the hike at the parking area near Anse Couleuvre.

Follow the old roadbed north from the parking lot. There are, in some places, the remains of the asphalt and concrete that used to pave the road. The path passes many reminders that the area was once cultivated and inhabited. Mango, coffee, and cocoa plantations used to thrive here and many of these trees still line the old road.

A number of small beaches are accessible from the southern section of this hike. The isolated shorelines of Anse-à-Voile and Anse des Galets are worth the side trips. Soon after passing through an old road tunnel, be on the lookout for the marked side trial to the right, which ascends along the Rivière Trois Bras. If you have the time and are in good physical shape, this two-hour (round trip) hike to some stunning falls is highly recommended.

The main trail continues northward past the ruins of an old sugar factory and rum distillery. It eventually passes through an area of virgin forest and vegetation before arriving at a present day banana plantation and, shortly thereafter, Grand'Rivière. The paved road (D.10) leads from Grand'Rivière to Basse-Pointe and highway N.1. From here it is possible to return to Fort-de-France by the Route de la Trace (N.3).

This is a moderate hike. The only difficulty is its length. There are few ups and downs, and they are short and not very steep. If you have the time, take this hike. Nowhere else on Martinique is it possible to walk so easily for such a length of time without passing through inhabited areas. Along the way, the trail goes by beaches, old plantations, savannahs, and one of the few primary rain forests remaining in the Caribbean. Do take note, though, that the river crossings encountered on this trip will be quite difficult if there has been heavy rain. Also, because of the length, be sure to start this excursion early in the day.

21. The Montagne Pelée Par Grand'Rivière Trail

Walking time: 4½ hours, one way, to the intersection with Walks #24 and #25

This long, but moderate ascent of Montagne Pelée is accessed by following N.3 north out of Fort-de-France for approximately two hours to its intersection with N.1 near the northeastern coastline. Bear left on N.1 to its end in Macouba. From this village, follow D.10 for almost five miles to the marked trailhead on the left side of the road. The trail is marked with white and red blazes.

Rising along agricultural lands, the route parallels the Rivière Potiche to its headwaters in the Savane Jalouise. The ascent soon meets up with the Savane Anatole Par Désiles Trail (see Walk #22) coming in from the left. Bear left and enter a mahogany forest, whose trees diminish in size as you gain elevation and approach the main ridgeline of Morne Macouba. Don't be surprised or disappointed if you have no views from these heights because you will probably now be walking through continual mist and rain to reach a hiker's shelter at the crater rim. Although the trail you have been following technically comes to an end here, it is possible to walk around the rim and up to Montagne Pelée's highest point by following the descriptions for Walks #24 and #25.

22. The Savane Anatole Par Désiles Trail

*Walking time: 2½ hours, one way, to the intersection
with the Montagne Pelée Par Grand'Rivière Trail*

To reach the beginning of this hike, which is an additional access route to Montagne Pelée, follow the directions to Macouba described in the first paragraph of Walk #21. A half-mile beyond Macouba you'll see the marked trailhead area on the left side of the road. The trail is marked with yellow and white blazes.

Ascending a ridgeline between Rivière Legarde and Rivière de Macouba, the route crosses through the Ravine Lacou and continues through cultivated lands to its terminus, where it meets the Montagne Pelée Par Grand'Rivière Trail (see Walk #21) in the Savane Anatole.

An easy route taking you half-way up to the summit of Montagne Pelée.

23. The Montagne Pelée Par l'Aileron Trail

*Walking time: 2 hours, one way, to the intersection
with Walks #24 and #25*

To reach the shortest, but steepest ascent of Montagne Pelée, follow the Route de la Trace (N.3) north from Fort-de-France and continue through the village of Morne-Rouge. Make a left onto the road marked for l'Aileron. Continue driving all the way to the television relay station where, even before you take a step upwards, you can enjoy a pleasant view. Directly below is the deep and narrow cleft of a gorge carved out by the Rivière Falaise, while farther east is Martinique's coastline near Sainte-Marie. The trail is marked with white and red blazes.

Almost immediately the steepness of the hike begins. At times the trail makes use of the slippery ravines stretching up the mountainside. At other points it is necessary to climb and scramble up and over large boulders. In 45 minutes a plateau is reached, l'Aileron. The view from here is superb. Not only can you see both the Caribbean and Atlantic coasts, but to the south (on clear days) are St. Lucia and even St. Vincent.

The trail now follows the ridgeline on a somewhat gentler slope along the Plateau des Palmistes and, in another 45 minutes, makes a short and steeper ascent up to the rim and a hiker's shelter. On the Office of the National Forest's map and brochures, the trail officially comes to an end here, but you may easily explore the heights of Montagne Pelée by following the route descriptions in Walks #24 and #25.

This is a strenuous hike and the physical stamina needed to complete it should not be underestimated.

24. Le Circuit de la Calderia Trail

Walking time: 2½ hours, complete circuit

Having reached the crater rim of Montagne Pelée (see Walks #19, #21, or #23), you may now circumnavigate the crater by following Le Circuit de la Calderia Trail. It continues along the rim, passing through an area of mountain pineapple, mosses, ferns and, interestingly, raspberries. It is possible to peer into the crater at the stunted growth of the forest and the lava formations left from Pelée's last eruption in 1902. Caution must be used while on this route, which is marked with green and white circle markings. The quickly growing vegetation often covers the trail, hiding pitfalls and other dangers right on the pathway. Be on the lookout for these!

As you round the crater, you have the option of taking a 30-minute sidetrip to the 4,580-foot summit of Montagne Pelée (see Walk #25).

25. La Chinos (the Summit of Montagne Pelée) Trail

Walking time: 1 hour, round trip

Having arrived at the crater rim via Walks #19, #21 or #23 and walking along the Circuit de la Calderia Trail (Walk #24), watch for La Chinos Trail, which ascends southward to attain the mountain's summit of 4,580 feet above sea level. It is marked with green and white blazes. You'll be at the summit in 30 minutes, passing by fissures and lava formations along the way. On a clear day, which is rare, all of the island and much of the Caribbean can be seen stretching out below you. To the east is Morne Jacob, the Presqu'Ile de la Caravelle and the Atlantic; to the west is Le Precheur and the Caribbean coastline; to the south lie the Pitons du Carbet, the Baie de Fort-de-France, and St. Lucia. Across the shimmering water of the channel to the north, are the emerald green, mist-encased peaks of Dominica.

26. The Gorges de la Falaise Trail

Walking (and swimming) time: about 3 hours, round trip

A narrow river canyon punctuated by crashing waterfalls and verdant tropical greenery, the Gorges de la Falaise is located off N.3 on a secondary road about five miles north of Morne-Rouge. Both the secondary road and the trail are marked with signs identifying the Gorges de la Falaise. The trail itself has yellow and white blazes.

The beginning of the trail passes through private property. Sadly, and against the wishes of the National Forest Office, the landowner has recently been collecting a fee from hikers to walk here. Yet, the cost is small enough and the splendors of the gorge exciting enough that this is only a minor annoyance. (There is no need, however, to be talked into purchasing the special "river walking" sandals from the information booth.) Please note that a landslide in 1994 caused enough concern for the National Forest Office to remove this hike from its official inventory. However, the local guides have constructed a re-route and still take people on this hike.

The trail takes off along the edge of a cultivated field and soon begins the descent to the Rivière Falaise. The drop is made easier by the use of switchbacks. The river is reached in 10 minutes. Turn left and follow the path upstream; in less than five minutes you'll come to the gorge. The walk now becomes a wade through the river. Although there is something of a path on the narrow banks, it is much easier and safer to walk along the river bed. As you go upstream, the gorge narrows to only five or six feet wide. At this point it is necessary to swim a short distance around a bend to reach the beautiful 40-foot waterfall. Sit in the water and enjoy the whirlpool effect of the cascading waters. Sunlight, filtered through the tropical growth, dances in the shimmering stream and along the vertical rock walls that tower above you.

When this was listed by the National Forest Office, it was a highly recommended journey; the actual hike still is, but you will need to make your own decision about the private landowner's fee, the re-route around the landslide, and the attitudes of the local guides. Except for the little bit of swimming, this excursion requires a minimum amount of physical exertion. For obvious reasons, swimming in the gorge during periods of high water should be avoided.

27. L'Aileron de la Pelée par Trianon Trail
Walking time: 1½ hours, one way

Marked with blue and white blazes, this route connects the elevated slopes of Montagne Pelée with the depths of the Gorges des Falaise. This easy hike may be reached from the parking area for the Montagne Pelée par L'Aileron Trail (see Walk #23 for driving directions).

Martinique

From the television relay station parking lot, walk downhill for a few yards to begin the marked pathway on the left side of the road. With wonderful vistas of the Falaise Valley, Basse-Pointe, and the northeastern coastline, the pathway gradually drops into an area of cultivated fruits and vegetables. Within 45 minutes, the route becomes a small rural road lined by fields of christophine plants. Another 45 minutes of walking on the pleasantly sloping land brings you to the end of this hike and the beginning of the Gorges de la Falaise Trail (see Walk #26). An easy hike.

28. La Pointe de la Caravelle Trails

Walking time: this is such an enjoyable, easy, and fascinating hike that you should allow at least 3 hours to fully explore

To reach the easternmost point of Presqu'Ile de la Caravelle, follow N.1 east out of Fort-de-France. Shortly after Le Lamentin, keep left and follow N.1 through Le Robert. Just before reaching Trinité, turn right on CD.2, pass through Tartane, and continue all the way to the parking area for the Chateau Dubuc. The trail is marked with yellow blazes and red blazes.

This once thriving 17th-century plantation is now in ruins, but much of the original structures remain in the area that is administered by the Parc Naturel. The ruins, the beautiful view out to the Atlantic, and a museum make this an area worth exploring. Wander around the grounds for a while and locate the marked trail leading to the Baie du Tresor. The bay is fringed by a mangrove forest which is really the only easily accessible mangrove thicket on the island. The dense grove is characterized by massive roots that extend above ground to support the trees in the moist, sandy soil.

Once on the shore, enjoy the antics of seabirds and the occasional blue heron. Be on the lookout for crabs and, perhaps, a few oysters in the shallow waters. Continue along the shore, crossing a number of small bays and points. Eventually you will reach the lighthouse, built in 1861, on the easternmost point of the peninsula. Turn uphill, following the marked trail back to the Chateau Dubuc. Along the way are views of the Pitons du Carbet and Montagne Pelée and, to the south, the rugged Atlantic coast all the way to Montagne du Vauclin in the southern plains.

29. La Trace des Caps Trail

Walking time: 8 to 9 hours, one way

On official National Forest Office brochures, La Trace des Caps Trail also includes the Grande Anse des Salines Beach and the Savane de Pétrifications areas, but they are, in themselves, such good walking areas that they have been described separately below (see Walks #40 and #41). This trail is marked with blue and white blazes.

The hike begins in the picnic area at the northeastern end of the Savane de Pétrifications. Easiest access is at the marked trailhead on highway N.6 about half-way between Le Vauclin and Le Marin. This southeastern Atlantic coast of Martinique is sparsely populated.

It is possible to walk from this point, near Macabou and Cul-de-Sac du Paquemar, all of the way south to the Baie des Anglais. Along the way there are roads coming close to the shoreline so your walk may be as long or as short as you wish. You'll pass beaches, cliffs, mangrove thickets, sea grapes, palm trees, manchineel, gommier, and the isolated house or two. It would take eight to nine hours to hike all the way from Cul-de-Sac du Paquemar to Baie des Anglais. With the roads coming so close to this hike, it can be split up into several days worth of enjoyable hiking. Remember that there is very little shade along this whole hike.

An easy hike, only made a little difficult because of its length and isolation.

30. The Morne Larcher Trail

Walking time: 2 hours on the trail from
Grande Anse-du-Diamant to Petite Anse

Take N.1 east from Fort-de-France, turn right at Le
Lamentin toward Duclos and Rivière Salée. Follow
D.7 south from Rivière Salée. After passing Méde-
cin, turn west and you'll arrive at the village of Le
Diamant and its accompanying beach. The trail is
marked with yellow and white blazes.

This coconut palm-lined stretch of seashore is a
popular swimming and camping spot. It has a view
across the sparkling water of the canal to the mountains of St. Lucia rising from the sea on the horizon.
The surf is a little rough here, but there is nothing
to prevent a long enjoyable stroll on this stretch of
golden sand.

At the far west end of the beach is a trail to the summit of Morne Larcher. The trail goes up gently
through a hardwood forest and, in an hour, the
clearing of the peak is reached. Here, there are even
better views of Diamond Rock and St. Lucia. To the
east is the southern Caribbean coast of Martinique
and the Ste.-Anne Peninsula.

The trail continues across the mountain and descends through the orchids and vine- and epiphyte-
covered gommier trees of a rain forest. The vegetation becomes less lush as you go down and, in an
hour from the summit, the beach and road (D.37) at
Petite Anse are reached. It is possible to drive this
road back to Le Diamant. A moderate hike.

31. The Fontaine Didier - Absalon Trail

Walking time: 1½ hours, one way

Bathing in the water pouring from the Didier
Spring has been an antidote for numerous ailments
throughout the centuries. In the beginning of the
20th century its naturally sparkling water – rich in
magnesium, calcium, potassium, and sodium – was

bottled for commercial sale. This easy hike follows the water's course as it travels northward along the Rivière Dumauzé. It is marked with blue and white blazes.

The trailhead is reached by taking D.45 northward (you may have to ask directions locally for this road) from Fort-de-France to its end at the Fontaine Didier. Following the watercourse through ravines and along heavily forested slopes, the trail comes to an end at the Station Thermale d'Absalon (see walk #1 for directions to this point).

32. The Pointe Tenos Walks

There are two short trails leading to viewpoints in this picnic area maintained by the National Forest Office. One leads to a view of Pain de Sucre, Anse Charpentier, and Marigot. The second is a shaded trail through pine and mahogany trees to a cliffside overlook of the Atlantic churning onto the shoreline below. Both are very easy walks. The Pointe Tenos Picnic Area is marked by a sign on N.1 just a short distance north of Ste.-Marie.

33. The Pointe Rouge Walk
Walking time: 40 minutes, round trip

Another picnic area maintained by the National Forest Office, this one has a short pathway which descends from highway D.2 on the Presqu'Ile de la Caravelle (see Walk #28 for directions). It goes through a pleasant wood and offers a good view of the peninsula from the point.

 Be forewarned that there has been repeated vandalism to cars parked in this picnic area.

34. The Anse l'Etang Walk

Walking time: 50 minutes, round trip

As you are driving highway D.2 toward the beginning of La Pointe de la Caravelle Trail (see Walk #28 for directions), turn left onto the road marked for the Anse l'Etang. The beach, which has a couple of small resorts, is pretty enough, but the most scenic walk is at the western end of the sand. Rising through lush grasslands, the trail will lead you past a couple of old ruins to a rewarding view from the Pointe de l'Anse l'Etang. A moderate walk.

35. The Pointe la Vatable Walks

This is another picnic area maintained by the National Forest Office. It is within easy reach of Fort-de-France and is a pleasant spot to escape the hustle and bustle of the city. Take N.1 east from Fort-de-France, turn right at La Lamentin toward Duclos and Rivière Salée. Just after Rivière Salée, take the exit onto D.7 and, just before Trois-Ilets, there is a sign identifying the Pointe la Vatable Picnic area. (An alternative would be to take the ferry from Fort-de-France. Pointe la Vatable is about two miles east of the ferry landing at Pointe du Bout.) The picnic area contains several short, easy, interconnecting trails that pass through mahogany and pine trees. The paths lead down to a number of spots on the waterfront with views across the sailboat-crowded Baie de Fort-de-France and to the mist-covered Pitons du Carbet rising high above the city.

This spot is a good place to enjoy an easy afternoon of walking in the shade to escape the tropical sun and the tourists at Pointe du Bout.

 There has been repeated vandalism to cars here.

36. The Pagerie-Anses d'Arlets-Galocha Trail

Walking time: 2½ hours, one way

Just past Trois-Ilets, turn left onto D.38 toward La Pagerie. (See Walk #35 for directions to Trois-Ilets.) Follow the road to La Pagerie. It is almost a requirement of a visit to Martinique that you tour the ruins of the homestead of Josephine, empress-wife of Napoleon. The foundations of the house, ruins of the sugar factory, spacious grounds, gardens, and museum in the former plantation kitchen make this a pleasant and informative stop.

Continue on the road past La Pagerie and leave your car where the road crosses the river. It may be possible to drive further, but the road deteriorates from here. Besides, it is an easy, level walk on the road in the plains of Trois-Ilets.

In 30 minutes the road ends and the pathway begins. Rise gradually as the trail enters woodlands and works its way around the side of Morne Bigot.

Continue through the forest and, in another 35 minutes, you'll reach a small clearing. Shortly after this you'll arrive at a trail junction. A turn to the left would soon come to a dirt road which leads to the main highway in Les Anses-d'Arlets. That hike from the intersection is a gently sloping one through the plains of Anses-d'Arlets and takes about an hour.

Your route continues straight at the junction to the summit of Morne Bigot on a sightly steeper, but still easy pathway. The peak should be reached in a half-hour. The views from here are to the north and east – Rivière Salée, La Lamentin, and the Pitons du Carbet soaring above the city and bay of Fort-de-France.

From the television relay tower there are views to the south of Anse du Diamant, Morne Larcher, and the island of St. Lucia. Continue on a gradual descent through the bamboo and rain forest and, in 45 minutes from the summit, you'll reach the road that leads to the main highway (D.7) at Galocha.

Martinique

This is a moderate hike with good views and is shaded as you walk through the forest.

37. Le Morne Champagne Trail

Walking time: less than 2 hours, round trip

To reach this pleasant hike on the Caribbean coast, follow R.7 past Trois-Ilets. (See Walk #35 for directions to this point.) Pass through the village and continue to the southernmost point on the beach of Grande-Anse-d'Arlets. The trail begins between the last two houses on the beach.

This easy path follows the gradual grade of the ridgeline of Morne Champagne. In a short distance you'll reach the savannah in the old crater of Morne Champagne. A good view back onto the beach and bay of Grande-Anse-d'Arlets can be had before coming to a popular picnicking spot and the end of the trail.

An easy hike recommended for those who do not have time for the longer trails.

38. Les Anses d'Arlets Beach Walk

This mile-long sandy beach is located south of Trois-Ilets (see Walk #35 for directions to Trois-Ilets). The attractive small village and the activity of local fishermen on the shore and out in the ocean deserve on-foot exploration and not just a quick drive-by.

39. The Piton Crève Coeur Hike

Walking time: 2 hours, round trip

A short, easy ascent to the highest point on the Ste.-Anne Peninsula, this hike is reached by taking highway D.9 south of Le Marin. In 1.5 miles, turn left on D.33 toward Cap Chevalier. At the first intersection continue right toward Cap Chevalier and after one mile turn right onto an unpaved road as the main highway makes a sharp bend to the left. The trail begins behind the parking area near the remnants of a sugar factory.

Ascend the mountain gradually, passing some old homesteads and a trailside shelter. The trail gets steeper before reaching an open area with views to the south. A short while later, you'll reach the summit of Piton Crève Coeur (660 feet). All of the southern peninsula is now before you – Ste.-Anne to the west, the open scrub land of the Savane de Pétrifications to the south, the Atlantic coast to the east and Le Marin to the north. An easy, popular hike.

40. The Grande Anse des Salines Beach Walk

Follow D.9 south out of Le Marin through Ste.-Anne and finally to its end at the southeastern edge of the beach. The Grande Anse des Salines may just be the best beach on all of Martinique.

Walk along this popular beach toward the northwest. Enjoy the sun sparkling on the grains of sand as it is filtered through the palms. Off in the distance Diamond Rock juts out of the Caribbean Sea and fishermen ply the waters in search of a catch. The farther you walk from the road, the less crowded the beach becomes. It is possible to stretch this walk even further by ascending two small points as you come to them and continuing along the sand on the far side of the points. Relax and take a swim. The sun, surf, and sand of the Caribbean won't get any better than this.

41. The Savane de Pétrifications Hike
Walking time: 2 hours, one way

A unique excursion, the Savane des Pétrifications begins where the paved road ends at Grande Anse des Salines. (See directions in Walk #40.) Follow the dirt road past the camping area and out onto open savannah.

There is no set trail here; just wander through the petrified remains of a forest and volcano, now long gone. Walk past the large salt pond and onto the sheer cliffs overlooking the rock-strewn shoreline. The cliffs are home to a number of salt water birds, the most notable being the frigatebird.

Continue north along the coastline, passing a couple of smaller beaches and taking care not to get too close to the unstable edge of the cliffs. In a little over an hour you'll arrive at Anse Traband. The beach is lined with sea grape and manchineel trees. Remember! The manchineel apples are poisonous, and the sap from the leaves and bark will cause a rash. (Generally, the National Forest Office marks these trees with a red blaze to make them easily recognizable on public beaches.) At the end of the long beach, turn uphill from the ocean, ascend gradually, and come to the Baie des Anglais.

An easy, recommended hike through a unique area of cacti, beach, salt ponds, rocks, and petrified wood (most of which, sadly, has been carried off by souvenir seekers). Be prepared; there is no shade along this route.

Suggested Readings and Field Guides

📖 Alevision, William S. *Pisces Guide to Caribbean Reef Ecology*. Houston, TX: Gulf Publications, 1994.

📖 Bentio-Espinal, E. *Birds of the West Indies*. Gustavia, Saint Barthélemy: Editions Du Latanier.

📖 Bond, James. *Peterson Guide to Birds of the West Indies*. Boston, MA: Houghton Mifflin, 1995.

📖 Damman. *Natural History Atlas to the Cays of the U.S.V.I.* Sarasota, FL: Pineapple Press, 1992.

📖 Davies, Hunter. *In Search of Columbus*. North Pomfret, VT: Trafalgar, 1992.

📖 Fanon, Frantz. *Wretched of the Earth*. New York, NY: Grove-Atlantic, 1988.

📖 Forsyth, J. & K. Miyata. *Tropical Nature*. NY, NY: Charles Scribner's Sons, 1984.

📖 Hargreaves, D and B. T*ropical Blossoms of the Caribbean*. Lahaina, HI: Ross-Hargreaves, 1960.

📖 Honeychurch, P. *Caribbean Wild Plants and Their Uses*. London: Macmillan Caribbean, 1978.

📖 Kingsbury, J. *220 Conspicuous, Unusual, or Economically Important Tropical Plants of the Caribbean*. London: Macmillan Caribbean. Ithaca, NY: Bullbrier Press, 1988.

📖 Lennox, G. and S. Seddon. *Flowers of the Caribbean*. London: Macmillan Caribbean, 1978.

📖 Magras, Michel. *Caribbean Flowers*. Gustavia, Saint Barthélemy: Editions Du Latanier.

📖 Mitchell, Carelton. *Isles of the Caribes*. Washington, D. C.: National Geographic Society, 1966.

📖 Morison, Samuel E. *Christopher Columbus, Mariner*. New York, NY: NAL-Dutton, 1983.

📖 Paiewonsky, Michael. *Conquest of Eden, 1493-1515*. Chicago, IL: Mapes Monde, Acad. of Chicago Publishers, 1990.

📖 Seddon S. A. and G. W. Lennox. *Trees of the Caribbean*. London: Macmillan Caribbean, 1980.

📖 Schwartz and Henderson. *Amphibians & Reptiles of the West Indies*. Gainesville, FL: University of Florida Press, 1991.

📖 Vernoux, J. P., M. and P. Magras. *Coral Fish of the West Indies*. Gustavia, Saint Barthélemy: Editions Du Latanier.

📖 Walton, Chelle K. *Caribbean Ways: A Cultural Guide*. Westwood, MA: Riverdale Company, 1993.

📖 Warmke, G. and R. Tucker Abbott. *Caribbean Seashells, A Guide to Mollusks of Puerto Rico and other West Indian Islands, Bermuda and the Lower Florida Keys*. New York, NY: Dover, 1975.

Index